VALUES AND ASSUMPTIONS IN

AMERICAN LABOR LAW

The University of Massachusetts Press

Amherst, 1983

Values and Assumptions in
American Labor Law

James B. Atleson

Copyright © 1983 by The University of Massachusetts Press
All rights reserved   Printed in the United States of America
Third printing
A portion of chapter seven has previously appeared in the *New York University Journal of Law and Social Policy* 11, no. 1(1983).

Library of Congress Cataloging in Publication Data
Atleson, James B.
Values and assumptions in American labor law.
Includes index.
1. Labor laws and legislation—United States—Interpretation and construction. I. Title.
KF3319.A84   1983   344.73'01   82–21993
ISBN 0–87023–390–4   347.3041

To Carol, Michael, and Jonathan

CONTENTS

THE PURPOSE OF this book is to investigate the seeming incoherence of American labor law doctrine. In many ways, the law is indeed incoherent whether we focus upon its analytical exposition or the legal results reached. Labor law is not, I believe, unique in this regard, but the problem may be aggravated because there are few widely shared values in this most volatile and emotional area. The National Labor Relations Act does provide a structure and a body of law to implement public policies, but it is widely acknowledged that legal decisions frequently depart from the statutory language, policies, or legislative history of the act.

The goal of this volume is to demonstrate that the decisions are incoherent only if viewed through the lens of the statute and its policies, the way in which lawyers tend to view coherency. Underlying American labor law is a set of rarely expressed values that, although illegitimate under contemporary modes of legal thought, help to explain the judicial and administrative decisions reached. These values and assumptions predate the statute and can be found in nineteenth-century judicial opinions.

This inquiry, employing historical and other nonlegal scholarly sources to critically analyze legal doctrine, is not the traditional way for a lawyer to view or write about a body of law. The risks of such an endeavor were significantly eased by friends and colleagues who supported me throughout the long gestation period leading to this book. I have gained much from the stimulating writing and ideas of Karl Klare, David Montgomery, Howard Lesnick, Clyde Summers, and many others. Most important has been the support of my colleagues here at Buffalo who have created a unique atmosphere that supports and encourages innovative and critical legal analysis. Various sections of this volume have been read by William Greiner, John Henry Schlegel, and Dean Thomas Headrick, who has also been very supportive throughout this long and often agonizing process. I wish to specially mention my good friend and colleague Fred Konefsky who generously read and reread the manuscript and whose ideas, insight, and repeated expressions of interest and concern were invaluable. Moreover, Fred offered constant aid and support and he cajoled and nudged when necessary. He proved always ready to listen to new ideas as well as new doubts and qualms.

Joyce Farrell prepared the manuscript in its many forms and her thoughtful assistance and unfailing good humor were of inestimable value. Herbert Eisenberg and Kim Crites provided valuable assistance, and I specially wish to express my gratitude to Mary O'Connell. Finally, I wish to thank my many students whose ideas and forbearance have aided me in reaching the conclusions set forth in this volume.

VALUES AND ASSUMPTIONS IN
AMERICAN LABOR LAW

IN A LABOR LAW CLASS some years ago I was asked how the courts could consistently restrict the rights of employees to take concerted action when those rights were clearly and unequivocally set out in the National Labor Relations Act and limitations were neither discussed in the legislative debates and reports nor expressed in the statute. I began to patiently answer with the verities I had been taught, that no statute or right is absolute and that all rights had to be balanced against competing interests. I could not continue. Suddenly, the traditional dogma no longer made sense. Removing blinders does not, in itself, create understanding. This book is an attempt to answer the question.

Scholarly writing in labor law has been overwhelmingly doctrinal, or rule oriented and analytical, typically involving the evaluation of a number of adjudicated disputes in a narrow subject area, criticizing the results reached, and usually proposing new rules or considerations to guide future decision makers. Analysis in professional writing, as well as in agency or judicial decisions, usually occurs within the context of a received wisdom which assumes certain values and norms and, especially, involves particular forms of argumentation. The operative "received wisdom" in labor law includes the notion that disputes should be resolved in light of the stated purposes and policies of federal labor laws, derived primarily from their legislative history and inferences from the text of the statutes. It is, then, a framework for legal thought and analysis. Conclusions are often based upon assumptions about relative economic power or responsibilities that employers and employees must possess and about the way people can be expected to respond to particular situations or to alternative legal rules. Economic or sociological data, however, is rarely used to critically analyze existing rules, to propose new ones, or to determine how rules actually operate.

Thus, traditional analysis generally begins by noting that the Wagner Act of 1935 (the National Labor Relations Act) was designed in large part to encourage labor peace by prohibiting many of the employer actions that caused economic warfare, by creating a specialized agency to enforce these prohibitions, and by encouraging collective bargaining. Effective bargaining, however, ironically required the right to strike or to threaten strike action. Employee collective action was protected for the first time because of its functional value in fostering the private resolution of workplace disputes. Employees could generally be expected to act rationally but, in any event, the rationality or wisdom of their action was not to be a matter of federal scrutiny. Although the Taft-Hartley amendments of 1947 explicitly prohibited certain kinds of union conduct, the statute nevertheless retained the notion that collective action should generally be protected despite the economic harm it might cause. In addition, the Wagner Act was designed to create greater potential for industrial democracy, a vaguely designed phrase with varying meanings in American history.

Legal criticism constantly exposes the failure of adjudicators either to justify coherently the decisions reached or to rationally place the decisions within the received wisdom. The possibilities are boundless, for many legal decisions are indeed inconsistent with the received wisdom, that is, the results seem inconsistent with the stated or inferred policies or purposes of the statute. These variations, however, as well as the perceived rational failures, are due to a much more serious and deeply rooted phenomenon than simply whimsical or faulty analysis. In brief, it seems clear that many judicial and administrative decisions are based upon other, often unarticulated, values and assumptions that are not to be found or inferred from the language of the statute or its legislative history. The belief in the inherent rights of property and the need for capital mobility, for instance, underlie certain rules, and some decisions turn on the perceived superior need for continued production or the fear of employee irresponsibility.

Often a particular decision or rule seems to be based upon assumptions that are not even stated. Should these values be articulated, such announcements are usually made without elaboration. Legal writers normally note the irrationality—based upon the traditional set of assumed values or assumptions—and attempt to devise a more rational approach. I do not wish to suggest that legal writers are necessarily unaware of these often unvoiced but operative assumptions and values, although some may perceive them only dimly. Instead, I wish to note that the writing of scholars (and judges) either tends to overlook such problems or, if recognized, fails to proceed much beyond the expression of such a perception. These hidden values, inconsistent with the received wisdom but determinative in many cases, are not part of the traditional legal mode of analysis and, as such, they can conveniently be ignored. Scholars can then attempt to fashion a new and more rational analysis which tries to accommodate the "irrational" results with the received wisdom as well as possible.

I have previously noted that the stated reasons for particular rules are often irrational[1] or inconsistent with social-science data.[2] In an article on the nature and causes of wildcat strikes, for example, I noted that the assumptions underlying the disdain for wildcat activity were inconsistent with social-science data on small group and workplace conflict. Many walkouts were not so spontaneous, irrational, or nonfunctional as one might assume from legal writing. The legal results seemed inconsistent with a statute that expressly protects concerted employee activity. It is quite conceivable that the common legal condemnation of such behavior is based upon certain, often unstated, assumptions about the expected behavior of employees, inherent obligations of employees to their employers, and the perceived needs of the economy. The legal decisions, therefore, may well be "rational," but only because they are consistent with those hidden values and assumptions. The presence of unstated but deeply held premises helps explain why social-science data is often treated as irrelevant.

Rather than analyzing one narrow area of labor law, which is the normal focus for scholarly activity in the field, a number of situations will be analyzed in an attempt to discover and articulate the assumptions made and values implemented by decision makers. I seek to decipher these values and assumptions and then try to relate them in a coherent way in light of recent historical scholarship. This is admittedly a dangerous mission into uncharted terrain by a perhaps too unsophisticated pilot. Nevertheless, such an endeavor is important because it will tend to broaden the scope of analysis to include basic issues currently being ignored, help set an agenda for empirical study, and, perhaps, lead to a more realistic understanding of the area.[3]

It will not be possible to pursue any one area of labor law in the depth to which law professors, at least, have become accustomed.

Each of these areas has received extensive analytical attention, some of which is extremely perceptive and useful and some of which is good, run-of-the-mill wrinkle-writing. The tracing of wrinkles or the following of all the minor tributaries flowing from the legal doctrines discussed here would only be distracting. Moreover, such "tradition-al" modes of inquiry tend to structure our focus by implicitly accept-ing the underlying assumptions and values of the doctrines analyzed. Thus, an effort will be made to avoid burdening the reader with more doctrinal development than seems necessary. Unfortunately, a good deal of doctrinal information will be necessary for purposes of exposi-tion, and normal legal analysis will be employed to demonstrate its inability to explain the legal doctrine. Much of the discussion will be a critique of doctrine, using legal and nonlegal materials. Such a mix-ture is untraditional in legal writing, but the relevance of social-sci-ence and historical material to legal analysis is, I believe, indisputa-ble. Legal doctrine is stressed throughout the text, not as an end in itself, but, rather, as evidence of values and ideology, or, if you prefer, consciousness. The lack of data to support most legal conclusions or empirical statements, moreover, is noted in part because such data would be useful but primarily because it further supports the notion that a set of underlying values exists. Even the judicial tendency to rely on "pop sociology" of the "everyone knows" variety masks ideo-logical views.[4]

The following examples briefly illustrate the premise that unex-amined values and unarticulated assumptions underlie much of labor law. These situations generally raise issues about the nature of pro-tected employee action and the scope of mandatory collective bar-gaining under the National Labor Relations Act. Other examples could be given, but these are the situations that have led me to the premise outlined here.

Section 7 of the NLRA broadly and unconditionally grants em-ployees the right to engage in collective action.[5] These rights, how-ever, have been limited in various relevant ways. The presence of a labor organization, for instance, effectively limits the permissible range of actions for employees. Unauthorized strikes, depending upon the forum, are either prohibited totally or permitted in only a narrow range of circumstances. Behind these results lie often unex-pressed assumptions that production must be maintained and that the integrity of the bargaining system must be protected even from expressions of employee outrage.

The courts have also refused to protect employees who engage in slowdowns, that is, employees who lessen their work effort can be discharged, even though courts would normally protect a full strike in the same situations. These policies seem to be based on notions, never articulated clearly, about innate obligations employees owe their employers to expend energy in accordance with prior levels irrespective of some employer action that alters employee expectations. Slowdowns are deemed "unprotected," which means employees who engage in such activity can be discharged, even though the employer may not have set a production standard and even though employees may be protesting a unilateral reduction in their pay. The reason for these results have never been clearly explored. A similar doctrine penalizes action deemed "disloyal," such as disparaging an employer's product during a labor dispute. These examples suggest that decisions are based upon deeply held judicial feelings about the contractual or status obligations of employees as well as the rights of property. The writing in the area, however, generally moves on after noting that some set of unarticulated assumptions must underlie such results.

Another set of rules protects certain collective activity but only if certain employee perceptions of reality are correct, even though logic or scientific knowledge would suggest the impossibility or irrationality of requiring correct perception. For instance, although employees may legally respect another union's picket line, it is usually believed that they can do so only if the picket line is lawful. Yet, such a determination is quite complex and even experts may not agree.

Similarly, the NLRA protects employees who cease work because of a good-faith belief that they are facing an abnormally dangerous situation threatening their safety or health. Yet, a recent Supreme Court decision held that such a stoppage of work is protected only if the employees' perception can be objectively supported, [6] a condition that is not literally part of the statutory language. Such a requirement places an obviously unfair as well as unrealistic burden upon employees. [7] The requirement, for instance, overlooks the paucity of knowledge on workplace health and safety risks. The decision is based, I believe, on an assumption that employees can be expected to behave irresponsibly and stop work even when no health or safety risk actually exists. In addition, it assumes that enterprises must be permitted to operate even if employee fears are indeed reasonable because management can be expected to act upon greater knowledge or, simply, because productivity is more important. In area after area, reasonable belief or good faith is irrelevant, and employees are protected only if they correctly perceive the legal or scientific situation.

Even if employees are participating in conduct that is *concededly* protected by Section 7, striking employees may nevertheless be permanently replaced. The law distinguishes between discharge, which is not permitted in this circumstance, and permanent replacement, which is allowed. To the striker, of course, the distinction is meaningless because in either case he or she has become unemployed due to the exercise of a statutory right. It would be difficult to find a greater interference with the right to strike than permanent replacement. Apparently, the law gives greater weight to the interest in maintaining productivity than to the statutory right to strike.

Two other examples are helpful because they specifically involve the extent to which the statute will permit employee interests to affect the mobility of capital and basic decisions concerning the scope and direction of the enterprise. In the famous *Darlington Manufacturing Company*[8] decision, the Supreme Court held that an employer could close its only plant even though the closing was motivated *solely* by a desire to punish employees for voting for a union. The Court thought the proposition too obvious for explanation, even though the National Labor Relations Board had only ordered the employer to pay the employees back pay until they could find substantially equivalent employment. Implicit in the Court's action is a belief that capital decisions should not be affected by vital employee interests even when the employer's action is not based upon "legitimate" economic considerations but, rather, is designed to punish employees for exercising explicit statutory rights.

Similarly unarticulated notions about the inherent rights of employers underlie the problem of defining the scope of mandatory collective bargaining. The courts and the National Labor Relations Board have long experience in dealing with the subjects over which employers and unions are legally required to bargain. Indeed, the courts have been somewhat more explicit about underlying concerns in this area. Certain subjects, at the "core of managerial prerogatives," are outside the area of mandatory bargaining.

As Clyde Summers has recently noted:

Decisions to continue subcontracting, to close one of several plants, to build a new plant, to liquidate assets, to sell part or all of the enterprise, or to become part of a conglomerate are all decisions which may be more important to the employees than wages or hours of work. Nevertheless, the courts have held that the employees have no right to be notified, no right to discuss, and no right to use their concerted efforts to affect these types of decisions. The impact on the employees' livelihoods and their futures may be far greater than the impact on the stockholders or management, but employees have no voice. They do not even have a right to know the business facts on which the decision was based; they are told only of the consequences which they must bear because of a unilateral management decision.[9]

I am less interested in the precise boundaries of the obligation to bargain, the focus of most of the writing in the area, than I am in the source of and reasons for the strongly held belief that boundaries must exist. What is clear is that the assumptions involved cut across the entire labor-management spectrum.[10]

These instances of doctrinal development suggest a hidden set of values and assumptions varying from the received wisdom. It is then necessary to discover and determine the nature of these premises. One of the most crucial assumptions that seems to underlie legal decision making is that continuity of production must be maintained, tempered only when statutory language *clearly* protects employee interference. Of course, no statement this bold would ever be found in a legal decision. Moreover, this assumption may seem ironic given that federal labor law has explicitly protected strikes and other kinds of concerted actions since 1935. But the seeming incongruity quickly disappears. The right to strike is granted because the threat to withdraw labor power, or its actual withdrawal, is the only employee action that will make collective bargaining effective, and collective bargaining, in turn, will encourage "industrial peace." Thus, strikes are statutorily protected in order to support a private method of resolving labor disputes which, it is hoped, will reduce the need for strikes. The statutory rights, however, have been limited in a variety of ways and especially when the concerted activity can be characterized as something other than a strike. The first section of the book, dealing with the rights of strikers, poignantly reflects the extent to which courts will protect an assumed inherent right of management to maintain production despite the serious impact upon statutory rights.

A second assumption implicit in the decisions, flowing from the first, is that employees, unless controlled, will act irresponsibly. Thus, for instance, the strong interest in continued production limits the extent to which employees may act to protect their health and safety. In general, employees face a difficult burden of proof when seeking to justify a work stoppage because of perceived threats to health. As already noted, many of the statute's protections are granted only to employees who correctly gauge the extent to which their action falls within the ambit of statutory protection. Reasonable behavior alone is insufficient. These holdings tend to assume that employees are irresponsibly strike-prone or that greater employee freedom will result in "anarchy," ignoring the fact that many employees already view their work situation as a state of anarchy.

The fear of anarchy suggests more basic concerns with productivity and a third assumption relates to the limited status of employees in the management of the enterprise. Therefore, in addition to an emphasis upon continued production, an analysis of American labor law would have to recognize the presence of status assumptions. Employees, clearly the junior partners in the labor-management partnership, owe a measure of respect and deference to their employers. This obligation of respect, involving both speech and nonverbal behavior, is employed to limit the scope of permissible concerted behavior. The Supreme Court has explicitly stated that the NLRA was designed to strengthen loyalty to the "common enterprise." Despite such communitarian notions, judicial decisions clearly assume that employees are a relatively minor part of this entity. These status or class assumptions are derived from classical master-servant law, in which the servant's deference or respect need not be earned but, rather, was implicit in the employment relationship. Employer freedom of action, however, has generally not been circumscribed on the theory that the "common-enterprise" notion involves corresponding obligations of employers to their employees. Only the act defines those areas in which employers are restricted, but limits on employee statutory rights stem from their inferior status.

Fourth, the "common enterprise" is primarily under management's control. Thus, an important focus is on the workplace as the property of the employer. The right of employees to communicate with each other and other statutory interests must compete with shadowy notions about employer ownership. Thus, employee rights to solicit and pamphlet for union organization on company property are limited by property interests, unrecognized in the statute, and rarely made subject to detailed analysis. Similarly, the employer's presumed property rights seem to support decisions that reject the legitimacy of employee efforts to regulate their work effort.

A fifth assumption involves the belief, often made explicit, that employees cannot be full partners in the enterprise because such an arrangement would interfere with inherent and exclusive managerial rights of employers. Again, statutory rights are restricted by pre-1935 notions of managerial freedom. The courts often assume, in the absence of supportive statutory language or legislative history, that the statute gives employees only limited participatory rights in the management of the "common enterprise." Thus, although the employers must bargain in good faith, the most critical decisions about the enterprise, such as its continued operation and location, are excluded from the scope of mandatory bargaining under the statute.

The deeper reasons for the assumption of managerial exclusivity lie hidden, but explanations often rely upon notions of property rights and the need for capital mobility. Capital decisions, for instance, are distinguished from other types of decisions in order to exclude employee participation in their formulation and implementation. Certain serious and far-reaching capital decisions such as the termination of the entire enterprise are permissible even if made to retaliate against employees for exercising statutory rights. Thus, employers have the right to direct and control labor power except in those cases where fairly clear statutory provisions prohibit such action.

In addition to delineating implicit assumptions, I wish to show that the problem is not a new one, and that similar undercurrents existed in the common law long prior to the enactment of the National Labor Relations Act. In interpreting the NLRA, courts seem to apply many assumptions held by judges prior to 1935. For instance, the common (nonstatutory) law of the nineteenth century applied an "unlawful means–unlawful ends" test to determine the legality of union or employee activity. The test, derived from the treatment of union activity as criminal conspiracies in the first half of the nineteenth century, meant that courts would enjoin activity that sought some unlawful goal or even a lawful objective by unlawful means. The test has been uniformly criticized by scholars because it is so vague and so lacking in articulated standards that judges could impose their own social and economic views. Scholarly writing, however, tends to assume that judicial excursions into law making somehow halts in 1935. Yet, the "means-ends" test, for instance, has been employed in various areas under the NLRA, sometimes leading to results similar to those reached by common-law courts. The "means-ends" test is still employed under the NLRA, and this is strikingly clear in the definition of "protected" activities.[11]

Another example of this historical continuation is the distinction between actions stemming from the promotion of self-interest, which would sometimes be found justified despite the economic harm caused, and activity arising from the assertion of altruistic, class-based or "sympathetic" feelings.[12] Similar distinctions exist under the NLRA. The basis of this distinction in law predates modern labor law, but it results in according selfish or self-interested economic action greater protection than attempts to aid employees or union organizational efforts elsewhere. The judges could perhaps understand and sympathize with economically based action but may well have been suspicious or contemptuous of class-based or sympathetic activity. Analysis will seek to draw connections or resonances between this distinction and other values or assumptions underlying legal rules.

The basic theme of the book, then, is that assumptions and values about the economic system and the prerogatives of capital, and corollary assumptions about the rights and obligations of employees, underlie many labor law decisions. Moreover, these assumptions permeate modern decision making just as they did prior to the passage of the Wagner Act. The presence of such values and assumptions, often only implicit or hinted at, helps explain many decisions which otherwise seem odd, irrational, or at least inconsistent with the received wisdom.

In the process of working on the manuscript, two other notions have arisen that both complicated and illuminated the original endeavor. First, the courts' reliance upon certain explicit or implicit values is often premised upon the belief that a cultural harmony of values exists, thereby ignoring the presence of a quite different working-class value structure. For instance, it is commonplace to note that different norms exist for determining what output is "fair" in a given set of circumstances. Similarly, the nature and meaning of time, especially the differences between employee time and employer or working time, varies by the interests and norms of the perceiver. In certain cases, a clash of cultural values clearly exists and legal decisions, although seeming oblivious to the fact, choose one cultural value over another. This realization is not discussed in order to suggest that cultural choices can be avoided, but to recognize that the "of course" statements by decision makers reflect not only underlying values, but often a particular set of cultural values. Recent writing in labor and social history dealing with class structures and relationships as well as cultural norms will be used to support this contention. These studies show that workers and entrepreneurs possess quite different cultural and economic views and that employers have been engaged in a systematic and highly successful effort to control the labor force.

The second notion stems directly from the realization that some underlying assumptions have remained the same under both common and statutory law. This continuation in some areas reflects the judicial interest in defining and regulating the employer-employee relationship. Ironically, this occurs even in NLRA cases where the presence of a union, not to mention the statute itself, drastically alters the relationship. In many cases courts seem to be composing or shaping an employment contract, a process similar to common-law dispute resolution and, not surprisingly, one that often leads to similar results. This suggests not only a contractual outlook but a melding of contract and status, a conjunction that also mediated common-law decision making.

The employment contract was always treated as being quite different from other forms of contract: "The purposive contract is the characteristic legal institution of an exchange economy. It is a contract made to complete a specific transaction or to further a discrete objective. Only a tenuous and temporary association is created. The purposive contract is infused with the spirit of restraint and delimitation: open-ended obligations are alien to its nature; arms-length negotiation is the keynote." The preindustrial period is often viewed as precontractual, but this view rests on a perception of contract that includes limited and specific obligations as opposed to more open-ended and diffuse commitments. A status arrangement, or "status contract," created a continuing relationship and usually was thought to affect the "total legal situation of the individual."[13] Such arrangements were generally not premised on the existence of explicit consent to particularized obligations. In theory at least, reciprocal rights and obligations under a contractual regime are limited to those in the contract.

For a variety of reasons, status or quasi-feudal arrangements were replaced by contractual ones in the nineteenth century.[14] Personal relations, traditional bonds, and community ties could underpin local transactions but not economic arrangements outside the local community in a system employing intermediaries and monetary measurements of exchange.

The labor contract, although arising during the same period as the general "triumph of contract," was not required by expanding market structures because most enterprises were still relatively small. Labor, however, was treated as a commodity, although concededly more unruly than other factors of production. The notion has become deceivingly trite now, at least outside formal economics, but it was sufficiently unobvious in 1914 for Congress to explicitly attempt to refute this view by stating: "The labor of a human being is not a commodity or article of commerce."[15] Nevertheless, although energy and skills were personal, they were alienable possessions which could be handed over to others for a price.[16] Personal relations, however, cannot be completely removed from the employment relationship, just as they cannot be fully removed in business transactions.

Although ideology might trumpet the employment contract as the "personal and voluntary exchange of freely-bargained promises," the mythological nature of such arrangements was clearly recognized.[17] Adam Smith, who has no doubt been more widely discussed than read, early recognized that "it is not . . . difficult to forsee which of the two parties must, upon all ordinary occasions, have the advantage in the dispute, and force the other into a compliance with their terms. . . ."[18]

The callousness of subjecting work relationships to the "law of the market" did not pass unchallenged by American workers, and expressions of concern can be found at the beginning of the industrial revolution. Labor leaders as early as the Jacksonian period, for example, challenged laws as "wicked instruments of oppression,"[19] and they were aware of notions of surplus labor.[20] In the United States, as in Britain, the working classes considered labor to be "exploited and impoverished by the rich, who were getting richer while the poor became poorer. And the poor suffered *because* the rich benefited."[21] The situation is dramatically expressed by Karl Polanyi:

To separate labor from other activities of life and to subject it to the laws of the market was to annihilate all organic forms of existence and to replace them by a different type of organization, an atomistic and individualistic one. Such a scheme of destruction was best served by the application of the principle of freedom of contract. In practice this meant that all noncontractual organizations of kinship, neighborhood, profession and creed were to be liquidated since they claimed the allegiance of the individual and thus restrained freedom. To represent this principle as one of noninterference, as economic liberals were wont to do, was merely the expression of an ingrained prejudice in favor of a definite kind of interference, namely, such as would destroy non-contractual relations between individuals and prevent their spontaneous reformation.[22]

Not only did the attributes and virtues of the employment relationship substantially diverge from reality but there was considerable ambiguity as to the definition of the relationship. Contracts of employment were rarely written, let alone precise, and they almost never spelled out the range of rights or obligations that might be involved in the relationship. In fact, to the employee the arrangement is much more like the all-encompassing status agreement than the express, limited regime of contract. Traditional contract notions might suggest that all the ambiguous sections or unanticipated questions dealing, for instance, with the level of energy to be expended, working conditions, disciplinary authority, and employee integrity, could not be exclusively and authoritatively interpreted by the employer. The employer could be granted the right to make rules under the contract or by law, but the employer would not have the sole authority to determine whether these rules were arbitrary or consistent with the scope of that authority.[23] Undoubtedly, the fear of an external adjudicatory agency would be highly disturbing to employers. The legal response was the fusing of the employment contract with traditional master-servant notions, thereby giving a legal basis for the power employers desired.

This inference seems consistent with nineteenth-century law in the United States as well as in England.[24] The language of master-servant, with its focus on bonds of loyalty, subservience, and one-directional joint endeavor, fitted nicely with the needs of enterprise. The older law was based on a society in which everyone was presumed to belong somewhere and in which in all spheres of life "subordination to legitimate authority was thought to be a natural, inevitable, even welcome accompaniment of moral grace and practical virtue."[25] The household provided the model, and the master had inherent power to prescribe for his family, as well as for his servants.[26] The household model seemed appropriate for the overwhelmingly predominant, agricultural family unit that hired supplementary labor, but the model also fit the pattern and training of skilled artisans who often worked in the home or nearby in a small shop. Some terms, such as duration and wage, could be contractual, but "it was never contemplated that the parties would design their own relationship."[27] The predominant aspects of the relationship were taken as given and were based upon custom, ideology, and law which defined expectations and obligations.[28]

Contract, when viewed as a system of social organization by Spencer or Maine, was a system of voluntary cooperation, and success was based upon one's own efforts and efficiency. Status, on the other hand, involved compulsory cooperation in which the individual has "his appointed place, works under coercive rule, and has his apportioned share of food, clothing, and shelter."[29] Except for the last phrase, most industrial workers would no doubt recognize their situation as being closer to a status than a classically defined, contractual relationship.

The merger of master-servant law and contract meant that the law never treated the employment contract as the result of free bargaining and mutual assent, despite dogma that this was indeed the case. Instead, the contract was deemed to include "implied" terms which reserved to the employer the full authority and direction of employees. A one-sided streamlining of master-servant occurred which clearly lessened the obligations of employers and purged the relationship of all bonds that might obscure economic calculation and impede the mobility of resources, including labor.[30] The Webbs put the situation succinctly:

The capitalist is fond of declaring that labor is a commodity, and the wage contract a bargain of purchase and sale like any other. But he instinctively expects his wage-earners to render him, not only obedience, but also personal deference. If the wage contract is a bargain of purchase and sale like any other, why is the workman expected to touch his hat to his employer, and to say "sir" to him without reciprocity, when the employer meets on terms of equality the persons (often actually of higher social rank than himself) from whom he buys his raw material or makes the other bargains incidental to his trade?[31]

During the act of hiring, the employer technically concludes a contract, but, essentially, it hires an asset that is expected to bring a return. Over the course of the work relationship, the employer has the power to seek to enlarge the return. The goal, of course, is to create the largest possible gap between the yield of this asset and the terms of its hire.[32] The law supported the employers' desire for this prerogative and, obviously, supported a highly unequal property system.[33]

Added to this picture of the nineteenth century was the notion of work as enabling and redemptive. Labor was treated not only as a commodity, but also as an obligation to social superiors and as a source of spiritual or secular enhancement of the self. For our purposes, it is important to repeat that by the end of the century "the employment contract had become a very special sort of contract—in large part a legal device for guaranteeing to management the unilateral power to make rules and exercise discretion."[34]

One theme, then, is that certain assumptions of obedience and obligation stem from master-servant law. There were reciprocal obligations, of course, and the law would protect the lesser groups from abuse[35] much as Southern states might impose some standard of civility upon slave owners.[36] But I believe that there is a set of obligations that define the employment relation which is inherent in categorizing someone as a servant. One could assume that some of these notions would carry over to the latter part of the nineteenth century when, despite the change in explicit law and economic arrangements, master-servant law was used to help define the contours of the contractual employment relation. One can hypothesize (prove is another matter) a fairly straight line that runs from master-servant beginnings, through the nineteenth century, and includes the NLRA cases discussed earlier.

Conceptually, managerial or paternal authority could be based upon property notions, as incidents of ownership, rather than upon contractual concepts. But it was contract and not property which lawfully gave employers power to direct the work force.[37] The alleged move from status to contract obscures the very special kind of contract that emerged.

An important aspect of the law of employment contracts is that employees have no stake, interest, or investment in the "common enterprise" other than the right to receive wages for the sale of labor power. The American common-law rule held that in the absence of an expressed term of employment, every contract of employment was terminable at will.[38] Because the employee could leave at any time, "mutuality of obligation" meant that the employer could freely discharge an employee without notice and on any ground. Given these assumptions, it follows that employees have little investment in the enterprise in which they work. With the exception of a few recent decisions,[39] the basic rule is generally intact even though the doctrinal underpinnings have been eroded. Indeed, courts have been reluctant to find implied promises of term employment, even in cases where permanent employment or a specified term *is* actually promised, and even if the promise is the quid pro quo for the employee's decision to forego employment elsewhere. The legal doctrines of mutuality and consideration have been used, often in bizarre fashion, to deny term employments despite explicit promises of such employment and acts of employee reliance upon such promises. As in the nineteenth century, judicial decisions repeat outmoded notions of individual bargaining power and the often illusory power of employees to quit.[40] Although these decisions normally deal with the law of contracts,[41] the underlying assumptions are nevertheless still reflected in NLRA and other labor decisions today.

PART ONE

COLLECTIVE ACTION

AND THE NATIONAL

LABOR RELATIONS ACT

1

THE RIGHT TO STRIKE: FALSE PROMISES

AND UNDERLYING PREMISES

Nor was it an unfair labor practice to replace the striking employees with others in an effort to carry on the business. Although Section 13 provides, "Nothing in this Act shall be construed so as to interfere with or impede or diminish in any way the right to strike," it does not follow that an employer, guilty of no act denounced by the statute, has lost the right to protect and continue his business by supplying places left vacant by strikers. And he is not bound to discharge those hired to fill the places of strikers, upon the election of the latter to resume their employment, in order to create places for them. The assurance by respondent to those who accepted employment during the strike that if they so desired their places might be permanent was not an unfair labor practice nor was it such to reinstate only so many of the strikers as there were vacant places to be filled.[1]

THE LANGUAGE ABOVE, quoted from one of the Supreme Court's earliest NLRA cases, drastically undercut the new act's protection of the critical right to strike.[2] Although this statement was unnecessary for the resolution of the issue facing the Court, the doctrine has survived over forty years despite vigorous scholarly criticism. The result is that although the right to strike means that employees cannot generally be refused reinstatement at the end of a strike and cannot be discharged, they have no right to reinstatement if they have been replaced by strikebreakers.

It is important to note at the outset the tone of the above quotation from *NLRB* v. *Mackay Radio & Telegraph Company* and the audience to which it is directed. The statement is designed to assuage fears, predominantly felt by employers, concerning the impact of the Wagner Act; it does not speak to employees or their unions, nor does it seem particularly concerned that the Wagner Act was designed to grant economic rights, and thus power, to workers.

The content of the statement, moreover, assumes a set of rights that allows the employer "to protect and continue his business." Such assumptions underlie many labor law decisions, even when as in *Mackay* the assumption drastically circumscribes the apparent meaning of the "right to strike." This body of implicit rights is seemingly unaffected by the Wagner Act unless employer action is, perhaps explicitly, "denounced" by the act. This chapter will illustrate the acceptance by decision makers of inherent employer rights to continue operations even though such actions have drastic effects on statutory rights and employee interests. The result is to alter the apparent meaning of the statute's goal of industrial peace, for the kind of peace here envisioned is to be gained by limiting the right of employees to impose economic sanctions on employers. Implicit also is the assumption that the NLRA recognizes and seeks to protect the employer's property, a property defined in terms long predating the NLRA's passage. Employees, as the result makes clear, have a right to return to their jobs, but only if they have not been replaced during the strike. Thus, any contract or property interests employees may feel they possess can be destroyed by the employer's act of replacing them. Ironically, therefore, an act seemingly created to radically alter economic power is used to institutionalize employer power.

I do not argue that statutory rights necessarily must be read literally. Generally, however, traditional legal thought requires that limitations on statutory rights stem, at least in their explanation or rationalization, from policies reflected in the statute or its legislative history. Alternatively, statutory issues may simply create the occasion for the same type of analysis and valuing found in common-law decision making. That is, the argument that one solution is more responsive to the resonances of the statute or its legislative history than another may have no real mooring. This is an intellectual debate of real importance, but this study will assume the belief, for better or worse, that relative and qualitative statements are possible in statutory interpretation. Admittedly, if we look at what decision makers do, we would have to conclude that statutes are often fairly hollow vessels. In any event, the judicially created limitations that will be discussed here do not radiate from explicit language, history, or other federal statutory policies. Rather, as the quotation that opens this chapter indicates, critical limitations on scope of the statute stem from a set of rights or prerogatives deemed to preexist the Wagner Act and which, if not clearly restricted by the statute, still exist. The catch is that the courts will decide if this body of "inherent" rights is limited by the statute. Thus, the statute is interpreted in light of a body of inherent rights and value assumptions whose source and scope is not clear. Such an approach makes prediction and advocacy difficult, for professors as well as practitioners, and leads to results that often seem inconsistent with the received wisdom. The approach, moreover, makes it difficult to rationalize labor law. The *Mackay* decision and the courts' attempt to live with it is perhaps the most significant example of this point. As a legal rule, moreover, *Mackay's* shadow falls across all of labor-management relations.

The background of the Wagner Act is discussed in the following chapter, but that discussion should be read in the light of *Mackay*, a decision that affects all that will follow. The facts of *Mackay* are not complex but they are revealing because of the stated goal of affecting imbalances in power. A nationwide strike had been called against Mackay operations, with the degree of success varying widely across the country. The San Francisco local was, apparently, the dominant local as well as the center of union activity. The employer needed radio operators on the West Coast for trans-Pacific circuits, and it met this need by transferring employees from other stations to San Francisco. Perceiving that the strike was lost after only a few days, the San Francisco local requested the employer to reinstate all strikers. The employer initially agreed as long as the strikers "returned in a body." At a subsequent meeting, however, the employer said eleven strikers would have to fill out reemployment applications to be subsequently reviewed by the vice president in charge of operations. Being apprised of this ominous procedure, the employees nevertheless voted to return to work.[3] By the following day all but four of the striking operators had returned to work. When these four applied for reinstatement, they were informed that no vacancies then existed.

During the strike, strike replacements had been promised that they could remain permanently in San Francisco. Evidence suggested, however, that although the company believed that some replacements would wish to remain at the conclusion of the strike, the choice of which strikers to replace was based upon discriminatory grounds. Thus, all four unreinstated employees were active union members or officers. Unfair labor practice charges were filed with the National Labor Relations Board, focusing upon the company's refusal to reinstate the four operators.

The NLRB noted that the absence of positions for the four operators was caused by the retention of four strikebreakers and, arguably, this constituted "discrimination in regard to hire or tenure of employment" in violation of Section 8(3) [now Section 8(a)(3)]. The employer, therefore, may have discriminated against the strikers in violation of the act by favoring replacements. The Board, however, did not decide this issue, finding that a decision "on the point is not necessary."[4] For the "sake of argument," it assumed that strikebreakers could be retained without running afoul of Section 8(3).

The Board did not even raise a more obvious possibility, e.g., that the permanent replacement of a striker "interferes" with the right to strike granted by Section 7 and enforced pursuant under Section 8(1) [now 8(a)(1)].[5] This section prohibits employer action which interferes with, restrains, or coerces employees in the exercise of Section 7 rights. One of the rights granted by Section 7 is the right to engage in concerted activities. The importance of such activities, especially strikes, is reflected in Section 13 which states that "nothing in this Act, except as specifically provided for herein, shall be construed so as either to interfere with or impede or diminish in any way the right to strike. . . ." Instead, the Board faced another question—did the employer discriminate in deciding which strikers it would reinstate? The Board answered in the affirmative and sustained the charge.[6]

On appeal, the court of appeals for the ninth circuit denied the Board's petition to enforce the order. The court initially had held the NLRA to be unconstitutional;[7] but a rehearing was directed after the Supreme Court's decision upholding the constitutionality of the act.[8] Again, however, the circuit court refused to uphold the Board's order, this time because it believed that the act of striking severed the employment relationship. An order of reinstatement, therefore, would create a new contract of employment and would exceed the Board's authority. Such a reading, presumably, would permit the employer to exercise complete discretion in rehiring strikers at the termination of a strike, an argument seemingly at odds with the act. The Supreme Court correctly held that strikers remain "employees" under the act and, thus, the act of striking was not to be deemed a "renunciation of the employment relation."[9]

The Court's reading of the scope of right to strike is both logical as well as realistic; striking employees do not intend to terminate their employment. Having thus added some vigor to the right to strike, the Court then imposed a restriction that made its initial conclusion irrelevant. Because the General Counsel had only challenged Mackay's discriminatory reinstatement policies, the right to replace strikers was not presented to the Court as an issue. Nevertheless, the Court's gratuitous statement is the case's most important legacy: "Nor was it an unfair labor practice to replace striking employees with others in an effort to carry on the business."[10] Even though NLRA Section 13 explicitly bars a reading of the act which would "interfere with or impede or diminish in any way the right to strike," it did not follow, said the Court, that an employer "lost the right to protect and continue his business by supplying places left vacant by strikers. And he is not bound to discharge those hired to fill the places of strikers, upon the election of the latter to resume their employment, in order to create places for them."[11]

The Court, however, went on to hold that the Board sufficiently sustained its findings that employees were discriminated against in rehiring. On the issue of hiring permanent replacements, however, nothing more was added except that no violation occurred when the employer promised replacements the possibility of permanent location in San Francisco. This was not an issue, however, as the NLRB had not decided the replacement question.

Although the Board's decision in *Mackay* states that a decision on the effect of permanent reinstatement is "not necessary to the final judgment in this case,"[12] the Board's brief on appeal did refer to the issue:

The Board has never contended in this case or in any other that an employer, who has neither caused nor prolonged a strike through unfair labor practices, cannot take full advantage of economic forces working for his victory in a labor dispute. The Act clearly does not forbid him, in the absence of such unfair labor practices, to replace the striking employees with new employees or authorize an order directing that all strikers are not "guaranteed" reinstatement by the Act. . . . Admittedly an employer is fully within his rights under the statute in refusing to reinstate striking employees when he has legally filled their positions prior to the commission of any unfair labor practice. The Board did not question that right in this case.[13]

Why the Board's General Counsel surrendered an issue with which the NLRB had refused to deal is not clear. The General Counsel's brief refers to the employer's "right" to hire replacements and then refuse to reinstate strikers at the termination of the strike as *clear*. The act, however, simply does not speak to the issue, and the implications of Sections 7 and 13 certainly tend in the opposite direction. Moreover, prior to the Supreme Court's decision, the NLRB had not spoken to the issue.[14] Thus, at this early date, both the Supreme Court and the

NLRB's General Counsel were reading the act to recognize employer rights even though none were explicitly set out and such "rights" drastically reduced the effectiveness of rights that were explicitly given to employees.

It is possible that because of the early date of the case, the General Counsel wanted to assuage possible Court concerns of the rights of nonunion workers. Early common-law cases also stressed the impact of concerted activities on nonunion employees or prospective employees,[15] although it was never clear whether these arguments were important or only makeweights, designed to mask pro-employer values. In any event, the dicta or unnecessary statements in *Mackay* have become settled, albeit uncomfortable, law.[16] No explanation was given, no policy justification enunciated, no legislative history asserted to support the conclusion reached. The Court's conclusion is stated as an "of course." As a colleague has stated, "of course" statements in labor law cases indicate where the corpses are buried. But what is the corpse?

The ruling not only flies in the face of the literal as well as the logical reading of Sections 7, 8(1), and 13, but it has bedeviled legal scholars ever since, creating serious intellectual obstacles to rationalizing much NLRA law. This conclusion, unfortunately, does not distinguish *Mackay* from other decisions, including many that will be subsequently discussed, even though *Mackay* is critically important. It seems worthwhile to detail some of the analytical problems created by *Mackay* to indicate the difficulties created by decisions based upon vague concepts of managerial prerogatives.

DOCTRINAL DILEMMAS

Section 8(a)(1) protects concerted activity such as strikes against "interferences," and Sections 7 and 13 make doubly clear the critical role of the strike in the congressional scheme. One can conceive of few interferences greater than permanent replacement for striking. The replaced striker has joined the ranks of the unemployed because of the exercise of the statutory right to strike and the situation may well serve to deter protected activity by other employees. The act of replacement itself obviously has an effect on the right to strike because it is the employer's attempt to weaken the strike and overcome the economic harm it has caused. Because of this, it has always been clear that strikers can legally appeal to strikebreakers to cease work. Moreover, when the employer favors a replacement over a striker seeking reinstatement at the end of a strike, the employer literally "discriminates" on the basis of the exercise of protected activity, a seemingly clear violation of Section 8(a)(3). If replacements have not been hired, the employer would clearly violate the statute should it refuse to rehire a striker. Why does interference not exist in the situation where a replacement has been hired during the strike?

"Interference" under Section 8(a)(1) has generally not been treated as a merely factual matter, but it has always been a label attached when the employer's interests have been outweighed by employee or statutory interests.[17] Nevertheless, the employer's interests in the replacement situation would seemingly have to be heavy indeed to overcome the obvious harm to the exercise of protected activity, yet the Supreme Court apparently felt that this interest needed neither clear nor full expression.

The Court's justification seems to be based upon its conclusion that an employer has the right to "protect and continue his business."[18] It is not clear from the opinion whether the Court justified the doctrine on the employer's understandable desire to maintain operations or the employer's need to hire replacements to avoid economic destruction. Although replacements may conceivably be needed for sheer survival in some situations, employers often operate with supervisors or nonstriking employees. Such continued operation has never been questioned, although strikers can legally appeal to neutrals crossing picket lines.[19] The Court's ruling, however, does not turn on evidence that the employer *required* replacements, permanent or temporary, because no showing of economic necessity was required. The purpose of strikes, of course, is to impose economic pressure upon an employer, but unions rarely engage in brinkmanship when a strike would threaten the survival of the enterprise. Later decisions, in any event, have not required proof that replacements are required to stave off bankruptcy or financial ruin. In addition, employers need not prove that the business could not continue with temporary (as opposed to permanent) replacements. Employers may hire permanent replacements—and thereby remove the strikers, and often the union, from the scene—even if other alternatives exist to avoid serious economic dislocation.[20] Thus, the language in *Mackay* and the current understanding of its scope is that permanent replacements can be hired even if the failure to do so would not lead to business destruction or even serious economic loss.

Not only is it difficult to understand the basis for *Mackay,* but the *Mackay* dictum has made it difficult to explain later decisions that demonstrate, for instance, that the employer's need to carry on business does not always justify any response to a strike. For instance, an employer who in good faith offered superseniority to replacements because it believed such an offer necessary to secure their employment during a strike was declared to have committed an unfair labor practice in *NLRB* v. *Erie Resistor.*[21] Because a large number of employees were on lay-off status at the time of the strike, the employer felt it would be difficult to obtain replacements if they feared their own displacement when laid-off workers returned or in the event of a subsequent layoff. The employer thus promised replacements (and returning strikers) twenty years seniority in any layoff or recall situation. The employer's bona fides was not questioned, and the result focused, at least in part, upon the long-term damage to union solidarity and future collective bargaining likely to result from the employer's action.

Superseniority renders future bargaining difficult, if not impossible, for the collective bargaining representative. Unlike the replacement granted in *Mackay* which ceases to be an issue once the strike is over, the plan here creates a cleavage in the plant continuing long after the strike is ended. Employees are henceforth divided into two camps: Those who stayed with the union and those who returned before the end of the strike and thereby gained extra seniority. This breach is reemphasized with each subsequent layoff and stands as an ever-present reminder of the dangers connected with striking and with union activities in general.[22]

The Court's conclusion is dubious only in its attempt to distinguish *Mackay,* because that doctrine also threatens future union cohesion by creating a work force that may consist of reinstated strikers as well as strike replacements. It would be difficult to generalize any empirically based rationale that one situation is necessarily more damaging to future union effectiveness than the other.[23] The result of *Erie Resistor* is that the employer's need to maintain operations is not necessarily decisive in every situation, but the basis of *Mackay* is no clearer.

It is settled dogma that although an employer may hire replacements, even permanent replacements, to continue operations during a strike, it may not replace in order to punish strikers. Such intent, if it could be established, would clearly violate the act. Serious evidentiary problems abound under the NLRA because the act makes intent rather than impact crucial in a number of situations. The harm to the strikers is the same, whatever the intent of securing replacements, and losing one's job for striking is not made less drastic by the knowledge that the employer did not seek to punish. So long as the employer does not selectively replace employees on the basis of union leadership or strike militancy, for instance, the theoretical violation vanishes given the difficulty of proof of motive.[24]

The potential impact of *Mackay* is as important as the resulting doctrinal confusion. It is, for instance, reasonable to assume that strike replacements will tend not to be union supporters or activists. The fact of replacement may well cement this reluctance and have a deterrent effect upon potential strike decisions in the future. Although current doctrine states that employers can replace but not discharge, employers are not likely to discharge strikers unless replacements can be found. Decent legal advice will avoid some pitfalls for the overanxious employer. Moreover, the replacement of a substantial number of strikers can predictably result in the destruction of the union's representational status. In brief, such a result is possible because strike replacements are entitled to vote in a decertification. Economic strikers who have been replaced may also vote, but even this right is lost after twelve months. As Schatzki has stated, the *Mackay* doctrine "is an invitation to the employer, if he is able, to rid himself of union adherents and the union."[25]

Doctrinal difficulties arise from *Mackay* in large part because the interests of employees, especially when the workers are engaged in conduct expressly protected by the statute, are generally accorded great significance in the act. The bizarre nature of *Mackay* is also apparent when contrasted with the Court's treatment of Section 8(a)(3), a provision barring discrimination to encourage or discourage membership, which at various times has been read to require proof of employer antiunion motivation. At certain times proof of motivation has been dispensed with because of the inherently destructive impact of the employer's action or because the Court, as in *Erie Resistor*, eschewed the search for motive and applied a balancing test, holding that the impact upon employee interests was more serious than the legitimate concerns of the employer.[26] The Court's constant fluctuations in this area are not relevant here, but it is significant that the current test enunciated in *NLRB* v. *Great Dane*[27] permits the Board to find a violation in "inherently destructive" situations without proof of antiunion animus and even despite proof that the employer acted pursuant to legitimate business considerations. The *Great Dane* doctrine has never been applied to the *Mackay* situation, but one can think of few actions more "destructive" of the right to strike than the permanent replacement of strikers.

Mackay has not only made impossible the attempt to intellectually rationalize much of the law that follows it, but its shadow falls across much of labor law. The dicta means, for instance, that the often troublesome issue whether particular activity is "protected," or encompassed under Section 7, is less significant than it first appears. Numerous articles have been written attempting to categorize or rationalize the kinds of employee activity included or excluded from the ambit of Section 7. *Mackay*, however, shows that the *functional difference* between "protected" and "unprotected" conduct is the difference between permanent replacement, on the one hand, and discharge prior to replacement on the other.[28] If employees are replaced, they need not be rehired at the termination of the strike irrespective of the protected nature of their activity. If striking employees are not replaced, they must be rehired if their activity is within the ambit of Section 7, for there is little justification for refusing to rehire strikers when they have not been replaced.

It is true that employers do not always replace strikers. The actual incidence of permanent replacement is unknown, but I think it occurs often enough to make the issue a serious one.[29] An employer's right to replace strikers will turn not only on the employer's views about the possible long-term effects of such action but also on other, nonlegal, considerations—the strength of the union and its ability to economically hurt the employer at the struck location or elsewhere, the norms and nature of the surrounding community, the tightness of the labor market and the skills of the strikers. An employer's "need" or desire to continue operations, therefore, does not guarantee that replacements either will be sought or will be found. It is likely, however, that replacements would be hired when the union is relatively weak, the community is not strongly prounion, the strikers are not highly skilled, and unemployed persons are available in the labor market. In short, the *Mackay* doctrine may well harm those employees in the weakest bargaining position.[30]

Possible justifications for *Mackay* have been asserted by writers attempting to rationally deal with its ramifications and to place it, however uncomfortably, within the received wisdom and traditional legal discourse. For instance, some suggest that the employer should be given the opportunity to attempt to operate during a strike. A possible factual premise for this conclusion, which itself contains certain unarticulated assumptions, is that employers are generally unable to find temporary, rather than permanent, replacements. Unfortunately, we simply have no way of determining how often and in what contexts this might be true. It obviously will not be universally true, and it might not operate in specific contexts at all times. Moreover, as a premise for a legal conclusion, it is of doubtful significance given the Court's rejection of this very justification for offering super-seniority in *Erie Resistor.*

Recognizing the modern emphasis on "balancing" of conflicting interests, an approach that realistically encompasses the balancing of economic weapons, perhaps the basis for *Mackay* is the notion that the right to replace is the employer's legitimate counterweapon to the strike. So strong is the modern emphasis on "balancing" rights that *Mackay* is often interpreted as giving some consideration to the impact upon strikers of their permanent replacement when the Supreme Court's own language shows that none was given. The "of course" of *Mackay* now is often interpreted to mean the employer's replacement of strikers is lawful because managerial interests outweigh those of the strikers to their job even though strikers engaged in activity expressly protected by federal law.[31] The seventh circuit, for instance, perceives *Mackay* as holding that the "employer's interest in continuing his business during a strike and the needed inducement of permanent employment to obtain replacements is a sufficient business justification overcoming protection for economic strikers."[32] Why the employer's interest is sufficient to destroy the statutory right to strike is not clear. The change from a classical mode of legal thought to the modern balancing mode has hardly affected Oliver Wendell Holmes, Jr.'s, dictum that the rules of law are based upon "considerations of policy and social advantage."[33]

A recent study found that operation during strikes is an increasingly common phenomenon.[34] The decision to operate, it found, was generally more economic than philosophical, occurring more often in periods of low rates of economic growth and of increasing competition for customers. The result, in decades such as the 1960s, for instance, was an increase in the cost of nonoperation. An important finding was that operation was basically a tactic designed to weaken the union or discourage organization elsewhere even though operation generally did reduce expected losses. The companies also avoided the loss of customers and nurtured their reputations as reliable sources of supply. Primarily, though, economic goals were joined with, or less significant than, tactical objectives. In either case, such gains are purchased by the destruction of the jobs of strikers.

No one would seriously question that employers possess significant countermeasures to union pressure, such as prestrike stockpiling, operating with supervisors and nonunion personnel, shifting work to nonstruck locations, subcontracting work, and perhaps even hiring temporary replacements. If the employer's opportunity to replace is seen as a statement of general economic policy, it should nevertheless be seen as an "opportunity" only—there is no guarantee that replacements will be found, no matter how economically important the enterprise may be.

Surely, under any notion of weapon balancing, a substantial case is necessary to support a doctrine that so substantially reduces the effectiveness of the right to strike. The "right to strike" upon risk of permanent job loss is a "right" the nature of which is appreciated only by lawyers.

In an irony of labor law, the explicit balancing of weapons is accepted, but only if the decision maker is the Supreme Court. Thus the Court can deny the "weapon" of superseniority because it could deal a "crippling blow to the strike effort" or approve the legality of a bargaining lockout,[35] but the NLRB is not permitted to "assess the relative economic power of the adversaries in the bargaining process and to deny weapons to one party or the other because of its assessment of that party's bargaining power."[36] The statement, based on a similar disapproval of Board weapon balancing in *NLRB* v. *Insurance Agents*,[37] assumes that textual analysis and legislative history resolve legal questions, a view seemingly at variance with experience. Given this view, however, *Mackay* would be wrong if it were based upon some notion of the need to equalize employer and union power. Yet, if the decision is not based on some calculus of relative power, or perhaps inherent managerial prerogatives, it is difficult to find any intelligible rationale.

In the world of labor relations, power and economic realities are often as, or even more, relevant and informative than legal rules. Although replacements, deemed "permanent," are hired, the pressure of the picket line may still cause economic loss and force employers to modify their plans. Sometimes the designation "permanent" is merely a bargaining stratagem, designed to weaken the union's resolve or alter its expectations downwards. Replacements, promised permanent status and risking the approbation of picketers and neighbors, often accept strikers' jobs only to be unceremoniously dumped when a strike settlement is reached. This may have been foreseeable or the employer's intentions may have been altered by stronger-than-expected union pressure. In any event, the status as a "permanent" employee is often illusory.[38] Poststrike contract settlements that return strikers to their jobs arguably discriminate against replacements because of their nonunion or antiunion activity in violation of 8(a)(3) and 8(b)(2),[39] although the NLRB has not so ruled. Strike settlements calling for the allocation of jobs on the basis of seniority normally remove the strike replacements effectively,[40] but unfair labor practice charges filed by replacements who are in turn replaced are routinely dismissed. Employer promises of permanency also seem worthless. Such promises are either unenforceable under state law, given the normal rule that all employment contracts are terminable at will unless a specific term has been set out in a written agreement, or the application of state law may be barred by preemptive effect of superior federal law.[41] The result is that replacements are often pawns in a labor-management struggle.

A replacement is "permanent" if the employer so designates the employee or manifests such an intent,[42] and, as noted, there is no legal necessity for the employer to prove the need to grant permanent, as opposed to temporary, status. The evidence would admittedly be difficult to obtain and would, in any event, be in the possession of the employer. Yet, as noted above, the employer may negotiate with the union to "depermanentize" the "permanent" replacement. Or, should the strike be deemed or become a response to the employer's unfair labor practices, all replacements are legally "temporary" in effect, for an "unfair labor practice" striker is rehired, generally, pursuant to the NLRB order remedying the employer's violation.[43] An economic strike may become an unfair labor practice strike; if so, the replacements legally become temporary.[44]

There is some feeling that when replacements occur, the NLRB may be prone to find some employer violation, a warping of the act stemming directly from *Mackay*.[45] The parties, moreover, may have difficulty in assessing their legal position. If the NLRB disagrees with the union's belief that employer actions that precipitated the walkout are unfair labor practices, the employees are deemed economic strikers and are legally subject to permanent replacement. Should the employer incorrectly view its actions as legal, it may subject itself to back-pay liability when it refuses to rehire strikers and decides to retain strikebreakers.[46]

The basic issue is whether the employer should be able to maintain production during a strike through replacements, an event which historically has been the cause of much violence and bloodshed and, at a minimum, poststrike bitterness.[47] Possible factual premises underlying *Mackay* have been soundly attacked. The doctrine's destructive effect upon attempts to rationalize much of the law under Sections 8(a)(1) and 8(a)(3) has been demonstrated as well as the doctrine's anomaly given rules in other areas, *e.g.*, the right to cross picket lines.[48] It is true that we do not know the incidence of permanent replacement,[49] although the fairly steady stream of unfair labor practice charges arising out of such events suggests some regularity. More important, we do not know how often the *fear* of replacement operates to deter "protected" conduct or to curtail existing and legitimate economic pressure. Empirical research, however, would not seem required in order to demonstrate *Mackay*'s destructive effect on rights seemingly granted by Sections 7 and 13 and not limited by the statute or by legislative history.[50]

The long tenure of *Mackay*, the impossibility of rationalizing the holding, and the hopelessness with which labor law scholars view the opportunity for revision, suggest the doctrine is based on some deep-seated notion of employer prerogatives and rights. Attempts to rationalize *Mackay* in order to attack the dictum have encounter difficulty because they have assumed a particular kind of rational model, one based upon the policies and language of the act.[51] The *Mackay* doctrine, however, seems to be directly related to common-law notions that an employer owed no duty to rehire employees who had left for any reason.[52] An employer's right to maintain operations, as noted, is not a determination of socially good economic policy because not all employers could or would avail themselves of the "right" to permanently replace strikers. Rather, the basic notion seems to be that employers can seek to maintain operations because the operations are *theirs*—to deny this right is to deny a basic property. Is such an argument overdrawn? Perhaps so, but compare the Court's recent *Barlow* decision which invalidated a section of the Occupational Safety and Health Act permitting warrantless searches because of the employer's property interests, a decision that completely ignores the health and safety interests of employees working in the facility.[53] *Mackay* is illogical only if our rational system is based upon the stated policies of the act and the seemingly clear import of its provisions. The *Mackay* doctrine, however, reflects values that are not easily subject to tests of conventional rationality.

Maintaining production may be a high—and unstated—value as other sections of this paper will show. But the basic value seemingly operative here involves more than production—it is the value implicit in the recognition that employers possess the *option* to maintain production during strikes. It is not the NLRA that grants employers this option; rather, the language of the Court indicates that the right preexisted and was unaffected by the NLRA. Despite Section 7, strikes are not to be fully protected. Although most strikes must be permitted to some extent as a political and statutory matter, just as in the late nineteenth century ordinary strikes were not enjoined as a matter of political expedience,[54] strikes do interfere with the prerogatives of capital, and employers may seek to overcome this political reality.

Mackay, therefore, reflects a historical continuity of values reflected in judicial opinions. The traditional judicial deference given to productivity, hierarchical control, and continued production has thus remained significant after, as well as before, the NLRA. *Mackay* can be viewed as the almost automatic responses of judges raised in an era of acknowledged managerial freedom.[55] The Mackay employees could legally strike, as they could prior to the Wagner Act. They were, after all, exercising their right to "dispose of one's labor with full freedom." We are told, however, that these employees had "no right to be protected against competition. ..."[56] Thus, one of the critical problems of union organization, the competition of employees among themselves, is used to limit the effectiveness of concerted action. The quoted phrases are taken from two nineteenth-century decisions, *Plant* v. *Woods* and *Walker* v. *Cronin*. Although the phrases actually refer to nonstriking workers and not to strikers, the point is nevertheless the same. Nonstrikers, strikebreakers, and prospective employees have a right to "dispose of their own labor," and, therefore, their economic interests (which may undercut a strike or union standards) will be legally protected.[57] The replacements in *Mackay*, and third parties in cases like *Plant*, are judicial surrogates for the employer. In the interests of continued production or "competition," the employer may *permanently* replace strikers. After all, as the Massachusetts Supreme Judicial Court could state in 1896, "an employer has a right to engage all persons who are willing to work for him, at such prices as may be agreed upon. . . ."[58] Presumably, such freedom is not affected by the fact that the availability of positions is caused by an ongoing strike. Thus, one can construct a sympathetic dialogue between benches separated by forty years and a supposed social and legal revolution.

2

THE WAGNER ACT AND

THE NEW DEAL

REVIEWS OF EARLY Wagner Act litigation often focus upon the substantial number of victories won by labor.[1] Judicial opinions limited the scope of judicial review of Board decisions and, on other fronts, employed the First Amendment to protect picketing from state interference,[2] restricted the application of the Sherman Antitrust Act to labor by generously interpreting the meaning of the Norris-LaGuardia Act,[3] and limited the substantive scope of the antitrust laws.[4] At the same time, a number of important decisions like *Mackay* restricted the scope and purpose for which concerted activities could be employed. These limitations are noteworthy given the broad literal scope of Section 7, the stated purposes of the act, and, especially, the assumed significance of the New Deal.

After the national election of 1932, a new administration and Congress tried to carry out their mandate to respond to the Depression. The outlines of the New Deal had certainly not been a part of the campaign nor did the Democrats have clear proposals on issues of labor relations. Organized labor was not a significant force, having been reduced in 1933 to less than half of what its strength had been in 1920. The New Deal began at a time when less than 10 percent of the work force was organized.[5] The weakness of labor might explain why the 1932 campaign involved little discussion about unionism, but it also seems apparent that the new president's view on unions was not clearly sympathetic. As governor of New York, Roosevelt had sponsored social welfare programs, evincing a "faith in direct legislation to assist the needy rather than a desire to nurture unionism as an instrument to raise their standards."[6]

Moreover, the New Deal, at least at its inception, was certainly not a radical reform movement.[7] There was a willingness to experiment, but, at the start at least, "the administration sought no basic changes in the structure of the American economy. In fact, it worked within the viewpoint and framework of the business community." Recovery more than reform was the goal and its basic measure, the National Industrial Recovery Act (NIRA), "wrote the aspirations of businessmen into national policy."[8] The NIRA was based upon a business recovery plan formulated by the Chamber of Commerce as early as 1931: modify antitrust laws to permit industry to limit competition, raise prices, and restrict production. The National Industrial Recovery Act,[9] which became law on June 16, 1933, was a joint endeavor by business and government to promote recovery. The antitrust statutes were relaxed to permit agreements or codes within industries, in the interest of increasing employment and purchasing power. Codes were to regulate wages and hours of labor, set prices, and control production levels. Organization by employers was encouraged and the protection of organization by workers was felt to be either a necessary corollary or a political necessity.[10] Accordingly, in spite of the anxiety of some employers, Section 7(a) was included, reminiscent of the protection given the right to organize by the War Labor Board during World War I and borrowing much of its language from the stated policy of the Norris-LaGuardia Act,[11] a federal anti-injunction statute passed in 1932. Except for Section 7(a), however, the act was addressed to the needs of business, and primarily large businesses at that.

Section 7(a) required that every code of fair competition or agreement or license approved or issued under the title should contain the following conditions:

employees shall have the right to organize and bargain collectively through representatives of their own choosing, and shall be free from the interference, restraint or coercion of employers of labor, or their agents, in the designation of such representatives or in self-organization or in other concerted activities for the purpose of collective bargaining or other mutual aid or protection.[12]

It also required that no employee or employment seeker shall be required as a condition of employment to join any company union or to refrain from joining, organizing, or assisting a labor organization of his own choosing. Unions took this as a green light for an organizing drive and began extensive and successful campaigns, especially in coal, clothing, textiles, and iron and steel industries. Many employers, on the other hand, quickly turned to the organization of company unions, often company sponsored and controlled, which they believed permissible under Section 7(a). This occurred notably in steel, rubber, chemical, and automobile industries.[13]

The NIRA's recognition of labor rights in Section 7(a) was of secondary importance to the new administration and was set out, some say, "largely to create the impression of balanced treatment of business and labor."[14] Section 7(a) was certainly not forced on the government by labor disruption nor by the political power of the AFL. Suspicions of the government's commitment to unions seemed confirmed by the narrow reading given to Section 7(a) by the administration and the lack of vigorous enforcement for violations. Moreover, employer opposition to that section was lessened because it soon became clear not only that company unions could be used to avoid real collective bargaining[15] but also that the National Recovery Administration (NRA) had no real interest in encouraging collective bargaining.[16]

Conflicts arose earlier over the meaning of the right of employees to organize and to be free from interference, and on August 5, 1933, the president established a National Labor Board consisting of Senator Wagner and representatives from labor and industry.[17] Not until December 16, 1933, however, was an executive order issued that formalized the power of the Board and approved and ratified actions already taken. The Board's broadly stated functions were to settle by mediation, conciliation, or arbitration any controversies between employers and employees that tended to impede the purpose of the NIRA. In February 1934 further executive orders authorized the holding of elections by which employees could choose representatives for collective bargaining and authorized the Board, if it found that an employer had refused to recognize such a chosen representative of the employees or was in any way in violation of 7(a), to report to the compliance division of the NIRA or to the attorney general for appropriate action.[18] The National Labor Board was charged with the responsibility of trying to settle strikes, including disputes over recognition, as well as with the quasi-judicial function of interpreting 7(a) and preventing its violation. Not only did it try to combine mediation with enforcement or compliance, but it also chose to rely upon case-by-case adjudication rather than setting out general policy statements. The head of the NRA, General Hugh Johnson, and Donald R. Richberg, NRA General Counsel, set policy during the early months by issuing a series of statements interpreting 7(a) to mean that the company unions were legal. Moreover, exclusive representation was not required, which meant that minority or proportional representation was permitted. Statements also recognized that workers were free to bargain individually, that the closed shop was contrary to public policy, and that employers were not obliged to accept or agree to a contract.[19] Most seriously, the Board had no effective means of forcing an unwilling employer to comply.[20] Enforcement was a special problem because much of industry simply refused to cooperate.[21]

Senator Wagner (and others) became convinced that if the policy of 7(a) were to be made effective, further elaboration and provision for enforcement would be required. He thus introduced a bill in 1934 that explicitly declared the right to organize and set out unfair labor practices of employers, giving a federal agency power to seek enforcement of its orders in the federal courts.[22] As expected, strong opposition was voiced by the National Association of Manufacturers and the Chamber of Commerce and other important employer associations, but the bill was also lost due to the disinterest or opposition of the administration and the Senate Labor Committee. The committee, through Chairman Walsh, prepared its own bill which reflected the administration's continued optimism concerning the benefits of mediation. The bill also rejected the principle of exclusive representation, permitted company unions, and did not provide for an employer obligation to bargain.[23]

Outside of Congress, desperation was growing and labor unrest finally erupted in 1934. As Irving Bernstein noted, 1934 was one of those few years in which there occur "strikes and social upheavals of extraordinary importance, drama, and violence which ripped the cloak of civilized decorum from society, leaving exposed naked class conflict." The 1,856 strikes, involving about one and a half-million workers, included the virtual general strike in San Francisco in support of the longshoremen, the equally dramatic truck driver strike in Minneapolis, and important strikes by auto workers at Auto-Lite in Toledo and textile workers in New England and the South.[24] It was in this context that a simple resolution, designated Public Resolution 44,[25] was transmitted to Congress by the president, quickly enacted, and signed on June 19, 1934. Under the authority of this resolution, the president on June 29, 1934, established a National Labor Relations Board with three full-time public members.[26] Public resolution 44 also authorized the president to establish a board or boards to investigate any controversies arising under Section 7(a) which obstructed commerce. The Board could act as an arbitration panel, select arbitrators, or appoint boards of mediation,[27] and it could also conduct elections, order the production of documents, or secure the appearance of witnesses. Except for orders in connection with elections, which could now be enforced or reviewed by courts, the Board could obtain enforcement of orders, as before, only through the compliance machinery of the NIRA or the Department of Justice. The resolution also did not settle some basic issues, one of which was the question of majority rule.

The new National Labor Relations Board was as powerless as the ineffectual National Labor Board,[28] and the resolution was clearly a stop-gap measure designed to postpone a congressional battle over the government's role until a newly elected Congress convened some six months later.[29] This compromise was to continue only until the end of NIRA on June 16, 1935, when the act was declared unconstitutional.[30]

The promise of Section 7(a) proved illusory because employers found nothing in the law inconsistent with the formation of company unions, and they defied the Board whenever it attempted to proceed against them. Whatever its original intention, the NIRA intensified labor conflicts. Although the administration of the act denied its promise to labor, the act may well have encouraged the wave of labor organization and helped create an accelerated strike wave.[31] The act also led to governmental support for unions which would eventually result in the passage of the NLRA in 1935. The NIRA's failure encouraged Senator Wagner, for instance, to develop more effective legislation, and it helped create a climate for governmental protection of unions and regulation of collective bargaining. Wagner had vowed, at the time Resolution 44 was adopted, to try again in 1935. His determination was no doubt strengthened because many of the principles he thought to apply throughout industry were enacted for the railroads in the 1934 amendments to the Railway Labor Act.[32] Roosevelt, however, was never greatly interested in labor-management relations and gave the Wagner Bill his support only at the last minute and then under considerable political pressure.[33] Thus, except for the timing of the act's passage, the NLRA or Wagner Act cannot be considered a part of Roosevelt's New Deal legislation. Indeed, Raymond Moley explained Roosevelt's last-minute adoption of the act on the grounds that the president "needed the influence in votes of Wagner on so many pieces of legislation and partly because of the invalidation of the NIRA."[34] Roosevelt's need to "salvage a labor policy from . . . the

NRA's wreckage prompted a White House statement pledging full support for the Wagner Bill" after it had already passed the Senate.[35] It is ironic that the Supreme Court's decision also convinced some that the Wagner Act was unconstitutional and, thus, there would be little reason to oppose the bill on the legislative floor. More important, perhaps, was the rising militancy of labor. The importance of these issues cannot be measured with exactness, but it can be said that the act's passage owes much to the shrewdness and tenacity of its sponsor and the hospitable congressional climate created by the stunning Democratic victories in the 1934 elections.

The most common argument in favor of the Wagner Act was that it would reduce industrial strife. This argument was no doubt framed with an eye to the constitutional hurdle the act faced before the Supreme Court (preparation for Supreme Court review would consume most of the energies of the new labor board until 1937). The draftsmen had to justify federal action on the basis of the government's right to control interstate commerce, and it was by no means clear that a law governing labor-management relations had anything to do with interstate commerce. This does not necessarily suggest that the sponsors were dishonest in their contention that industrial strife would be reduced, for this surely was the overall goal of New Deal labor policy. They never contended that more than 25 percent of all industrial disputes were over union recognition, the principal area affected by the legislation. Beyond that, they could have believed that friction would be reduced by the mere act of bargaining. Such an article of faith is common even today.

The new National Labor Relations Board would gain from the experiences of its predecessors. A list of unfair labor practices was specified, barring in both general and specific terms employer actions thought harmful both to the organization of unions and to their effective participation in bargaining. These violations, set out in Section 8, were based upon a set of rights enunciated by Section 7, the ultimate source of all rights under the act. The numbering and wording of Section 7 could hardly be coincidental, and it was obviously designed to build upon the symbolic importance of Section 7(a) of the NIRA. The new Board was empowered to investigate charges, file complaints, hold hearings, subpoena testimony and other information, and issue complaints. In addition to being empowered to remedy unfair labor practices, the Board also could hold representation elections in order to determine whether employees desired to be represented by a union who, upon winning, would become the exclusive representative of all employees in the unit deemed appropriate by the NLRB. Thus, the act would encourage the peaceful resolution of representation disputes, bar those employer actions thought most disruptive, and, most important, compel employers to bargain in good faith with unions who were selected by employees to represent them or were designated as the representative via a NLRB-sponsored election.

Another theme was that the economy would be strengthened by independent unions which could insist upon more equitable division of profits, thereby maintaining high purchasing power. Therefore, the act was thought of, at least in part, as an anti-Depression device whereby private groups would raise wage rates and pump money into the economy. Wagner and a large portion of the Democratic party viewed the Depression as the result of underconsumption. This analysis was clearly set out in the introductory section of the Wagner Act: the "inequality of bargaining power between employees who do not possess full freedom of association or actual liberty of contract, and employers who are organized in the corporate or other forms of ownership association substantially burdens and affects the flow of commerce, and tends to aggravate recurrent business depressions, by depressing wage rates and the purchasing power of wage earners in industry and by preventing the stabilization of competitive wage rates and working conditions within and between industries."[36] Unionization would, therefore, require state support to balance the concentrated power of employers. Unionization was seen to possess positive social functions, and the state would support and encourage their growth while simultaneously restricting corporate power.

It is significant that political democracy should be given deeper roots by encouraging democratic processes in the work life of employees. Industrial democracy was vaguely defined, but the concept primarily involved a collective, and thus fairer, representation of individual employees and the joint creation of private law through collective bargaining. Vaguely, democracy in industry as well as in government was to be achieved, and "democracy in industry must be based on the same principles as democracy in government."[37] A New York Times article of April 13, 1937 (p. 20, col. 1), stated "democracy in industry means fair participation by those who work in the decisions vitally affecting their lives and livelihood; and . . . the workers in our great mass production industries can enjoy this participation only if allowed to organize and bargain collectively through representatives of their own choosing."[38] Through collective bargaining, employees would have an effective voice in determining the rules and conditions of their work lives, thereby achieving a higher level of human integrity and dignity.

The concept of industrial democracy then current certainly did not contemplate joint determination or representation on managerial boards as is found today in some European countries. Nevertheless, Senator Wagner ardently believed that industrial democracy was as essential as political democracy to the preservation of the American heritage.[39] When evaluating Senator Wagner's devotion to the proposition that democracy in the shop was an important ingredient in preserving political democracy, one must consider that many thought that American government was in great peril in 1935 from both internal and foreign threats.

Yet the most important theme in all Wagner's speeches was that the act would effect a greater economic stability through the creation of a better economic balance. Collective bargaining would promote both a higher level of real wages and a better distribution of the national income. Genuine collective bargaining could be carried on only by unions that were free from any domination by the employer.[40] Thus an avowed objective of the act was to promote the growth of a free and independent labor movement. Although both Section 7(a) of the NIRA and Section 7 of the NLRA were said merely to reflect previously established federal policies, the NLRA's strong endorsement for unions and their social and economic advantages had no legislative precedent.[41]

The federal government's expanded role in industrial relations and in the economy was caused, in part, by union economic and political activity during the Depression. The government, already deeply involved in labor relations alongside state, municipal, and judicial authorities, responded to economic conditions and union activity by encouraging collective bargaining and by subsidizing economic growth.[42] The growth of unions in this period should be seen as the result of worker initiative, but government played an important role in molding and directing this burst of energy.[43]

Yet, according to one view, the New Deal primarily represents a series of stratagems designed to strengthen and revitalize American capitalism. Business opposition is viewed as basically a small-firm phenomenon, while large corporations are seen as proponents of greater state intervention in an economy threatened by economic collapse as well as by working-class militancy. This view is based on a reversal of perception about twentieth-century liberalism; it is, under this view, a "movement of enlightened capitalists to save the corporate order."[44]

As Theda Skocpol perceptively notes, some facts do support this thesis. Business leaders were involved in the New Deal, and the New Dealers were committed to saving capitalism through reform.[45] Skocpol stresses, however, that the NIRA failed to bring about economic recovery, and this can be "attributed to the strong and misdirected political influence of (by corporate-liberal criteria) *insufficiently* class conscious capitalists."[46] Support for labor and the weak National Labor Board came from within government, primarily from Senator Wagner and his staff. The influence of the AFL was certainly negligible. Moreover, the opposition of the National Association of Manufacturers cannot be dismissed as the reaction of small business, because the organization was dominated by large businesses by the early 1930s.[47] The measures of the New Deal were accepted by business later as aiding the smooth growth of economic development and the stabilization of labor relations, but these measures were neither planned nor promoted by capitalists. There was little evidence that the ultimate effects of these actions would be beneficial. Instead, business feared the "immediate ill-effects of increased government power within the economy."[48] Thus, the New Deal cannot be explained as the result of careful strategies of corporate leaders to control the political process.

Even in the short run, New Deal legislation seems to have encouraged rather than lessened the incidence of strikes. Although causation can hardly be established, the incidence of strikes increased after the passage of the NIRA in 1933, tapered off after the congressional elections of 1934 and Public Resolution 44, but then increased dramatically in 1937—two years after the NLRA.[49]

A seemingly more helpful analysis might be that in times of crisis the state tends to act to stabilize or rationalize capitalism through an expansion of state power despite the opposition of business. Concessions may be granted to workers, but only in ways that can concurrently increase the power of the state as well.[50] Pressure from below combines with a desire to increase the institutional power of the state at crisis times, and, concurrently, such crises weaken the power of capital to block change.

3

SITDOWNS, SLOWDOWNS, AND THE

NARROWING OF FEDERAL PROTECTION

A GOOD DEAL of the debate on the Wagner Act concerned its "one-sidedness," in that only employer actions were proscribed. This argument had strong appeal to many opponents of the act even though it overlooked the long, hard-fought hearings on the bill. The act's proponents, relying on past judicial behavior, responded that the courts could not be trusted to interpret concepts such as "coercion" if they were applied to the activities of labor organizations. Senator Huey Long, for instance, stated that Congress had never "been able to draft a law yet which has not been whittled down. . . . By interpretation the laws have always been cut down."[1]

Nevertheless, and despite the breadth of Section 7, certain types of collective action were early deemed "unprotected," that is, outside the zone of the act's protection, by the courts or NLRB. Slowdowns and sit-ins, for instance, are types of strike activity or concerted action for "mutual aid or protection" within the apparent scope of Section 7. In most of the cases, a normal, full-scale strike would clearly be lawful. Nevertheless, it has long been clear that the section would not be given its literal scope—"concerted activities" would be a legal, not a factual, definition. The functional meaning of such a formula is that the scope of protected activities can be widened or narrowed by factors that need not respond to statutory policy, language, or history.[2] The choice of a subjective rather than an objective test for the scope of Section 7 encourages the use of subjective views by decision makers, as the common-law decisions of the late nineteenth century demonstrate. Moreover, neither the act nor its legislative history provides standards or even much illumination from which standards can be created. The foreseeable result is the creation of vague or unarticulated standards which are based upon premises that also are often unexpressed (or perhaps unperceived).

The condemnation of slowdowns seems based predominantly

upon a rejection of the belief that employees have an equal right to set their level of effort. The management of the workplace is assumed to be hierarchical and authoritarian. The treatment of sitdowns is based, in addition, upon the employer's status as owner and the rejection of employee property interests in their jobs or working conditions. Rather than reflecting community values, these decisions choose to support the values of only part of the community.

Just as the Board and courts have ruled that certain conduct, not necessarily unlawful, is nevertheless unprotected, it has also ruled that conduct illegal under federal law is unprotected.[3] Even employees who are striking in response to employer unfair labor practices, generally granted greater protection than employees seeking economic goals, may be refused reinstatement in certain situations if they have violated state law. It can be conceded that illegal conduct presents the least attractive case for granting Section 7 protection, but ordinary legal remedies do exist, and society's interests do not necessarily also require job loss in addition to normal criminal penalties in situations where illegal activity occurs. Thus, it is not inevitable that illegal activity by employees should lead to private penalties in addition to public sanctions or that employers should be able to act as private enforcers of social policy. Admittedly, there may be reasons for holding certain types of activity unprotected. It is difficult to make a strong case for protecting activity that constitutes a union unfair labor practice, thus violating Section 8(b) of the NLRA, or one that tries to induce the employer to violate Section 8(a).[4] Yet it is important to remember that the difference between unprotected and protected conduct is only the fact of replacement, and neither the striking employees nor the struck employer can generally be certain that the activity does indeed constitute or urge a violation of the act. Moreover, the resources and remedies of the NLRB are available to handle these cases.[5]

Cases like *NLRB v. Fansteel Metallurgical Corp.*,[6] which held that illegal conduct removed the otherwise proper right of reinstatement, adds a private punishment in no way related to the act's remedial scheme. The Court's expression of moral outrage is understandable although it was wrong-headed.[7] The sitdown that outraged the majority of the Court in *Fansteel,* for instance, was the arguable result of the promises of the Wagner Act and the New Deal and the inability of unions to enforce the act.

Broken promises color much of labor history in the 1930s. The initial growth of industrial unionism following the passage of the NIRA, for instance, was quickly thwarted by the actions of AFL unions, which were unwilling to countenance industrial unions or take militant action, and by the indifference of the federal government.[8] Organization rose dramatically again after the passage of the Wagner Act in 1935, but hopes were suspended by the vigorous constitutional attack directed at the new act. The battle for recognition, consequently, initially focused on concerted action rather than on the administrative procedures of the NLRB, and one of the first dramatic events was the rubber workers' sitdown in 1936. This job action, soon followed by the more famous sitdowns at General Motors, ultimately led to the establishment of union status in two basic industries.[9] By the end of 1936, the sitdown had become a full-blown labor weapon with significant advantages.[10]

From September 1936 through May 1937, sitdown strikes directly involved 484,711 workers and closed plants employing 600,000 others.[11] In March 1937 alone, 167,210 people engaged in 170 occupations of employer property.[12] Sitdowns occurred primarily in unorganized industries, and recognition was the critical goal.[13] The basic grievance was generally the refusal of employers to observe the NLRA and engage in collective bargaining.[14]

The movement began in the mass production industries where sitdowns could be an effective response to many kinds of workplace grievances. Sitdowns often seemed spontaneous and they were relatively easy to begin, although considerable skill and planning were required to continue the effort.[15] Significantly, the incidence of sitdowns declined after the Supreme Court's 1937 determination that the Wagner Act was constitutional.[16]

Historical accounts generally refer to public condemnation of the sitdown. Although public statements of opposition generally stem from newspaper editorials and anti-NLRA congressmen, liberal congressmen also doubted the sitdown's legality. Neither the AFL nor the CIO formally adopted the sitdown as a labor weapon, yet the CIO attempted to take advantage of it and even AFL unions engaged in sitdowns. The AFL did officially reject the appropriateness of the sitdown, perhaps because of interunion rivalry or because AFL president William Green is said to have feared that its use might lead to compulsory arbitration and other repressive legislation. The United Auto Workers and the United Rubber Workers, on the other hand, sanctioned the use of the rank-and-file weapon, but each sought to require international approval prior to its use. The CIO disfavored the use of sitdowns after bargaining was established, favoring the bargaining process instead of self-help actions during the term of an agreement.[17] The UAW's attempts to centralize decisions concerning concerted activity may have stemmed more from the perceived institutional need of a fledgling union to gain control and integrity than from a distaste for the sitdown as a weapon. In addition, leaders may have felt that poorly considered sitdowns threatened the gains already won. Thus, leaders might have said that "now that we are a fully legalized organization, we don't need to engage in guerrilla tactics, even when the cause is just." Strikes might endanger the "fruits of our struggle," and unity might be undercut by "well-intentioned but uncoordinated" actions at local levels. These statements are attributed not to UAW leaders in the 1930s but to Lech Walesa in November 1980, who was facing pressures different from, but not unlike, those of CIO leaders in the 1930s.[18]

The declaration that such activities are "unprotected" responds perhaps to one of the main themes of the New Deal, that is, the need to direct and focus worker activities in ways that "would not threaten the economy's basic market and profit mechanisms."[19] Moreover, unions began to discourage such actions in order to win favor with the government which, after all, had created agencies to aid unions, and, in turn, union officials. In addition, agencies and procedures that could help secure contracts also strengthened union officials.[20]

The narrowing of the Wagner Act was supplemented by the Taft-Hartley amendments of 1947 which, among other things, barred certain secondary strikes and boycotts and some sympathetic economic pressure. The result, especially after the Supreme Court's and the NLRB's glorification of, and deference to, grievance and arbitration procedures, was to limit collective activity primarily to the specific relation of employer and certified or legally recognized bargaining agent. Activities that were based on class or worker solidarity or that existed outside the contractual regime were often defined as outside the protective ambit of the law.[21]

There is little in the legislative history of the NLRA dealing with concerted activities that could be deemed unlawful. A reference to illegal employee activity is found in a Senate Committee response to the charge that the Wagner Act referred only to *employer* violations. The Senate Committee on Education and Labor noted that the Wagner-Connery Bill did not "prohibit fraud or violence" by employees.

"The Bill is not a mere police court measure. The remedies against such acts in the State and Federal courts and by the invocation of local police authorities are now adequate, as arrests and labor injunctions in industrial disputes throughout the country will attest."[22] Congress, moreover, explicitly rejected proposals in 1935 that the act should include prohibitions of coercion or violence by employees or unions.[23] Admittedly, it does not necessarily follow that because Congress refused to enjoin illegal employee action, employers were prohibited from punishing such activity. The argument seems fairly strong, however, that illegal activity should be punished by public authorities rather than serve as a limitation on the scope of Section 7. The argument, of course, seems more compelling for conduct that is not illegal, but only deemed "disloyal" or "indefensible."

Actions that are "unprotected" are not illegal in the sense that some civil or criminal penalty will necessarily follow from their performance. But such actions are also *not legal* in the sense that government will not protect workers engaging in such activity from employer retaliation. The designation "unprotected" removes any legality from the conduct it might otherwise have. Such a determination is a "legal" sanction even though penalty might only be felt via employer discipline. Thus, the NLRB's refusal to reinstate employees guilty of conduct thought beyond Section 7 is an affirmative governmental act not greatly different in effect from an express governmental prohibition of the conduct. The *lack* of federal protection permits employer discipline, and this is the employment sanction employees fear most. In effect, the employers' power to discipline activity that is in fact concerted is a far greater deterrent than a federal prohibition (leading to a cease-and-desist order, for instance). One difference, of course, is that employer discretion determines whether activity, concerted in fact, leads to discharge. Nevertheless, refusing to protect activity within the literal scope of Section 7 as a means of *punishment* seems inconsistent with the original statutory scheme. It is true, however, that the legislative history is fairly unhelpful, as can be seen by the continual failure of courts to refer to such history.

The issue was in doubt until *NLRB* v. *Fansteel Metallurgical Corp.*,[24] in 1939, after which employers could discharge or refuse to reinstate strikers for serious violence or destruction of property during a sitdown strike. Thereafter, the Board had to decide in each case whether the line had been passed or whether the purposes of the statute would be effectuated by requiring orders of reinstatement to all the strikers.[25] Even in cases involving conduct that violated federal statutes, repeated warnings were sounded by Board dissenters. In *American News Co.*,[26] for instance, a majority of the Board in 1944 held that strikers were not protected when they struck to compel the employer to grant wage increases without prior approval of the War Labor Board. The NLRB pointed out that it would have been unlawful for the employer to have granted the increases. Moreover, the federal price control act expressly enjoined the NLRB and other agencies "to work toward a stabilization of prices, fair and equitable wages, and cost of production." This was, therefore, the kind of statute to which the NLRA should be accommodated if it could reasonably be done. The Board conceded that Congress in 1935 had rejected proposals to include explicit regulation of employee misconduct, but it noted that misconduct had nevertheless been held to justify the discharge of employees. Although the Board conceded that it possessed no broad discretion to determine proper objectives of concerted activity, it held that Congress could not have intended it to ignore the character of a strike if its purpose was to induce a violation of federal law. *American News*, therefore, was the first decision to hold that protection could be withheld from strikers, not because of improper strike conduct, but because of the goal of the strike.[27]

This conclusion was not clearly compelled in 1944, and Harry Millis, the former Board Chairman, dissented. After studying the congressional reports and debates, Millis concluded that Congress could not have intended any limitation of the right to strike, especially given the broad language of Sections 7 and 13. Congress had specifically rejected numerous proposals to deny statutory protection to employees who strike for an unlawful purpose based on broad considerations of policy because it did not consider the act "a fitting instrument for the regulation of coercive conduct by employees or labor organizations . . . ," and it "did not intend to vest the Board with authority to inquire into the objectives of employee concerted activity in determining substantive rights under the Act." Millis argued that Congress, by adopting the unrestricted language of the Norris-La-Guardia Act, clearly meant to "guard against the revival of the discredited legality-of-object test." He distinguished *Fansteel* and similar cases on the problematic ground that they involved actions that were in themselves unlawful, apart from purpose. If widely applied, he felt the majority's view would motivate employers to continue disputes rather than encourage prompt settlement and a return to work. The Board in the exercise of discretion could adjust the remedy to the facts without removing all protections from concerted activity.[28]

Thompson Products, Inc.[29] indicates that the issue was still debatable after the war. The UAW struck for exclusive representation in disregard of a Board certification previously issued to another union. The Board upheld the discharges, yet a dissenter argued that the phrase "concerted activities" was intentionally borrowed from the Norris-LaGuardia Act in order to foreclose any inquiry into the purposes for which employees acted. The fear was that a "legal" definition would reintroduce "a convenient device whereby a judge might outlaw union conduct which was contrary to his own economic or social philosophy."

Certain cases, of course, avoid the fear expressed above by the Board dissenters. The act, especially Sections 8(a) and 8(b), provides standards which create a situation different from that existing under the open-textured common-law. The distinction, however, turns out to be more theoretical than real. The material that follows indicates the costs of venturing beyond statutory standards to limit the scope of Section 7, clearly demonstrating the legitimacy of the concerns of the Board dissenters.

One case graphically reflects the judicial attitude, involving worker attempts to control the pace of work and, thus, is highly significant for the major theme in this book. Unlike sitdowns (as in *Fansteel*, for instance), the slowdown does not violate state or federal law and, thus, employees who engage in such tactics cannot be deemed lawbreakers. If such activity is to be proscribed, it must be because there is some social or economic insidiousness inherent in slowdowns that Congress surely did not mean to countenance.

In *Elk Lumber Co.*[30] the employer lowered the pay rate of car loaders from an average $2.71 per hour on an incentive basis to $1.52½ an hour because of improvements that allegedly made car loaders' work easier and steadier. Because of the pay-scale change, which was a unilateral reduction in pay, the loaders decided to load one car per day, although they could have done more. Employees believed that one car per day was the quota at other plants in the same area and that it was a "good day's work at a dollar and a half."

The case reflects the classic battle over the amount of work to be done. What an employer buys in the labor market is a right to labor power, the worker's *capacity* to do work. Actual labor must be extracted, urged, or compelled from labor power. The classic conflict occurs because employers believe it is their interest to wring out of the employee the greatest amount of labor possible. Predictable conflict arises over how work is to be organized, the conditions and pace of work, the rights and obligations of each party, and the level of remuneration. A worker's interpretation of a "fair day's work" would not be the same as the employer's, which might in some cases more nearly reflect Frederick Taylor's view that a worker should perform all the work he or she can do without injury to health. Under this view, which will be more fully treated later in this volume, fairness tends to be defined as physiological maximum output and effort, while a worker's view might more closely equate the amount of labor to be expended as an amount "necessary to add to the product a value equal to the worker's pay. . . ."[31]

Efforts by employees to limit or regulate production have a long history which predates unions. The efforts of craft and unskilled workers should be seen as stemming from a quite different culture than the values underlying decisions such as *Elk Lumber*.[32] Workers traditionally maintained their own norms and customs of work which have undercut the expectations and formal rules of employers.[33] One machinist, for instance, was recorded protesting the stopwatch timing procedures of Taylorism: "We don't want to work as fast as we are able to. We want to work as fast as we think it's comfortable for us to work. We haven't come into existence for the purpose of seeing how great a task we can perform through a lifetime. We are trying to regulate our work so as to make it an auxiliary of our lives."[34] It is true that many examples exist of individualistic, success-driven workers who dissented from the "ethics of group solidarity."[35] Nevertheless, there seems clearly to be more than one work ethic.

In labor parlance, the employer's expectation of work output is called a "production standard," a goal to be reached. Workers' attempt to define the level at which they will expend energy, however, are called "output restrictions" or "slowdowns." The language may mean that Taylor's notion of output has become accepted, so that any production at a lesser pace than humanly possible must be a "restriction."[36] Also involved in the negative connotation of "output restrictions" is the notion that such matters are inappropriate for worker consideration, discretion, or participation in the first place.

The employees' determination of their work level in *Elk Lumber* was a response to the employer's unilateral reduction in the pay scale and, apparently, a change in the method of compensation. Moreover, the employer had never set a production quota nor had car loaders been warned that they would be discharged unless production was increased. Nevertheless, the employees who had "continued to work at their own pace" were discharged, and the NLRB upheld the discharges. The Board held that the car loaders' action, usually referred to as a "slowdown," was not a protected concerted activity, although their action clearly fell within the literal scope of Section 7.

The Board did not explain what the employees were slowing down *from*, although presumably it was from their prior work level. It was irrelevant that the employer never set a production standard or that the employees' action was an attempt to tailor their output to the new, lower-wage scale. The Board technically did not find the slowdown, as such, to be the problem. Instead, the Board's test was whether the action of the employees was "so indefensible" as to warrant discharge. The protections of the act could be lost if the employees had an unlawful object or adopted an "improper means of achieving it. . . ." The statement hearkens back to the common-law conspiracy test, later applied in torts and injunction cases when labor regulation shifted to the civil jurisdiction of courts.[37] Despite an act designed to free labor activity from legal regulation and to modify common-law restrictions, the Board's test focused on "improper" means, a test not defined by criminal law or the act, but, rather, the views of the decision makers. The result is painfully ironic, for common-law judges were most criticized for reading their own political and economic predilections into the law,[38] and the improper means-ends test was criticized as permitting arbitrary, unbounded judicial discretion. The repeated use of such a test despite changes in formal law may indicate that no better doctrine is available, relevant, or appropriate or that the underlying notions of American labor law have not significantly been altered by the passage of the Wagner Act.

The focus in *Elk Lumber* was upon the *means* used by the car loaders because their *end* was clearly lawful. The test, similar to the one applied in nineteenth-century cases,[39] led to the same kind of result. The Board's views are clearly seen in the following statements: "To achieve this objective, however, they [the employees] adopted the plan of decreasing their production to the amount they considered adequate for the pay they were receiving. In effect, this constituted a refusal on their part to accept the terms of employment set by their employer without engaging in a stoppage, but to continue work on their own terms."[40]

This quotation speaks volumes about the state of labor-management relations in the United States. Although the employees could have struck, they could not remain on the job and "continue work on their own terms," even though the employer could unilaterally alter the process of car loading and subsequently reduce the pay scale. Thus, employees are not permitted to determine the amount of labor they can expend, even when no work quota has been set previously.

The NLRB's General Counsel unsuccessfully argued that a slowdown should only be condemned, if at all, after there has been a deliberate refusal to follow employer's orders or guidelines. Even this position, of course, assumes the employer's power to determine the appropriate amount of labor to be expended. The Board's response was that the workers knew their loading rate was perceived as unsatisfactory by the employer. The reduction in output was no doubt a bargaining tactic and, as such, employer knowledge and dissatisfaction would obviously have been required. Nevertheless, neither the absence of a set quota nor a warning was deemed critical given the fact that the workers "continued to load fewer cars a day than they could have loaded, or than they would have loaded, for more money." The teachings of Frederick Taylor apply—employees are expected to work at peak performance, even when there is a unilateral reduction in their pay scale.

Ironically, decisions of the Supreme Court have held that the use of unprotected activity does not constitute bad-faith bargaining and, recently, the Court decided that state courts could not enjoin unprotected activity. After the Supreme Court's decisions in *Insurance Agents*,[41] holding that slowdowns do not constitute bad-faith bargaining and in *Lodge 76, IAM*,[42] holding that state courts cannot enjoin unprotected partial strikes, why can it not be argued that partial strikes should be protected? If such activity is to be left free from any regulation, state or federal, as the Supreme Court has held, why is it that the employer can punish for these actions? If states may not regulate such conduct because their intervention will deter activity meant to be protected, is it not possible to argue that the employer's power to discharge or to threaten discharge would be a far greater deterrent to partial strikes than a state court injunction? The answer seems to be clear, suggesting that some other explanation exists for the result, because it seems likely that slowdowns and other partial strikes will continue to be deemed unprotected.

One possibility, of course, is that although neither the federal agency nor the state courts can intervene or enjoin such activity, private parties nevertheless can exercise their economic power. That is, the two cases mentioned above arguably suggest that these matters should be resolved through private economic warfare rather than through the intervention of law. But if that is the case, why not simply call these activities protected rather than unprotected? The battle could then rage on in a private way without the law playing a role. After all, the only difference between protected and unprotected conduct is that in one case replacement must precede discharge and in the other it need not.

What is the most rational way to analyze the traditional condemnations of slowdowns as in *Elk Lumber* and similar job actions? My students and I have wrestled with this problem for years, with little success. Why not, for instance, permit a less economically harmful action like a slowdown in situations where a strike would be permissible? Do the rules of the game require that both parties must bear economic hardship in order for employees to engage in protected activity, so that employees should bear the risks of a full-scale strike? This, of course, might limit the number of strikes because it forces employees to use the ultimate—and most risky—weapon or none at all. A strike subjects workers to a loss of pay, related economic harm, and mental anxiety, as well as to the risk of replacement under *Mackay* (although this is true of all job actions). Although some strikes will be deterred, others will nevertheless occur, causing economic harm to employees and their employer. Why should the law encourage this result?

It may be that slowdowns, being covert in nature, are difficult to pinpoint, leaving the employer few adequate responses. The Supreme Court had earlier suggested that an employer has no way to respond to a slowdown: certain weapons cannot be permitted for "the management would be disabled from any kind of self-help to cope with these coercive tactics of the union except to submit to its undeclared demands."[43] Similar sentiments have been expressed by Archibald Cox: slowdowns "cost employees nothing and, if they were protected activities, management would be helpless to resist. Hence such weapons are too effective to permit them to be part of the employee's arsenal."[44] This argument assumes, however, that some notion of fairness or equivalence of bargaining power is required by the NLRA, a suggestion negated by common experience and ruled out for express consideration by the Supreme Court itself.

Cox acknowledges, moreover, that the employer possesses countermeasures. Employees engaging in slowdowns need not be treated better than economic strikers[45] and, thus, they can be replaced. The employer may also be able in most cases to reduce pay to match the reduction in output.[46] Thus, because countermeasures are present, it would arguably seem better in general to expand the scope of protected activities and leave the conflict to private economic struggle.

If the Supreme Court meant that an employer has no *effective* responses, it may be merely saying that these weapons give unions too much power and, thus, such weapons "unbalance" the proper relationship between the parties in some abstract way. But this argument involves a determination of the proper balance of power and puts the Court in the position of allocating economic weapons. Yet, the Court, in two decisions already referred to, made clear that the Board (at least) is not to be the "arbiter of economic weapons" and is not to make decisions based on what it believes should be the proper balance of power between the parties.[47]

The argument that slowdowns "cost employes nothing" also seems doubtful. Any concerted effort involves the expenditure of time and energy, and its failure could "cost" the union in terms of future willingness to act in a concerted manner. Presumably, however, Cox meant that a slowdown does not "cost" in the sense that no pay is lost. This is not the case for employees working on incentive systems, however, and, in any event, this argument presumes that employers cannot or will not act to counter a slowdown by creating their own economic pain.

If employers can discharge employees for "quickie" strikes or slowdowns, there would seem to be little harm in permitting the employer to seek state injunctive aid. In the recent *Lodge 76* decision, however, the Court found that Congress intended such employee activity to be free of state regulation even though it was neither protected nor prohibited by federal law. In referring to the relative deterrent effect of injunctions, the Court felt than an injunction might not be the less potent recourse but, rather, could be the result of the employer's inability to overcome union tactics by "its own economic self-help means." The Court clearly did not confront the "protected" issue, although it seemed to accept the notion that such action was unprotected, for it listed discharge[48] as an available self-help option. If self-help is unavailing, however, no federal or state remedy exists. The argument raised here is that if such activity is to be free of *any* regulation, it arguably should also be free of what may be the most potent response—discharge.

These arguments and responses parallel portions of the *Mackay* analysis. Labor law scholarship contains many areas where similar point and counterpoint positions are based upon empirical assertions without empirical evidence. Nevertheless, and unhampered by this concern at this point, it seems reasonable to assert that the employer's presumed lack of countermeasures is mistaken. Moreover, the stress on the slowdown's effectiveness suggests a balancing of weapons that the Court has ruled improper in other contexts.

Many of these issues have been forcefully argued by Julius Getman,[49] leading to a revealing response by Kenneth Lopatka. Lopatka rejects any argument based upon the employer's ability to respond, a response of some potential force, but, revealingly, he states that the question is whether the conduct "deserves federal blessing and encouragement."[50] Except for citing precedent, however, Lopatka gives us little information as to how that determination is to be made.[51] Lopatka's principle is simply a restatement of dogma which assumes the underlying value without dealing with it. Thus, he argues that "a refusal to confer federally enforced job security on employees who pick and choose among their tasks or hours, work at their own pace, or work sporadically, rests on a comprehensible and confinable principle." The "loss of protection inheres in the fact that the employees presume to work on their own terms . . . when their employer has offered remuneration and continued employment only for full service." Even though employees may strike or picket while *off duty*, Lopatka argues that there is a great public consensus supporting the view that the "employer, not the employees, sets the terms of employment; the former has the right to expect full service on those terms if the latter chooses to work at all."[52]

But the asserted "principle" is hollow. It does not really separate strikes protected under Section 7 from less than full strikes except by assuming in a circular fashion that only "full strikes fall within section 7." If employers pay for full service, then arguably a strike is also inconsistent with employment, for the employer may not expect, and certainly abhors, strikes or any kind of work action. Second, "quickie" or intermittent strikes, for instance, are strikes—employees do cease work, albeit for short periods. Why should length or duration of a stoppage be relevant to protection?

Third, Lopatka overlooks the fact that the battle is not over "job security" at all, for calling the activity *protected* hardly protects employees—it merely restricts employer response by requiring a replacement before discharge. Thus, except for penalizing employees for certain conduct, there is little "productivity" reason for permitting discharge *prior* to locating a replacement.

Finally, we have no empirical evidence as to the incidence of partial strikes and there is little evidence of any "consensus." Lopatka assumes that unions refrain from partial strikes,[53] as does Getman, although the evidence is not in. Even so, there may be tactical reasons for such restraint. Indeed, the fact that such action is unprotected at present may be the chief reason for such forbearance!

The entire debate exemplifies the extent to which legal writing eschews the discussion of basic value conflicts. Lopatka, like the Board and the courts, states his principle as *ipse dixit*. The "principle" assumes certain values without discussing them and is not intellectually sound as expressed. Principles built upon such tenuous bases cannot help causing continued litigation and a series of unprincipled decisions.

The opposition to partial strikes, then, seems not to rest on a perceived imbalance of bargaining power or upon a presumed inability of employers to respond. It is true, of course, that if the only options are striking or not striking, employees might hypothetically strike less often than they might engage in lesser actions such as slowdowns. Moreover, a strike economically hurts the employees as well as the employer and, thus, encouraging full-scale struggle may lead more quickly to a resolution of the dispute. Again, little empirical evidence exists to support or criticize this sometimes-mentioned rationale. It is possible that by encouraging only full-scale strikes, the law would lengthen those strikes that do occur because each carries an emotional backlog. In any event, why force employees to opt for a total strike which hurts them, as well as their employer, more than a partial strike?[54]

It may be more rational to argue that there is something else that condemns partial strikes, something that cuts closer to the bone and is perhaps clearly involved in other protected activity cases. In slowdown situations like *Elk Lumber*, for instance, there may be some substance in the Board's statements that employees cannot remain at work and work "on their own terms." The key to the legal condemnation of such activity is the rejection of the notion that employees have an equal right to determine their level of effort. Thus, the Board has quoted approvingly from a seventh circuit decision: "We are aware of no law or logic that gives the employee the right to work upon terms prescribed solely by him." Employees could strike but could not "work upon their own notion of the terms which should prevail."[55] Employees who are unwilling to strike, of course, must work at terms prescribed solely by their employer, but such an authoritarian structure is simply accepted. The message thus far seems clear, clearer than most of the writing in this area would suggest. Strikes are permitted, but employer control over production and the production process remains paramount.

The notion that employees may not "continue to work and remain at their positions, accepting the wages paid them, and at the same time select what part of their allotted tasks they care to perform of their own volition, or refuse openly or secretly, to the employer's damage, to do other work"[56] has been applied with varying degrees of explicitness in a variety of cases that involve the employer's hegemony over the production process, e.g., refusing to work overtime, to process orders from a struck plant, to obey work orders, or engaging in intermittent work stoppages.[57] Such rulings, Cox notes, may "reflect an apparently deep-seated community sentiment. Despite their obvious effectiveness neither the slowdown nor similar practices have taken hold in the American labor movement, and there can be little doubt of the general public condemnation of occupying a job and taking pay while simultaneously refusing to perform the services required."[58] The actual incidence of slowdowns has not been empirically measured, although the creation of intragroup norms by which employees create and enforce group production standards has long been noted. Production levels have been the subject of tacit negotiation between employees and employers or tacit agreement among employees for centuries. In any event, we are here talking about slowdowns or other actions, not as a way of life, but as a tactic used in a particular dispute either to pressure the employer or to respond to an employer action.

The extent of "social condemnation" is also not clear, and such a perception seems based on the views of only part of the community. "Deep-seated community sentiments" are sometimes cited to justify results that reflect the views of only portions of the community, yet, ironically, the very same writers often acknowledge the lack of a broad consensus over labor goals and values in the United States.

Nevertheless, it seems that refusals to work overtime, slowdowns, partial strikes, or intermittent work stoppages are perceived as interfering directly with the employer's power to plan ahead and to direct the work force. Intermittent work stoppages or refusals to work overtime, for instance, make production planning more difficult and are thought by employers to interfere with their right to control the work process. Slowdowns involve employee participation in determining the rate at which they work. Legal decision makers must be saying that this invasion of the employer's "prerogative" to control the pace and programming of work is improper. These weapons are clearly attempts by employees to gain control over the production process and over their work lives, even though they may only be used as bargaining weapons. Again, inherent prerogatives exist that seemingly remain unaffected by the passage of the NLRA.

These prerogatives could be based upon property or contract notions, although the language of contract seems more accommodating. A concerted refusal to work overtime, for instance, is also deemed unprotected[59] even though it may be a nonpermanent device aimed at gaining bargaining concessions. Like the other weapons discussed, it is "part and parcel" of the bargaining process and is not subject to a state court injunction. Yet, participation can result in discharge. Why is it assumed that employees are obliged to serve overtime despite the absence of any contractual requirement, so that a refusal to serve may lead to discharge? The result assumes an implied obligation that has the effect of creating an express contract clause mandating overtime.

It seems that the Board and courts are defining the employment agreement or, alternatively, defining the employees' *status* in the enterprise. This status involves, in part, a particular conception of workers' time. The Court has stated that "working time is for work," leading to decisions permitting employers to validly prohibit union solicitation on working time.[60] "Time outside working hours, whether before or after work, or during luncheon or rest periods, is an employee's time to use as he wishes without unreasonable restraint, although the employee is on company property."[61] However, as the quotation suggests, such "free" time is qualifiable by special circumstances that make restrictions necessary "in order to maintain production or discipline."[62]

Thus, "working time is for work," but nonworking time may also be "for work." Such a recognition is based, first, upon the presence of the employee on the plant property and, second, upon the superior needs of production. Cases raising questions concerning employee and employer time, e.g., union solicitation cases, are often treated as "property" cases, but such a focus is not completely satisfying. Admittedly, such a basis may help explain to some extent why nonemployee organizers (not employed by the target company) can be barred from plant property altogether unless no reasonable, alternative channels of communication exist.[63] In addition, a conception of employer ownership may explain those surprising decisions holding that even an off-duty employee is to be treated as a nonemployee for purposes of the solicitation rules.[64] As will be noted subsequently, property plays a large role in explaining the basis of many decisions. Yet, presumed employer control does not explain why, for instance, nonworking-time solicitation by employees is generally protected. The employer's "invitation" to employees to enter the plant probably does not include the right to engage in union solicitation, to use the language of torts. Property, however, is inextricably tied to the interests of productivity, and concerted action or solicitation that does not clearly interfere will not be proscribed.

Employee refusals to work overtime, like union solicitation on working time, challenges the notion that employers have the power to control all employee actions, especially the level and timing of labor. Employees quickly learn that working time is for work, so that a conversation with a coworker can lead to discipline, although the employer may freely order the employee to forego or move a lunch or break period.[65] Similarly, refusals to work overtime, even when used as a pressure device, suggest that employees believe they have or should have control over their nonwork time. Such actions not only interfere with unfettered employer planning (unilateral planning, that is), but raise questions of relative power. The legal rules effectively fill in the employment contract—the employer may expand the scope of working time, or negate free time, in the interests of unilateral production planning.[66]

Even in those areas in which property notions are preeminent, such as solicitation on company property, the Court seems confused between some notion of inherent, absolute property rights and rights to manage the enterprise which inhere in possession. Justice Powell, for instance, has recently explained that the union organizers in *Bab-*

cock & Wilcox, who were not employed by the firm, "sought to trespass on the employer's property, whereas the employees in *Republic Aviation* who were permitted to solicit on nonwork time did not."[67] A "different balance was struck when the organizational activity was carried on by employees already rightfully on the employer's property, since the employer's management interest rather than his property interests were there involved."[68]

Babcock-Wilcox was decided in 1956, long after the original passage of the Wagner Act and, indeed, after the Taft-Hartley amendments, yet the Court's new explanation seems close to the mark. The *Babcock-Wilcox* Court had said that the distinction between employees and nonemployees is "one of substance" and that access of nonemployees is "governed by a different consideration." What that consideration or that substance was, however, was stated only obliquely: "Organization rights are granted to workers by the same authority, the National Government, that preserves property rights. Accommodation between the two must be obtained with as little destruction of one as is consistent with the maintenance of the other."[69]

These comments reveal much about basic assumptions underlying labor law. The statute obviously has an impact because union organizers would otherwise never have any access rights, at least under federal law. "Employees" are granted solicitation rights, however, even though the employer might well argue that such activity is outside the scope of its "invitation."[70] This modification of common-law trespass law only goes so far, however, as solicitation and distribution rights of employees can be limited in various situations where "managerial interests" are at stake. Nevertheless, the existence of the statute suggests that the application of trespass or common-law "invitee" notions to these questions is highly problematical.

First, the basic right involved, as the Court implicitly recognizes, is the right of employees to *receive* information about unionization. Even the Court recognized that the "right of self-organization depends in some measure on the ability of employees to learn the advantages of self-organization from others."[71] Nevertheless, the right is transformed from the interest of employees to *receive* information to the right of organizers to *present* information, and the Court then develops categories based to some extent on common-law property notions, which historically distinguished between classes of persons on private property.

Even at this point, however, there is an important irony, for statutory rights are given to "employees" which "shall include any employee, and shall not be limited to employees of a particular employer. . . ."[72] This clear recognition that statutory rights are given to persons who may not be employed by the relevant employer is the result of congressional reaction to decisions such as *Duplex* v. *Deering*,[73] and was ultimately reflected in similar language in the Norris-LaGuardia Act.[74] This history strongly supports the argument that "nonemployee" organizers are protected under the statute, not solely because "employees" of a particular employer may need their assistance, but because nonemployee organizers, as statutory "employees," have rights of their own to "form . . . or assist labor organizations."[75] The Court, however, feels free to apply common-law property notions without any felt need to respond to either the language of the act or its history.

Second, the language quoted from *Babcock* indicates that whereas organizational rights are "granted," property rights are "preserved" by federal law. The language used suggests that the necessary accommodation should aim at as "little destruction" of statutory rights as necessary in the interests of the "maintenance" of property rights. Such valuing thus explains why the difference in organizers' status is "one of substance." In fact, federal law does not protect property or the right to exclude but only the right to compensation when property is "taken" by the state for some public purpose, pursuant to due process and under its power of eminent domain.

Third, when employees are "rightfully" on the premises, only the employer's management interests rather than its (presumably more profound) "property interests" are involved. Perhaps some significant notion underlies this distinction,[76] but, in any event, the language again suggests that certain common-law property notions have not been altered by the passage of the act.

The Court's perception of employer property rights in the above cases helps to explain the reaction to slowdowns and similar activity. The normal analysis of these cases focuses on the *kind* of activity involved, for run-of-the-mill strikes for similar goals are generally protected. The difficulty in rationalizing the decisions may stem from the fact that the perceived problem is actually one of improper objective rather than improper means. It is the challenge to the employer's control of production, and the state's unwillingness to sanction such challenges, which seems to underlie these cases. True, strikes for similar objectives are protected, but such strikes are clearly protected by statute and there is little room for judicial maneuvering. Cases like *Elk Lumber* are important, for they show that the purported NLRA goal of industrial democracy, vague and elusive as it may be, is not to be gained by the adoption of a participatory or codetermination model. Perhaps the "divine right of kings" was dead, but the result is closer to a constitutional monarchy than a codetermination model.[77] Answers were required for questions on which no consensus or general understanding existed, and the open-textured nature of the statute opened the door to judicial creativity. The choices made tended to be based upon the echoes of the past rather than the reverberations of the present or the possibilities of the future.[78]

Another significance of decisions like *Elk Lumber* is the implicit assumption that worker attempts to control the work environment is somehow novel and violative of long-standing practices. Yet, one of the primary sources of labor-management strife in the late nineteenth and early twentieth century was the struggle for control of work. Employers sought to break any barrier that limited their freedom to control and direct new technology as well as labor. A key obstacle was the norms of craft or skilled employees and the "legislation" of craft unions. Skilled employees and unions had been able to impose upon management a variety of shop rules dealing with the introduction of new machines, techniques or technology, apprenticeships or wage determination methods.[79]

Work rules, such as the machinists' one man–one machine rule, obviously had an effect on production levels, a desired goal for employees concerned with maximizing employment levels. But employees were also concerned about the speed of the work process and new methods of wage determination such as piece work. The general discussion of these rules, referred to objectively as "restrictive practices," usually ignores that the rules sometimes protected workers against socially undesirable or unsafe conditions. Efficiency, even if we could always predict when it would occur, is not necessarily the only value in the employment relationship.[80]

Much of the skilled workers' influence or power over production in the mid- to late nineteenth century was based upon their knowledge of the work processes rather than upon collective power alone. These employees were not first-generation factory workers maintaining preindustrial life patterns, but second- and third-generation factory employees.[81] Craftsmen were often highly autonomous, having wide discretion, for instance, in the performance of their work or in the hiring of helpers to be paid out of their own wages.[82] Moreover, groups of workers, not necessarily formally organized in unions, might negotiate a price for work, allocate rates of pay and work among each other, divide up the level of output, and determine hiring and job progression procedures.

Employers consistently sought to simplify jobs, reduce skill content, thereby "rationalizing" work, in order to wrest control of production from skilled workers. At the same time, the introduction of new technology profoundly affected social relations in the workplace. In 1920 Myron Watkins, a political economist who worked in Detroit's automobile factories, concluded that "the consequence of the rigid application of standardization in production has been the standardization of labor. Along with the interchangeability of parts goes the interchangeability of producers."[83] Indeed, auto factory managers and production engineers went far beyond the mere dilution of skills; skills were homogenized so that it became impossible to differentiate one set of skills from another. A new definition of skill came into existence, emphasizing the attributes of dexterity and speed.

There is evidence to suggest that in the late nineteenth and early twentieth century the structure of work relationships in the carriage and wagon shops, the steel industry, small automobile factories, and machine and metal-working shops retained an essential artisanal character. Generally, skilled mechanics directed the labor process and performed the principal productive operations in the workshop or factory. Skilled artisans often supervised unskilled workers or helpers who assisted them and did the more strenuous tasks in the shop.

Nevertheless, as mechanization advanced through the late nineteenth century, the specialist began to emerge as an important figure in the shop or factory. The nineteenth-century specialist still retained significant productive skills. Although the division of labor might have narrowed the range of skill or the number or range of machines operated, these workers still retained the crucial combination of mental and manual skills that characterized the skilled workers' routines. The new workers at the Ford plant, however, were shaped to meet the demands of fairly rigid machines. The new specialist, unlike his nineteenth-century predecessor, possessed few traditional skills. Skills now could be easily transferred to other machines or other work situations. As Watkins lamented, operating a machine now required virtually no thought or judgment.[84]

Employer success in the twentieth century broke this last vestige of preindustrial artisan independence, but we should not assume that worker attempts to gain some measure of control over production somehow ceased. As David Montgomery has noted, "some degree of worker restriction of output remained, but on a guerrilla basis—as defiance of management's will and instructions, as sabotage. The small informal work group persisted, not as an agency of explicit control, as it had been under craft unionism, but as a submerged, impenetrable obstacle to management's sovereignty."[85] Nor should we assume that the victory of employers, perhaps achieved by the 1920s, was necessarily enshrined in the NLRA as a social value.

Finally, cases like *Elk Lumber* reflect the conflict of cultural norms present in many areas of employment. Whereas management efficiency is seen in terms of the lowest per-unit cost of production, worker perceptions of fairness and justice is quite different. "Throughout the industries workers maintained their own work norms and work customs, which effectively undercut the formal factory masters."[86] The long battle over piece work reflects this conflict, and the conflict is quite similar to the situation in *Elk*. Piece work was viewed by skilled workers as not only a "threat to their power over working conditions," but also as "pure and simple theft."[87] As a union officer noted: "A change in method of work in a shop whereby each workman will have to expend 50 to 100 percent more energy, which in turn will produce 50 to 100 percent more product for the same pay, fully merits . . . the idea of robbery."[88] As employees increased production to take advantage of piece-work rates, the rates were routinely cut back, a process recognized even by employers. It is this kind of conflict of "efficiency" versus perceptions of fairness that underlies cases like *Elk Lumber*. The legal decision must be based upon a choice among conflicting cultural norms.

A similar area of contention which cuts, perhaps, even deeper is the conflict over time. The phrase "working time is for work" is routinely accepted, but the conflicts subsumed by the phrase are usually ignored. There is, as noted, a constant tension between employee and employer definitions of work and nonwork time, just as conflict exists over the appropriate level of work effort over a specified period of time. The phrase, as usually used, assumes that employers may determine the appropriate *level* of work to be expended.

In the nineteenth century, the conflict was usually referred to in terms of efficiency and morality. The industrial revolution caused a serious conflict between the concept of working time held by a first generation of industrial workers and the views of owners. The need to impose the rigor of factory time on people more used to irregular or natural rhythms of work was referred to as the need for "discipline."[89] The existence of "St. Monday" and other similar habits were a constant concern of entrepreneurs: "Monday is Sunday's brother: / Tuesday is such another. . . ."[90]

In modern employment, these conflicts are reflected not only in high rates of turnover or of absenteeism on Mondays and Fridays, but in worker attempts to alter the mind-deadening rhythms of assembly-line work. Thus, it is not uncommon to learn of workers, often working on piece rates, speeding up for certain periods of time and then resting, a pattern common both to many self-employed persons and, as E. P. Thompson has noted, to seventeenth-century workers: "The work pattern was one of alternate bouts of intense labour and of idleness, whenever men were in control of their own working lives."[91]

The notion that "working time is for work" is closely related to "time is money." Although generally perceived as trite, it is actually one of our most commonly accepted notions. Punctuality, discipline, and industriousness are virtues stressed in our schools as well as in office or factory. Many aspects of life become valuable in terms of money, and it is not surprising that time, or other human experience, is reduced to money as well.

"Working time is for work" because "the employer must *use* the time of his employee's labour, and see that it is not wasted: not the task but the value of time when reduced to money is dominant. Time is now currency: it is not passed but spent."[92] Thus, time is, indeed, money.

4

THE DEFINITION OF EMPLOYEES'

REAL INTERESTS: THE CONTINUITY

OF LEGAL VALUES

EVEN WHERE EMPLOYEES are engaged in actions with deep roots in the union movement, legal protection is often hedged or grudgingly given. The law relating to the right to engage in sympathy strikes or to respect another union's picket line, for instance, reflects this inclination. Before and after 1935, the legal system, as the relevant legal doctrines will demonstrate, assumes the ability to define the real interests of employees. These doctrines are affected by the assumption of an employer's superior status position, the employer's ownership of the enterprise, and the fear that control must be maintained to guard against employee irresponsibility. Explicit protection of the right to strike has not barred judicial limitations on certain types of strikes, normal components of strike activity, or other types of concerted pressure.

Affirmative protection of the right to strike may seem to be an ironic component of an act designed in large part to encourage industrial peace. But it was hoped that the strike or threat of strike would encourage collective bargaining, a process that would ultimately restrict the need or incidence of strikes. Perhaps the aim was to permit unions to "clobber . . . backward employers into submission, permitting the Court to cut back on the right to strike once the purpose was realized."[1] One need see no necessary relationship, especially since the CIO was unforeseen in 1937, and a serious restriction such as *Mackay* arose as early as 1939. Strikes were necessary to make collective bargaining work, and strikes would also serve as private means to carry out social objectives.[2] One social goal, like that of other New Deal legislation, was the strengthening of unions so that the purchasing power of workers would increase, thereby avoiding future economic depressions.[3]

By 1935, the option of prohibiting strikes was probably not within contemplation. Late nineteenth-century state courts would not enjoin ordinary strikes, apparently for practical political reasons, even though strikes could not intellectually be justified under their definition of competition.[4] A strike by Elk Lumber car loaders, for instance, would probably be protected pre- or post-1935. A reduction in their rate of effort while remaining on the job, however, would be seen as an attempt to challenge employer hegemony over employment and, thus, receive no protection either before or after 1935. According to the Massachusetts Supreme Court in 1905, competition between "employers and the employed, in the attempt of each class to obtain as large a share as possible of the income from their combined efforts in the industrial field" was only "so-called competition."[5] The court determined that this kind of struggle was not necessarily "competition" because it involved a conflict of different kinds of interests operating on different levels. Real competition, on the other hand, existed when businesses competed for the same customers or unions for the same jobs.[6] The categorization was important because "competition" was a justification or defense for inflicting economic harm.

[T]he Massachusetts court did not believe that workmen competed with their employers but were rather engaged in a joint productive effort with them to turn out goods which neither of them could produce alone. In its opinion, employers and their employees were not striving against each other on the same plane of endeavor and for the same thing. . . . Believing all this, the Massachusetts bench could not justify a single strike for higher wages as competition especially as it could not overlook the early judicial decisions holding strikes for wages unlawful because they are the very antithesis of competition. Actually, it did not try to do so. In spite of its feeling for classical theories of competition, the Massachusetts judges knew that strikes for wages and other direct benefits—in brief, all collective bargaining strikes—had to be made lawful as a matter of political expedience.[7]

A version of the common-law "means-ends" test distinguished between attempts by employees to seek "direct" benefits, a proper goal, and attempts to secure "indirect" benefits, which would be an improper, enjoinable aim. The "indirect" purpose was not strictly unlawful but was somehow insufficient to justify the economic harm caused. What was direct or indirect, of course, turned primarily on judicial attitudes. No legislative standards existed, and courts did not limit themselves to existing categories of criminal or tort law. Moreover, even if one matter is less directly involved with the defendant's vital interests, such an observation does not explain at all why it should be without legal protection.

In *Plant* v. *Woods*,[8] for instance, Judge Holmes differed from his colleagues in believing that an attempt to secure exclusive representation (or perhaps a closed shop) was justified. The case provides rich insights into judicial views. An injunction was granted against attempts by a union to induce a splinter group to return to the fold and was based on the Massachusetts court's determination that "the necessity that the plaintiffs should join this association is not so great. . . ." Obviously, the employees' concerns were deemed sufficiently "direct" to cause them to act concertedly. The court apparently felt that it, and not the employees, was the best judge of whether the goal was in the workers' interest.[9] The case is sometimes explained by a perversely narrow view of self-interest or an ignorance of reality, but the Massachusetts court may well have understood that the closed shop was perceived by unions to be a vital condition of bargaining power. Thus, in a later case, the Massachusetts court refused to enforce a closed-shop clause, there used as the union's defense to a damage action brought against it by a discharged employee. The court stressed again that the union acquired no "direct" benefit from a closed shop but, significantly, felt that the union secured "only" increased bargaining power. Such an object is "too remote to be considered a benefit in business . . ." in order to justify the infliction of economic harm.[10] But the court obviously had a broader concern than merely delineating a standard based on "directness" or "remoteness." The court barred the enforcement of closed-shop agreements because such promises could give unions "complete and absolute control of all the industries of the country." For then, "employers would be forced to yield to all their demands, or give up business. The attainment of such an object in the struggle with employers would not be competition, but monopoly." The court, however, actually feared not monopoly *per se*, but only *labor* monopoly, for concurrent decisions justified all kinds of monopolistic practices by employers and entrepreneurs as lawful "competition."[11]

The "justification" doctrine recognized the pursuit of self-interest or gain as socially important. The court viewed self-gain only in immediate pecuniary terms,[12] for it professed an inability to perceive employee self-interest in situations where something other than immediate economic gain was sought. The doctrine applied beyond the union-management situation, and it was sympathetic to strands in the common law that recognized one's pursuit of pecuniary gain while being indifferent or hostile to altruistic or class-based behavior. Johnny Weissmuller, law students were traditionally told, need not stoop to save a drowning child. Volunteers are disfavored. In the labor area, however, the notion has a special function that clearly presents issues of class solidarity.

Assume that employees seek to aid workers who are employed elsewhere. Their action may be considered "sympathetic," a term used to distinguish such actions from perhaps more understandable, economically self-interested actions. Sympathetic action may entail vocal or monetary support or actual concerted assistance, such as the refusal to cross a picket line. Although such activity is quite normal for American unionists, courts have had a fitful time dealing with such situations.[13] Because such action generally violated no existing criminal statute or category of tort law in most states, and because it would be legal for one person to so act, a few common-law courts actually protected such action.[14] Most state courts, however, required some "justification," with the range of justification varying in each state.[15] Defining justification in terms of the pursuit of self-gain means that sympathetic activity would not be protected in some states. The workers, it would be held, have no "stake," no economic interest, that would justify the economic harm caused by their support of workers elsewhere. A "sympathetic" judge, more imbued with this American labor tradition, might argue that self-interest *is* involved because those you aid today may return the favor tomorrow or because workers simply have a felt interest in protecting their brothers and sisters employed elsewhere. Whether or not workers think in these terms is not at all clear, and empirical data, as for most labor questions, is lacking. But it is interesting that protection for action basically noneconomic in nature may be sought by resorting to the underlying basis of the economic-stake notion itself, that is, that men or women basically act for economic motives, and it is this kind of action that should be recognized.

Charles Gregory rejected this attempt to circumvent the economic-stake requirement, stating that "courts seem to be correct in holding sympathetic strikes to be unjustifiable because of the absence of direct economic advantage." Gregory appreciates the "dangers" of such a position because he notes that many feel that the right to refrain from work is "a sort of civil right, not to be questioned on the basis of its purpose or objective." Indeed, Section 7 of the Wagner

Act, on its face at least, would seem to suggest such a wide scope of freedom for collective action. Nevertheless, Gregory feels courts should accept this "conceptual position" as the "basic principle from which they may grudgingly make concessions out of deference to the existing practical needs of the community as against the asserted economic needs and self-interest of the strikers in question." Although the meaning is not readily apparent, Gregory supports the common-law disdain of sympathetic action, and he does so in revealing language. He recognizes that sympathetic strikes (he does not expressly deal with other forms of sympathetic action) could be defended by stressing altruism rather than self-interest. But, says Gregory, courts "seem rightly to have made no allowance for sentimentality in this respect."[16] Support of coworkers, however, or of class interests, if you will, seems something more than "sentimentality" or altruism. Obviously sentiment and sympathy have "soft" connotations, opposed to "harder" terms such as "self-interest" or "economic advancement."

The issue is why self-interest should be the linchpin in the first place, and this is rarely explained, if at all. Gregory only tells us that in applying the self-interest "maxim," courts "have assumed that people will mind their own business . . . , realizing that the general run of people will place their own interests first and will go to considerable lengths to advance these interests." Why courts *should* foster this individualistic spirit, and thereby reject the expression of collective interest, is not explained.

Federal statutes, however, have not been kind to the common law's notion of limited self-interest. Section 20 of the Clayton Act, for instance, barred injunctions in certain types of disputes whether the dispute was between an "employer and employees, or between employers and employees. . . ." Situations falling within Section 20 were not only nonenjoinable but also not to be treated as "violations of any law of the United States." Although this language was drastically narrowed in the infamous *Duplex*[17] decision, the language was given new vigor in Frankfurter's tour de force in *Hutcheson.*[18] That decision used the broad definition of interest in Section 13 of the antiinjunction Norris-LaGuardia Act to reverse *Duplex* and revive the substantive portion of Section 20 of the Clayton Act. Although Norris-LaGuardia was premised upon a requirement that participants in labor dispute have a "direct or indirect" stake in the dispute, the statute was defined in extremely broad—and clear—terms. Many sympathy strikes would be included if carried on by employees who are "in the same industry, trade, craft, or occupation . . . or who are members of the same or *affiliated* organization of . . . employees. . . ."[19]

Similarly, the NLRA grants rights to "employees," defined broadly in Section 2(3) so as "not to be limited to the employees of a particular employer, unless the Act explicitly states otherwise. . . ." Moreover, the wellspring of employee rights, Section 7, grants employees the right to engage in concerted activities for the purpose of collective bargaining *or other mutual aid or protection.*"[20] The last phrase means that employees may engage in collective action beyond that focused solely on collective bargaining.

Older notions of self-interest and "directness" constantly arise despite this statutory history. Perhaps one example will suffice. No notion is more strongly embedded in trade-union consciousness than the respect for another union's picket line. Even an individual's respect for a picket line is "concerted" in the sense that the employee joins with other employees for "mutual aid or protection." This has long been the position of the NLRB and most appellate courts, even though, analytically, the situation is not unlike a slowdown or other job action where an employee "chooses" what part of the job will be performed.[21] Some courts are more doubtful and some are opposed. In language echoing common-law decisions, the first circuit court of appeals believes that such activity is at least "arguably unprotected" because the "employees' self-interest is not directly or indirectly implicated in the primary strike."[22]

Similar views were recently expressed by Justice Stevens, although in dissent. In *Buffalo Forge Co.* v. *United Steelworkers,*[23] the Court rejected what many thought was the most reasonable accommodation between the policy of enforcing collective agreements, primarily under NLRA section 301, and the anti-injunctive provisions of the Norris-LaGuardia Act. The Court held that federal courts could not enjoin a union's refusal to cross another union's picket line even though its collective agreement contained an arbitration clause under which the scope of the contractual no-strike clause could be determined. Justice Stevens's dissent is based, at least in part, upon his valuation of such activity:

Furthermore, a sympathy strike does not directly further the economic interests of the members of the striking local or contribute to the resolution of any dispute between that local, or its members, and the employer. On the contrary, it is the source of a new dispute which, if the strike goes forward, will impose costs on the strikers, the employer, and the public without prospect of any direct benefit to any of these parties. A rule that authorizes postponement of a sympathy strike pending an arbitrator's clarification of the no-strike clause will not critically impair the vital interests of the striking local even if the right to strike is upheld, and will avoid the costs of interrupted production if the arbitrator concludes that the no-strike clause applies.[24]

Stevens's view is supported by a number of writers. For instance, Arthur Smith accepted the notion that sympathy actions "do not directly benefit the participants and may well be contrary to their own best interests."[25] The notion of "direct benefit" stems directly from the common law in the late nineteenth century and suggests that public, not private, decision makers should decide questions of self-interest. Because public decision makers have no intimate relation with the dispute at all, they can often, and more freely, decide on broader grounds. As under the common law, such decisions will only result in haphazard and uneven law making.

Smith's second point is even more disturbing. Whether sympathy action is within a union's "real" interests, however that may be determined, he suggests that such action can be limited in "their own best interests." Of course, it is easy to see how the view that permits a decision maker to decide a union's "best interests" could easily slip over into the view that once those true interests are discovered, the law can be used to "protect" unions from their false consciousness. Thus, the result is not antiunion at all, but rather benevolently designed to protect unions from themselves.

In a case not involving picket lines, the Supreme Court recently dealt with the long-standing recognition of employee action taken to support employees generally. The Court in *Eastex* ruled that employees could distribute a newsletter which in some sections urged political action against the proposed incorporation of the state's right-to-work statute into the state constitution. The newsletter also urged workers to register to overcome situations such as the veto by the president of a bill to increase the minimum wage. The employer had refused to permit the union to distribute the newsletter, ostensibly because the "political" sections had no relationship to a dispute "over an issue which the employer has the right or power to affect."[26]

The Court easily disposed of the contention that "mutual aid or protection" was restricted to matters involved in a particular employment relationship, and it broadly supported the phrase's coverage of action designed to aid *other* employees, citing a number of appellate decisions that had protected refusals to cross picket lines.[27] It noted, however, that it was not approving these decisions. Ironically, although refusing to commit itself on group self-help through collective respect of picket lines, the Court had no difficulty in supporting employee action to improve their lot as employees through channels outside the employee-employer relationship. Thus, the Court easily recognized the legitimacy of union attempts to secure advantage through legislative or administrative channels.[28] It noted, moreover, that "mutual aid or protection" was modeled after Section 2 of the Norris-LaGuardia Act,[29] which recognizes the "right of wage earners to act jointly in questions affecting wages, conditions of labor, and the welfare of labor generally. . . ."[30] At least one appellate court had limited Section 7 to matters over which the employer had some control, but the Supreme Court clearly rejected such a limitation.[31]

The Court also rejected the notion that the distributed material could be deemed unprotected merely by calling it "political." On the other hand, it left open the possibility that some material might be "so purely political or so remotely connected to the concerns of employees as to be beyond the protection of the clause."[32] Unlike the Court's reluctance to sanction respect for picket lines, a question not technically before it, the Court's seeming circumspection here responds to something more than simply a narrow view of proper judicial law making.

The argument the Court seems to be sensitive to—that employee activity becomes subject to discharge when the employer's direct interest declines—has always seemed strange. When the employee's concerns and subsequent action, the argument goes, extend far from, or have little relation to, his or her employment relationship, the activity is outside of Section 7 and, thus, discipline or discharge will not violate the act. Yet, by definition, this is a situation in which the employer has seemingly little legitimate interest in disciplining the employee involved. It is possible, however, to argue that such "nonrelated" activity is unprotected without basing such a conclusion on the ironic ground that the employer lacks interest or control over the object of the employee's concern. Thus, Julius Getman explains that because the employer is not a party to the controversy in these cases, "there is no reason why he should be forced to permit his business to be used as a battleground."[33] But the argument seems circular. The reason why the business should not be a battleground over *this* matter is the alleged remoteness of the specific concern involved to the immediate employer-employee relationship. Because the ambit of Section 7 extends well beyond the employer-employee relationship, what activity is without and what within the protected zone? In addition, the "battleground" reference is overdrawn. Getman recognizes that walkouts in such cases tend to be brief, and in *Eastex* the issue merely involved the distribution of a newsletter. A case-by-case approach suggested by both Getman and the Court subjects all parties to doubt and uncertainty about the scope of protected speech and may have the effect of deterring protected action. Perhaps material totally irrelevant to employment conditions should be excluded, but is it wise to permit a decision maker to determine what is "purely political" or "irrelevant" to workers' interests.[34]

The key to the belief that the employer's interest is "likely to outweigh the employees' " is, again, the notion of the battleground at "his business." As long as the enterprise is deemed to belong solely to the employer, only limited recognition will be given to the interests of employees who spend a large part of their lives there. The language, and its underlying assumptions, are particularly appropriate here. The Court has recently stressed that the rights of union access to employees on company property and the scope of union activity on private property are limited.[35] As Mr. Justice White stated in his *Eastex* concurrence, "[o]wnership of property normally confers the right to control the use of that property."[36]

Similar notions are found in the picket-line cases and, as already noted, in cases dealing with the right to solicit on company property. The first circuit, for instance, has only expressed doubt about the protected nature of such conduct, and it has established a test which makes it difficult to establish that respecting a picket line is protected. The test initially requires a "balancing" of the employee's rights against "the right of the employer to conduct his business." How this weighing is to be made is far from clear. Again we see that the rights in Section 7 can be "balanced" against implicit norms involving productivity and employer control. Thus far, however, the test is no different from the normal approach in almost all 8(a)(1) situations. The Board, however, tends to place the burden on the employer in this type of case to show that the discharge was predominantly based upon business motives. How the Board can sift these motives is itself a dilemma, and in any event, antiunion and business motivations are often simply two sides of the same coin. Moreover, because these cases are treated under Section 8(a)(1), motive would seem to be irrelevant.[37] Nevertheless, the first circuit has held that in these 8(a)(1) cases, the NLRB, rather than the employer, has the burden to show a predominant antiunion motivation. Because the facts will always show an employee's refusal to perform part of a regular job, it will be difficult for the NLRB to meet this test. The important point is that this court has used implicit employer interests to outweigh explicit statutory protections and read an intent requirement into a section that is generally believed not to require proof of intent.

The fourth circuit and others, on the other hand, will find "sympathetic" action protected, but only if employees are acting out of principle. The court thought it "now fairly well established" that employees who refuse to cross a picket line out of principle have "plighted [their] troth with the strikers, joined in their common cause, and [have] thus become . . striker[s] [themselves]."[38] Despite the Victorian prose, the court is aware that

respect for the integrity of the picket line may well be the source of strength of the whole collective bargaining process in which every union member has a legitimate and protected economic interest. And any assistance by a union member to a labor organization in the collective bargaining process is for mutual aid or protection of the nonstriking unionist even though he has no immediate stake in the labor dispute.[39]

Thus, this court acknowledges that employees have an interest in respecting picket lines, but it defines "stake" in a narrow economic sense. Nevertheless, it is willing to protect such action despite the absence of pecuniary interest.[40] It is the existence of a picket line that distinguishes this kind of case from slowdowns or refusals to perform part of one's job. Strikes and picket lines are central to the act, and these rights mean little if picket lines could be respected only at the risk of losing one's job.[41]

Giving other types of assistance to employees elsewhere, however, despite the absence of an economic stake in the "foreign" dispute, has long been protected.[42] Such decisions provide support for the "generally accepted" notion that activity supporting employees of another employer is "for mutual aid or protection."[43] Learned Hand referred to sympathetic strikes, among other actions, as clearly within "mutual aid or protection" and stressed employee interest "in a solidarity so obtained. . . ."[44] Judge Hand thought that the statute "put an end" to any doubt on this score, but the cases referred to above suggest that the optimism of 1942 was premature. Hand believed that it was generally understood that the Wagner Act protected the use of pressure in support of the employees of another employer. Indeed, the Taft-Hartley debates indicate that respecting picket lines and other secondary pressure was protected.[45]

Again, the specter of *Mackay* looms over this area. For even if a "respecter" engages in protected conduct, *Mackay* tells us that the employee can be permanently replaced! There is, after all, no inherent reason why a respecter of a picket line should be better treated than a striker. Again, the difference is between discharge and replacement preceding a discharge. A meaningless distinction? Perhaps so, but the legal struggle to obtain judicial support for basic trade-union norms again highlights some of the implicit values employed by judges.[46]

Respecters of picket lines, therefore, are generally given modest protection, but it is also often limited and grudging. This type of job action can be distinguished from other types of refusals to perform part of one's job because of the importance of picket lines in trade-union consciousness. Nevertheless, despite the importance of the picket line, substantively and symbolically, it is conceptually difficult to separate the act of respecting another's picket line from other types of refusals to perform part of one's job or, indeed, a slowdown. The explanation, therefore, may simply be expedience because the normal rationale hardly explains how the two types of activity can be distinguished. The justification for condemnation is usually stated in a conclusory way. As Robert Gorman notes, "the major reason appears to be that employees who remain on the payroll are believed obligated to discharge in full the work responsibilities embodied in their contract of employment and are not entitled to pick and choose the work they wish to do."[47] Although a more lenient attitude to "quickie" strikes or refusals to perform strikers' work seems to be developing,[48] the core of the argument rests upon a notion of the employee's obligations to the employer, an obligation that generally can only be legally breached by a full-scale walkout or, perhaps, by respecting a picket line.

Not even all full-scale walkouts will be protected. The most obvious example is a wildcat strike, a strike otherwise legal yet not authorized by the union. Wildcats are deemed unprotected activity in some circuits, although the Board and some circuits will protect those unauthorized walkouts which do not "derogate" from the union's status as exclusive representative.[49] Wildcats run afoul of the "unlawful means test" for a variety of reasons, reasons that are often unsupported by the evidence. As I have argued previously, empirical data does not support the common legal and sociological notions that wildcats are irrational, generally spontaneous, or even necessarily unjustifiable. Nevertheless, judicial condemnation is apparently growing,[50] although wildcats show no indication that they are a disappearing phenomenon.

The Board's test focuses upon the need to protect the unions' status as the exclusive representatives, but this test is rejected by many appellate courts who tend to deny protection to any wildcat. Wildcat activity often represents the failure or inability of the collective bargaining structure to deal with employee concerns. Yet courts continue to criticize wildcat strikers for failure to use grievance procedures[51] and the bargaining structure. Although many courts do refer to the harm to the union's status, the common judicial rejection of the Board's "derogation of union status" test shows that interests other than the union's institutional integrity are controlling.[52] For many courts, the critical interest is *not* the protection of the union's status but, rather, the protection either of institutionalized bargaining structure, or, simply, of the employer's economic interest in being free of disturbing economic pressure. Only these latter interests would justify employer discipline in any case.

The treatment of wildcats and other areas justifies George Schatzki's belief that the legal system tends to deny protection "whenever there are any legitimate institutional considerations competing with the protection suggested by section 7."[53] When courts either reject totally the NLRB's approach[54] or accept the Board's basic notion but give it a restrictive reading,[55] they must assume that the NLRB's approach[56] is based upon an overly narrow view of the relevant interests. The judicial concern, therefore, must be focused upon something other than the protection of the union or its integrity as the exclusive representative.

Like the *Mackay* rule, the often unprotected status of wildcat activity benefits employers who are relatively strong and can find replacements. Highly skilled "key" workers may engage in fractional bargaining, independent of the bargaining agent, without the need for overt job actions, for studies show that relatively low status, unskilled workers engage in wildcats.[57] Moreover, a wildcat is a signal that management, the union, or both have neglected an important area of worker concern, and discipline acts not on the problem but on an effect of a workplace problem. The institutional interests of the contracting parties and the structures created may be both a cause of wildcats as well as an obstacle for fair resolution of the underlying disputes.

As labor-management relations become formalized and routinized, each side will be concerned with constraining "unruly" members on the other side. Each side acts as disciplining agent for the other, and both discipline malcontented elements. Management and union leadership, for instance, often collaborate to eliminate a minority of "trouble-makers" from employment and union positions so as to main "amicable relations." Thus, agreement often exists between union and management to protect the relationship against disturbances led by unauthorized spokesmen.

The development of joint institutional interests suggests that arbitral proceedings aimed at discovering whether "just cause" for dismissal was present do not necessarily provide strikers with sufficient protection. Even a neutral arbitrator is limited by the contractual context, by the parties who have hired him, and by the presentations made before him. The grievance system forces the employee to in effect turn over his grievance to the union, as the union normally has full control over employee grievances. If the matter reaches arbitration, the arbitrator is jointly recompensed by the formal parties to the agreement. Finally, the legal possibilities of overturning an arbitrator's award are slim.[58]

The role of wildcats as communication devices or as enforcement devices for the protection of contractual or customary rights is rarely acknowledged because, perhaps, of the current stress on dispute resolution through grievance procedures. Yet, the Supreme Court has not always been solicitous of formal resolution procedures. In *Mastro Plastics*,[59] for instance, the Court held that a strike in response to an employer's unfair labor practices would not violate a standard no-strike promise in the parties' collective bargaining agreement. The holding was an early use of the notion, later to have greater significance,[60] that no-strike clauses were related to the scope of arbitration clauses.[61] Given that such strikers, unlike "mere" economic strikers, cannot be permanently replaced, significant protection is given to a strike over a matter which could, ironically, be peacefully resolved through the procedure of the NLRB. Indeed, one purpose of the act was to channel disputes to the NLRB in order to resolve some of the causes of economic conflict. If unions can act to enforce the NLRA, it becomes trickier to simultaneously condemn employee attempts to enforce contractual or customary rights.

Schatzki views the wildcat problem as being caused by the exclusivity doctrine,[62] but the courts that reject or restrict the Board's "derogation" doctrine obviously see the problem as involving more than the need to protect the union's status. Moreover, the bar against certain kinds of activity, such as slowdowns, applies to unorganized workers as well as to those in unions.[63] The real objection to wildcats may be that they upset expectations and assumptions about power relationships, causing problems that in the eyes of the institutional parties should not have arisen—at least in this form. Of course, and this is rarely mentioned, a wildcat, like a slowdown, causes economic harm to the employer.[64]

Although it is obviously critical for a union to be present in order for wildcat activity technically to occur, it is not clear that the union's presence is the *reason* for legal disapproval. Wildcats are usually a form of grass-roots action, occurring outside of formal institutional structures. They are often attempts by workers to affect their work life without the union's institutional support. Indeed, some wildcats are directed at a union action or are a reaction to perceived union hostility or indifference. The treatment of wildcats, then, although generally explained by the presence of the union and the existence of a bargaining structure, falls into place with the attack on "unconventional" concerted activity such as slowdowns or partial strikes. In either case, employee action reflects the assertion of worker control, an interest receiving little protection by the courts.

Cox favors the protection of wildcat strikes, despite his belief that they are a "harmful and demoralizing form of industrial strife" which may "disrupt plant relationships and interfere with the normal process of collective bargaining." On the other hand, wildcats stimulate union leaders, and perhaps it may not be "sound policy to submerge the interests of minority groups into the policies or inertia of the union hierarchy until the collective agreement is negotiated—or at least until the union has formally adopted a position." Cox recognizes that a determination of the issue requires a policy judgment about how bargaining should operate. To make "this kind of judgment the basis for an interpretation of section 7 cuts the court or . . . agency adrift from the statute, for no provision of the Act supplies a standard by which the choice can be made."[65]

Although I agree, the statement surprisingly suggests that most other statutory issues do not involve policy judgments. Moreover, Cox's support for a "legal" rather than a "factual" definition of concerted activities is a policy judgment in itself and, in addition, operates to permit the kind of policy judgments that courts make in situations such as wildcat-strike cases.[66]

The purpose of Section 7 is often stated as designed to take the "conspiracy weapon away from the employer in employment relations which affect interstate commerce."[67] The doctrine that labor activity was a criminal conspiracy had faded by the middle of the nineteenth century, and labor regulation had shifted to the generally more advantageous civil side of courts. The doctrine, however, referred to here as the unlawful means-ends test, remained in full force. If Section 7 were designed to overturn the use of this test and its value as a funnel for judicial biases, then the doctrines discussed here seem strangely out of tune, for it is clear that the restriction on wildcats and slowdowns, for instance, turns on the application of an "unlawful means" test infused with unstated assumptions and values.

Although scholars acknowledge the use of an unlawful means-ends test, there is a tendency to regard Section 7 as creating a statutory bias in favor of concerted activities and thereby reducing the possibility of judicial valuing. Exceptions, suggests Cox, are to be created "only when the employees' conduct plainly deserves condemnation." The function, then, becomes to fashion standards "by which the wholly egregious factors can be eliminated and the subjective attitudes and administrators reduced to minimum roles."[68] Viewing "concerted activity" as a legal rather than a factual description makes such a task dubious. The decisions restricting the scope of Section 7 do not apply only to activity that "plainly deserves condemnation." Indeed, in many cases, such as *Elk Lumber*, there is no evidence of an attempt to reduce "subjective attitudes" to a minimum. Often, the need for restriction is treated as obvious and, therefore, there is no necessity for explanation.

Finally, the beauty of Cox's statement is in the conjunction of the statement that "egregious" factors must be reduced but some conduct "plainly deserves condemnation." Some implicit set of values or assumptions must exist in order to determine what activity "plainly deserves condemnation," but neither the courts nor writers are very clear as to the source or content of such standards. As noted, the language of the act and its legislative history are notoriously silent on such values. Because no guides exist for determining how "exceptions" from broad statutory protections are to be made, it is virtually impossible to ascertain which factors are "egregious" unless, as is not the case, all agree on some inherent set of values and assumptions.

To call attention to judicial legislation or to the narrowing of seemingly clear statutory language is not necessarily to criticize the fact of judicial valuation. Nor should we be surprised that courts make "policy," whether in a common-law or a statutory context. Such judicial gloss does not always restrain unions. Supreme Court decisions in the 1960s, for instance, recognized that certain of the Taft-Hartley amendments of 1947 could not possibly be given their literal scope. The result was a narrowing, for instance, of the secondary boycott prohibitions. Some decisions were easily justifiable because the broad wording of Section 8(b)(4) would have barred any strike because most strikes intend, as one of many possible goals, to create secondary pressure.[69] In other cases involving the arguable prohibition of peaceful picketing, the Court refused to bar picketing unless "there is the clearest indication in legislative history" that Congress intended to do so. . . ."[70] This concern was motivated by the vague extent to which the First Amendment might protect picketing in the aftermath of the judicial retreat from *Thornhill* v. *Alabama*. The "silence of the sponsors" and the lack of discussion in regard to particular kinds of pressure permitted the Court to protect action seemingly covered by the broad scope of Section 8(b).[71]

The critique here is not directed to the impropriety of the judicial role so much as to the route taken. Whereas the union prohibitions of Section 8(b) were judicially limited because of First Amendment concerns or the clearly over-broad language, no such considerations were present in the narrowing of Section 7 rights of employees.

Again, it should be noted that a finding that particular conduct does not fall within Section 7 does not *prohibit* the conduct but merely removes any federal protection from the activity. Yet, there is no other body of law to protect the activity or to bar employer retaliation. Removing activity from the protective ambit of Section 7 permits private punishment of that activity. Although the NLRA may not prohibit the action in question, in the sense that no federal regulatory action is taken against the employee, the legal result *permits* punishment.

The restrictions on the scope of Section 7 do not arise from constitutional considerations or from concern with potential conflict with other portions of the act. Rather, the Court has created limits that are not justified by statutory language or legislative history. Courts have "balanced" broad statutory protections with considerations based upon the Court's own views of the necessities of the economic system. This is the very role long criticized in American labor-management relations whose continuation was sought to be avoided by clear, broad enactments such as the Norris-LaGuardia and National Labor Relations Acts. Karl Klare is correct in finding that the "Act did not produce a fundamental transformation of the premises and institutions of capitalist society," and, as the collective bargaining section of this volume suggests, the act did little to enhance the workers' "decision-making roles regarding the use of society's means of production, the organization of the work-process, and other decisions that affect their industrial lives."[72]

5

STATUS ASSUMPTIONS AND THE

"COMMON ENTERPRISE"

SUPPOSE DURING THE course of a dispute, employees attack or criticize the worthiness of the employer's product. The goal of such activity is clear—to administer pain that will stop when the employer becomes more "reasonable." Thus, it seems no different from other pressure devices or, for that matter, the strike itself. Yet employees generally engage in unprotected, "disloyal" activity when they criticize the employer's product. The key assumption here is that employees owe certain obligations of deference and respect to their employer. This chapter will demonstrate the extent to which the NLRA has been used to define the employment contracts in terms of nineteenth-century master-servant law, a process that recognizes the lower status of employees in the employment context.

In the most famous decision, technicians working for the Jefferson Standard Broadcasting Company picketed after successive breakdowns in negotiations. During the dispute, several technicians launched a "vitriolic attack on the quality of the Company's television broadcasts through the distribution of handbills."[1] The handbills criticized the company for poor quality programming as well as for owning insufficient equipment for local programming and for providing "second-class" television service. Moreover, the handbills questioned whether the station deemed the community a "second-class city." Ten technicians were subsequently discharged for sponsoring or distributing the handbills.

The company's discharge letter to each employee carefully stressed the distressing nature of the handbill attack and the fact that the technicians had not struck. The latter point could have been relied upon, as in slowdown situations, to argue that employees must strike and face the possible risks rather than engage in concerted activity while remaining at work. The picketing, however, occurred while employees were off duty and was concededly protected, so the focus of legal attack could not be the fact that concerted activity occurred but, rather, had to be directed to the nature of that activity.

The Board found that the employees sought deliberately to alienate the employer's customers and that the handbills did not refer to an ongoing labor dispute or to any particular bargaining demand. In addition, the subject matter of the handbills was not related to their interests as employees. If the employees had coupled the same handbills with a conventional appeal for public support, the Board suggested that a different result might be possible. Because, moreover, any legal job action causes economic harm, the basis of the decision cannot rest solely upon the resulting harm to the employer. Instead, the Board stressed that the product disparagement was related neither to the dispute nor to legitimate employee interests. Obviously, the handbill was conceived as a pressure device related to the ongoing economic dispute even though its content referred to other matters. It is also surprising, but perhaps revealing, that the Board would feel that quality of equipment and programming would be irrelevant to the station's technicians. Moreover, the employees were raising questions of community interest about the practices of a federal licensee.

The Supreme Court agreed with the NLRB that the handbills were unprotected and, thus, that distributors could be discharged. Referring to Section 10(c)'s prohibition against reinstatement for anyone discharged "for cause," the Court stated that "there is no more elemental cause for discharge of an employee than disloyalty to his employer."[2] This is another of the "of course" statements in the area that betrays a notion of the employee's relative "place" in the employment relationship.

The decision creates a vague standard, "disloyalty," with no inherent guideposts. The employees distributing the offending leaflets probably did not believe their action would warrant, legally at least, the penalty of discharge, but the employer may well have believed that *any* action, even picketing or striking, was disloyal. Terms such as "disloyal," "indefensible," or "irresponsible," which are sometimes used, fail to illuminate any standards pursuant to which conduct can be judged. The Court's explanation, after it noted that disloyalty is an "elemental cause for discharge," was that "it is equally elemental that the Taft-Hartley Act seeks to strengthen, rather than to weaken, that cooperation, continuity of service and cordial contractual relation between employer and employee that is born of loyalty to their common enterprise."[3] Although the act hardly comes freighted with the Court's view of its purpose, it is no doubt correct that the Wagner and Taft-Hartley Acts sought to induce some degree of peace and stability in workplaces. On the other hand, the statute explicitly protects strikes and other concerted activity and does not indicate that particular types of concerted activity are excluded from protection.

The most striking aspect of the statement is the notion that cooperation and continuity naturally arise from loyalty to a "common enterprise." The notion of a common enterprise enlists employees into the assumed support of employer goals. To some extent, of course, goals do intersect. But one could have a belief in a common endeavor and nevertheless differ on strategies and tactics. Moreover, other goals of employees, such as currently perceived economic needs, may conflict with the employer's estimate of future needs and present realities. The act itself recognizes that conflicts will occur, and the Court simply chose the interest it wished to protect in a product disparagement situation.

The Court's choice is the focus here, although scholarly attention is generally directed to the ambiguousness of the "disloyalty" standard. Even the General Counsel has stated in an appeal memorandum that a "clear test for resolving such 'disloyalty' issues could not be readily discerned from an examination of various Board decisions in this area. . . ."[4] Nor is the issue the truthfulness of the disparaging remarks, for the Board has stated in another case that "statements made by employees to the public which deliberately cast discredit upon their employer's product or service are no less disloyal and a breach of confidence because they are truthful."[5] Apparently, as the saying goes, "the greater the truth, the greater the libel."

Ironically, disparagement will be held unprotected even though true, but it could be protected even if false. The critical issue seems to be the nexus between the issues involved in the concurrent dispute, the employees' "legitimate" interests, and the subject matter of the written or oral statements. Such a vague standard would not be permitted if this were a constitutional matter, and we are here dealing, after all, with questions of free expression. Nevertheless, the legal results parallel those in areas already discussed. When disparaging words are tied to current disputes, they will apparently be deemed protected. The protection of concerted activities in Section 7, then, has real effect, but activity that can be separated from ongoing disputes or distinguished from full-scale strikes can be removed from statutory protection.

DEFINING THE CONTOURS OF THE EMPLOYMENT RELATIONSHIP

The *Jefferson Standard* decision could be viewed from two vantage points. Initially, the decision may be seen as defining the content of the employment "contract" by reading the obligations of loyalty into the employment arrangement. Although the "triumph of contract" in the nineteenth century presumably left the actors contractually free, and the employment situation "at will," notions stemming from older master-servant law are often read in, to fill the gaps. A similar process has been noted in both American and English practice preceding any labor legislation.[6] The result is a combination of contract and status notions.

It is commonly said that the industrial revolution dissolved ties of status or obligation that had previously existed between workers and their employer. These "ties," of course, were often created out of necessity, and relationships were structured by law. Slaves, apprentices, redemptioners, and indentured servants made up a large part of early America's work force.[7] One estimate is that 80 percent of English immigration prior to the Revolution consisted of redemptioners,[8] and Eric Foner has suggested that there were at least as many bound laborers and slaves as there were free laborers and journeymen in Philadelphia in 1775.[9] Indentured servitude was primarily an arrangement to increase the mobility of labor from England to America. Some of these forms of bound labor, not slavery alone, treated the individual as property that could be assigned or sold. Often, servants were "purchased" from the ship captains who were responsible for their passage. Moreover, contracts for work could be specifically enforced, that is, courts could order unwilling laborers to work. The history of these arrangements reveals that, first, the unemployment relationship has always been regulated. There was no idyllic, free-market period when employment relationships were not directly affected by law. Individual servitude was a device to increase labor mobility but, like other forms of bound labor, was intended to increase labor supply as well. Runaway servants, some prisoners, and even workers who abandoned contractual relationships would be ordered to work. Debtors were also an important source of labor. The supply of workers is often a problem for newly developing territories, but increasing the supply has the surely not unintended effect of weakening the bargaining power of free workers.

The second theme, and the one most relevant here, involves the effect of bound labor on the American conception of the employment relationship. It is possible that the fact that many early laborers were bound, unfree to leave or change circumstances, affected the way Americans viewed the employment relationship even after such forms faded away. Some forms of bound labor began to disappear, not because such forms were inconsistent with democratic principles, but because in periods of excess labor and, especially, economic depression, the market was substituted for status-contractual relationships. The American view of the employment relationship may intuitively have been affected by the substantial number of bound workers that had previously existed.

The basic problem is that possible connections between bound labor and conceptions of the modern "free" worker have not been explored. Many forms of bound labor seem to have faded away after the American Revolution,[10] but this does not mean that assumptions had not already been formed about the obligations and status of all laborers. Slavery in the north, after all, existed for some time after the Revolution. Northern legislators were extremely conservative on this issue, and freedom only came slowly to northern slaves. The legislators of the northeastern states rejected what David Brion Davis refers to as the "most cautious proposals for gradual abolition." Between 1784 and 1804 emancipation acts "won grudging assent in Connecticut, Rhode Island, Upper Canada, New York, and New Jersey." New York's first emancipation act in 1799 left all existing slaves in "perpetual servitude," and New Jersey's statute of 1804 was "so conservative and slow in operation that the state still contained slaves, euphemistically called 'apprentices,' at the time of the Civil War."[11] Thus, not only did slavery itself exist in northern states into the nineteenth century, but a clear connection existed between slavery and at least one form of bound labor, i.e., apprenticeship.

Because of the structure of antislavery opinion, Davis argues that the existence of slavery affected perceptions in an ironic way. "[A]ntislavery ideology served to isolate specific forms of human misery, allowing issues of freedom and discipline to be faced in a relatively simplified model. And by defining slavery as a unique *moral* aberration, the ideology tended to give sanction to the prevailing economic order."[12] The slave could not be held responsible for his status, and people could sympathize and criticize the institution while at the same time affirming an order that depended upon assigning people to unequal positions.

Thus, a society valuing freedom, but based upon property, was consistent with the existence of a "dependent class of workers."[13] Although slavery might be abhorrent, even northerners moved slowly to alter such "property relations." Thus it was possible for proponents of a revised form of paternalism toward laborers to be outspoken opponents of slavery.[14]

After the Revolution, forms of bound labor and indentured servitude seem to have ended, and nineteenth-century law emphasized the contractual rather than the social ties between master and servant. Workers were to be left to their own devices, to drive the best bargain they could, but they possessed no claims beyond those growing out of the employment contract. These changes may have speeded the rate of economic growth, but the system increased the risks of survival for workers. The risks of unemployment due to injury or economic downturns were shouldered by the employee and, eventually, partially shared by the community.

Like American law, English law rests the relationship of worker and employer upon the common law of contracts.[15] We should not assume, however, that this legal relationship is the most important factor touching the relationship. Social and economic relationships are no doubt more important, and the parties rarely stand upon or enforce legal rights.

English law also rests upon the assumption, based only upon lawyers' reality, that individual contracts of employment are the result of freely bargained arrangements. Judicial interpretations of "agreement" or "intention" in order to determine the rights of the parties "frequently resulted in a legal consolidation of the superior disciplinary and other powers of the employer."[16] It could be argued, of course, that the results were preordained by the initial assumptions. This law in England was developed in the eighteenth and nineteenth centuries and involved agricultural labor and domestic servants, although the initial assumptions may have been just as unreal then as when the same doctrines were applied to industrial workers.

At some point in the nineteenth century the designation of the parties as master and servant were replaced by the more egalitarian sounding "employer" and "employee," although many legal treatises have not yet caught up. The employee's contract is still routinely referred to as a contract of "service." "Many aspects of the master's quasi-proprietary interest in the service of his servant have shown considerable vitality even in our own time."[17]

Workers, however, do "in fact tend to regard themselves as having some right of possession in a job and to devise institutions which wrest control over incumbency from the hands of the employer and which express objectively a vesting of property rights in the worker."[18] This conception is still referred to as "novel," despite the evidence that such beliefs are widespread and historically entrenched in the working class. Although such views obviously do "impinge upon established conceptions of society and of management,"[19] the error is to define "society" as the views of only management and the courts. A cultural or class conflict of values clearly exists. For instance, evidence of sub rosa arrangements by employees which set limits for speed or productivity have long been noted, although such arrangements are inconsistent with the legal obligations thought inherent in the employment relationship.[20]

When we are told, therefore, that an employee's action is unprotected because it is "disloyal" or "indefensible," the result is to structure or fill out the scope of the employment relationship. What is covered by the employment contract? One way to view the decisions discussed here is as if the courts through the NLRA are defining the range of obligations present in the employment relationship. Although the decisions technically decide only whether the actions of workers fall within the parameters of federal protection, no other body of law generally exists. The application of state law will normally be preempted. Even if some parts of state contract law could be validly applied, employment contracts rarely exist in written form, and the traditional rule is that employment will be deemed to be "at will" unless arrangements to the contrary exist.[21] Thus, the statutory context masks what is primarily a contractual or status-defining function.

In all these situations involving unprotected activity, the employer's action does not violate the prohibitions of Section 8(a), and the employee's conduct does not fall within Section 7. Yet, there is rarely any support in either the statute or the legislative history for finding employee conduct unprotected. Admittedly, some easy cases do exist. It would not, perhaps, serve the statute's purposes to protect employees who violate Section 8(b) or who attempt to persuade employers to violate Section 8(a) or, perhaps, other federal laws. Fuzziness begins when action is said to violate "fundamental policies of the act," such as the sanctity of collective agreements or the integrity of the grievance process. These policies seem to underlie the proscription of strikes in breach of contract or unauthorized (wildcat) strikes. More must underlie these determinations because these job actions are "concerted" actions for collective bargaining or "mutual aid or protection" and, thus, are literally protected under Sections 7 and 13 of the act. Moreover, there are many statutory purposes and, in a particular case, they may conflict. Courts rarely explain why or how in a wildcat situation, for instance, the policy of protecting private dispute resolution systems is actually threatened, let alone why this policy outweighs *explicit* statutory protection of concerted actions.

As noted, the courts' use of "of course" rationales tells us where the ghosts are buried. The existence of these shadowy notions becomes even more obvious in those cases where courts do not even rely on "statutory policies" to find employee collective action unprotected. In these cases courts tend to rely upon vague terms of opprobrium such as "disloyal" or "indefensible." These cases are clearly defining the scope of the employment relationship and, I think, give us the clues to the identity and locations of those hidden assumptions. In sum, the ghosts will be certain values or presumptions about the role of management and the place of employees deemed by many decision makers to be inherent in our industrial society.

EMPLOYER CONTROL OVER PROPERTY AND WORKERS

[Employers in the nineteenth century] . . . all shared an almost psychopathic fear of having to meet the representatives of labor on a footing of equal authority, and a similar fear of labor gaining a position strong enough to influence management. "I do not believe," said President Meisel of the Kidder Press Company, "that a manufacturer can afford to be dictated to by his labor as to what he shall do, and I shall never give in. I would rather go out of business." This was the old conception of the employer as the host inviting the worker to come and make use of his property, but only on conditions that the owner of the property should dictate.[22]

A second perspective on *Jefferson Standard* stems from an understanding that the notion of a "common enterprise" also conveys notions about the employer's power over its property and, of course, over its employees as well. In many areas, courts explicitly use prop-

92 Collective Action and the NLRA

erty notions to overcome employee assertions of statutory rights. Indeed, the use of property notions, limited to the employer, destroys notions like the "common enterprise." A recent case that does not involve the NLRA highlights the problem. In the *Barlow's* decision, the Court held that federal OSHA inspectors, enforcing a statute designed to protect employees, must nevertheless seek warrants before entering the "common enterprise."[23] The decision, although involving constitutional rather than statutory provisions, ranged far from any notion of a common enterprise. Indeed, the interests of the employees were not mentioned. The enterprise was referred to as the employer's "private commercial property," and warrantless searches would infringe upon the employer's "privacy interest." The hiring of employees, said the Court, does not throw open the areas where employees are permitted to the "warrantless scrutiny of government agents."

The Court in *Barlow's* noted that prior decisions had held that warrantless searches were proper, but these decisions were limited to unique circumstances. Those situations involved industries that had such a "history of government oversight that no reasonable expectation of privacy . . . could exist for a proprietor over the stock of such an enterprise," and the Court listed liquor and firearms as "industries of this type." In these cases, the proprietor has "voluntarily chosen to subject himself to a full arsenal of governmental regulation."[24] As the *Barlow's* dissenters note, the Court's notion that an owner of a regulated industry ("one with a long tradition of close government supervision") "in effect consents to the restrictions placed upon him" is a fiction. Owners no more consent by entering into business subject to regulation than Barlow's did by continuing electrical and plumbing installation after the passage of OSHA. The validity of the regulations does not depend upon consent of those regulated but on the existence of a statute embodying a congressional determination that the public interest outweighs the business owner's interest in preventing an inspection.[25] The Supreme Court dissenters stressed that the issue was the reasonableness of the search, since some searches are constitutionally proper even if no warrant has been obtained. The *Barlow's* majority assumed, seemingly contrary to precedent, that a warrant was always required, except in certain industries, but nevertheless it stated that it would permit some searches without probable cause. That is, although judicially approved warrants would be necessary, and the agency would be normally required to show that there was reasonable cause to inspect, the Court would permit a relaxation of this standard if "reasonable" agency standards existed. The effect is to require warrants, creating administrative costs for OSHA, with no apparent gain to employers. The dissenters accused the majority of "substituting their judgment for that of Congress on what inspection authority is needed to effectuate the purposes of the Act."[26] The "new-fangled" warrant, permitted by the Court, provides little protection to employers except, first, to make the already over-strained search process of OSHA more time consuming and costly and, perhaps second, to provide advance notice of an inspection. Neither "advantage" to employers seems constitutionally required, nor is the Court's stress on the employer's "privacy" convincing in a case where the purpose of inspections are to protect employees working on the site. The decision represents another in the current line that protects rather abstract property rights of employers against rather clear statutory interests of employees.

Turning from *Barlow's* to NLRA cases, we can see that property notions affect both areas in much the same way. The cases on union access to company property for purposes of union solicitation, for instance, also must be read in light of implicit notions of employer property rights. For instance, the Supreme Court's decision in *Babcock & Wilcox*[27] found a crucial distinction between the access rights of nonemployee organizers and organizers who are employed by the firm to be organized, even though the basic statutory concern is the interest of employees in *receiving* information about unionization. The Court held that "nonemployee" organizers do not have the same rights of access and speech as organizers who are employees. Nonemployee organizers could be barred unless the union's ability to reach employees through "other available channels of communication" was ineffective. The little town of Paris, Texas, the site of the *Babcock & Wilcox* case, illustrates a textbook example of a situation that requires outside organizers to at least initiate organization. In cases like *Babcock & Wilcox*, however, there is typically no discussion of the property or other social interests that justifies a limitation on union access.

The current stress on property rights can be seen in the recent shopping mall cases, in which, after a promising beginning by the Warren Court, malls were held to be private property, thus barring solicitors from acquiring access rights under the First Amendment.[28] In each of the recent cases the Court placed great weight on rather abstract property interests without any felt need to specify those interests precisely.[29]

The labor-property cases assume either that the interests of the common enterprise are to be defined exclusively by the employer or that there is simply no conflict of interest. As in cases like *Jefferson Standard*, courts sometimes adopt a unitary view of the enterprise assuming common interests and objectives and shared values. A unitary view assumes that workers acknowledge the legitimacy of norms they are actually defying so that their action becomes a breach of promise. In a contractual sense, this view confuses passive acquiescence with active consent. Yet, courts assume that workers, needing jobs, acquiesce in an authoritarian structure regulating their work life.[30] In the employment context, interests do converge, and employer and worker share an interest in the success of the enterprise, although the parties might not define success in the same manner. But it is a peculiar American myth that confuses a limited, often tactical, merger with a commonality of interests.

The NLRA seems to accept a conflict of interest model, suggesting the need for worker participation, since conflict is inherent in the relationship and, perhaps, even functional. But the cases show the stubborn retention of a unitary model, combining aspects of contract and status, so that courts can condemn actions like slowdowns or product disparagement as violating implicit consensual norms. These assumptions accept the employer's view of the content of the relationship, one clearly rejected, at least to some extent, by the NLRA.

Loyalty or deference is also enforced by a set of rules or norms enforced by the Board and neutral arbitrators requiring respect for supervisory personnel. Employees may generally not use insulting, derogatory, or obscene language toward their supervisors.[31] None of these cases requires that employers create a parallel set of rules for supervisors. Moreover, as might be expected, the standards are exceedingly vague given the "rough" language often found in workplaces. "A certain amount of salty language or defiance will be tolerated in bargaining sessions with respect to grievances, in recognition of the fact that the sessions are usually held behind closed doors and that 'passions run high in labor disputes and that epithets and accusations are commonplace.' "[32] Passions run high in the workplace, too, but a distinction is nevertheless often made between workplace defiance and insults in grievance meetings.[33] Even so, "if the employee's conduct becomes so flagrant that it threatens the employer's ability to maintain order and respect in the conduct of his business," the speech will not be protected. The same sentiments are expressed by arbitrators who tend to face more of these cases than the Board: "[The grievant's comment] shows a willful disregard for constituted industrial authority, a challenge to the dignity and character of the foreman [and] a derogation of the authority necessary to direct the working forces."[34]

If the act permits the discharge of employees otherwise engaged in protected conduct, the conclusion must be that deference or "loyalty," vague and undefined, is an obligation owed to employers. There is, after all, little practical difference in holding that "disloyal" handbills fall outside the protective ambit of Section 7 and holding that Section 7 rights imply some obligation to the common enterprise, even though only the former reading is technically appropriate.

If bonds of loyalty and community are implicit in the act, though, would this conclusion not suggest that certain obligations are also owed to employees? After all, the original Wagner Act restricted only employer actions. One expression of "loyalty" to employees might be prohibition of the permanent replacement of strikers engaged in statutorily protected conduct. The common enterprise, after all, is not apparently upset by the employee's decision to engage in a federally protected strike. It is a strange form of common enterprise that rests exclusive control in one party, for instance, (1) to impose work orders that must, except in rare cases, be obeyed; (2) to unilaterally decide crucial matters of plant size, product line, the location or continuation of the enterprise despite the impact on the other parties; and (3) to impose these changes generally without warning.[35]

The conclusion is that although some obligations are imposed on employees to foster and support a joint productive enterprise, there are no or few corollary obligations upon employers to recognize participatory interests of employees, at least beyond express statutory prohibitions imposed upon employers. The absence of mutual obligations of honesty and deference, however, simply highlights the basic message of the disloyalty cases—employees should demonstrate deference and the enterprise should be productive, a goal that, presumably, management will seek without legislative intervention. Thus, the act's purported goal of promoting the "cooperation, continuity of service and cordial contractual relation between employer and employee that is born of loyalty to their common enterprise" is a one-way street.

The requirement of deference to employers and their property would have been clearly understandable to early nineteenth-century employers. Members of the managerial class in early America clearly expressed the desire and intention to maintain a quasi-status relationship with their employees. Thus, "managers wanted to maintain social control over the workers and at the same time they wanted to maintain the doctrine of equality before God and the Law; they wanted intimacy and trust in their relationship with them and also a recognition of hierarchy."[36] Such assumptions of junior status are still reflected in American law.

6

MANAGERIAL CONTROL AND THE

FEAR OF ANARCHY

THE SCOPE OF protected activities has received substantial scholarly attention. With the exception of the observation that certain activity seems to run afoul of deep-seated community sentiments, however, there has been no attempt to delineate the values underlying this body of law. This failure may be due to a natural hesitancy of lawyers to discuss values, although the ferreting out of underlying assumptions is said to be a particularly lawyerlike skill. It certainly cannot be said that these underlying values, whether social, economic, or whatever, have nothing to do with law. Whatever their origins, the effect of these values and assumptions upon existing law has been profound. And in no area is the presence of these values or assumptions more significant than in cases of work stoppages in the face of perceived threats to health and safety. This discussion again involves the employer's right to expect continued effort and production, even if employees face health and safety risks, and also reflects the assumption of employee status and irresponsibility. This chapter reveals the extent to which courts have accepted employer control over the production process.

Like all the activity discussed in these pages, a strike over perceived health and safety threats is clearly concerted in fact. Unlike the activity discussed up to this point, concerted activity in response to health and safety threats is protected by Section 7. The protection, of course, applies only to stoppages that are concerted and, even if they are concerted, the protection can be lost in situations where the union has contractually waived the right to strike. Despite a commonly existing imbalance of power, unions are permitted to surrender or waive statutory rights by agreeing, for instance, to a no-strike clause. It is this situation that makes Section 502 of the NLRA highly significant although until recently this section was virtually unknown. This section provides in part that "The quitting of labor by an

employee or employees in good faith because of abnormally dangerous conditions for work at the place of employment of such employee
or employees [shall not] be deemed a strike under this [act]."[1]

Because a strike over safety or health conditions would be clearly
protected under Section 7, the significance of Section 502 must be
that it protects some work stoppages that would be otherwise unprotected. The function of Section 502, therefore, must be to protect
stoppages that would otherwise violate a contractual no-strike
clause[2] and, for this reason, be unprotected. Employees who, for instance, cease work due to perceived threats to their health and safety
or refuse to cross a picket line because of the fear of personal harm arguably violate a broad no-strike agreement. It is somewhat ironic that
an employee who refuses to cross a picket line because of fears for
personal safety will not be deemed to have engaged in protected activity in some circuits. Yet, if the safety risks are so serious as to fall
within Section 502, the refusal is then protected. The difficulties of
such determinations are magnified by the Supreme Court's interpretation of Section 502.[3]

The Supreme Court first ruled on the scope of this section in its
1974 *Gateway Coal Co.* v. *United Mine Workers*[4] decision. I have
previously written at length on the subject of employee self-help in
cases of perceived health and safety threats,[5] and it is sufficient to
note here that despite the absence of helpful legislative history and in
the face of contrary implications of the statutory language, the Court
ruled that an employee's "good-faith" belief in the presence of "abnormally dangerous conditions" was not sufficient to bring such
stoppages within Section 502. The Court read the section to require
not only good faith, but also "objective evidence that such conditions
[abnormally dangerous conditions] actually obtain."[6] The nature and
persuasiveness of such "objective" evidence was not discussed.

The most rational, as well as literal, interpretation of Section 502[7]
is that the provision requires a motivational test (a good-faith belief
that *abnormally* dangerous conditions exist) and a causal test (the
perceived condition was the *cause* of the walkout). No real function
is served by penalizing employees who stop work out of a good-faith
belief that they are confronted by abnormally dangerous conditions
but who are later proved to have been factually mistaken by a tribunal
far away, in time, place, and temperament from the situation.[8] The
effect will be to penalize employees because they lack knowledge
about industrial disease or safety they often cannot be expected to

possess or because they did not have the proper equipment to scientifically test the accuracy of their perception at the crucial moment.

The counterarguments accepted by the Court, however, stress the "chaos" and "anarchy" that would result if employees could choose when to work.[9] These arguments underplay the restrictions that clearly exist in Section 502 and exaggerate the tendency of workers to cease work and risk discipline or discharge. Despite this, courts continue to argue that the use of a subjective test would expose employers to disruption by "naked assertion" or "attitudes, fancies, and whim."[10]

The effect of *Gateway Coal* on Section 502 is not easily determined, for it is quite possible to interpret the Court to require objective evidence supporting the employees' perception, rather than evidence proving that an unsafe condition within Section 502 exists in fact. Objective evidence can demonstrate that it is reasonable to perceive risk, but risk itself is a subjective determination. The success of this argument may be doubtful because the Court did state that the section required "objective evidence that such conditions actually obtain."[11] Nevertheless, the decision again represents the extent to which the Court will go to protect against the fear of "chaos or anarchy" in the workplace. The Supreme Court and some appellate court judges have made clear their disdain for employees who might make "naked assertions" that their lives or health are in danger.

The alleged fear of strikes caused by "whim" or "naked assertions" denigrates the integrity, honesty, and intelligence of workers, ignores the low propensity of workers to strike, and intentionally understates the actual effect of the rejected subjective test.[12] Whimsical strikes would seem adequately deterred by the need for good faith and a causal relationship between the walkout and the abnormal hazard as well as by the normal employment risks inherent in all strikes. Nevertheless, the judicial hostility to workers who might strike upon "naked assertions" is clear. Implicit is the notion that workers cannot (or should not) be expected to discern when they face workplace dangers. Because of this fact, it is apparently better to err on the side of deterrence and restriction, despite serious risks to workers, rather than to protect some good-faith but factually mistaken safety actions. The only reason, other than perhaps paternalism, to punish reasonable but objectively unfounded behavior is to protect the orderly flow of production by making employees think seriously before walking out. But further, the function is to deter walkouts when employees only subjectively fear risks to their health or safety or to punish those who act reasonably but who cannot support their actions by objective evidence. This aim is hardly sufficient to support the requirement of objective evidence.[13]

There seems to be a feeling that industrial relations cannot be conducted efficiently unless an objective test is applied. This test obviously provides the trier of fact with a broader discretion, for the court must decide whether there is factual support for a perception of danger as well as whether the danger is "abnormally hazardous." Arguments focused upon production efficiency, on the other hand, need no supporting evidence.[14] Obviously health and safety strikes interfere with the production process, but this is true of any protected economic weapon. Given the additional ubiquitousness of the contractual no-strike clause, it is not surprising that the drafters of Section 502 would impose conditions upon the scope of the right granted. Nevertheless, the Court saw fit to read into the section a requirement neither literally present nor supported by any legislative history. As in many areas of the labor law, the function of a standard is to shift certain risks. In this area, the issue is who should bear the risks of a good-faith walkout that, it ultimately appears, was not in response to an objectively established "abnormally hazardous" condition. A Board trial examiner expressed the dilemma: "[the objective evidence requirement] places a heavy burden on employees, who must act without the benefit of medical advice and whose choice places either their jobs or their health in jeopardy."[15] The Court chose to place the "risk" upon employees because of the value of continued, uninterrupted production and the assumption that employees are unreliable and irresponsible judges of workplace safety.

It may be that employees will often balk when they believe in good faith that safety hazards exist, and, thus, it may be unlikely that legal doctrine will actually deter many stoppages. There is often little time to contact legal counsel or union officials, who may themselves be unaware of the appropriate legal rule. And even if the rule be known, few have the temerity to firmly state a legal conclusion as to the application of Section 502 in a concrete case. The conclusion is critical in a case like this for if the walkout falls within Section 502, it is protected; if not, the employees are subject to immediate discharge.[16]

The interpretation of Section 502 is not the only legal doctrine that places a considerable burden on employees to be correct in their assessment of their legal position. Thus, for instance, should an employer commit a violation of the act, a resulting strike becomes an "unfair labor practice strike," and employees can be reinstated despite the hiring of "permanent replacements." Should employees incorrectly characterize the employer's actions as illegal, however, the strike is merely "economic," and strikers, although engaged in protected activity, can be permanently replaced. The risk is considerable, yet an administrative alternative to the unfair labor practice strike ironically exists.

In other situations, however, employees act at their peril even though administrative alternatives do not exist. A good-faith belief that certain activity is protected by Section 7 is thought to be no defense should that assessment prove incorrect. Yet, to choose one example out of many, determinations whether literature is too "political" to be safely distributed turn on a highly technical analysis of content. If the law is thought to provide guidance and deterrence functions, it places a heavy burden on employees to secure legal advice. Often there is no time for such assistance, and action is taken, if at all, in the absence of legal knowledge. In these cases, employees may be penalized for not correctly assessing the result of an NLRB proceeding. One consequence of this situation, assuming law actually guides behavior, may be the deterrence of protected activity.

The risk of inaccurate prediction could be lifted or lessened for employees by granting protected status for conduct that was "reasonably perceived" to fall within the scope of Section 7 or by broadening Section 7 so as to exclude unprincipled judicial decision making. For the reasons discussed, this is unlikely to occur. Poignantly, the Court has recently used the existence of ambiguity over the scope of mandatory bargaining as one reason to exclude unions from participating in decisions involving partial closings of the enterprise.[17]

Aside from concerns of predictability, the requirement of "objective" evidence in a situation involving the nonobjective perception of risk,[18] for instance, represents a clear example of decisions based upon unstated premises. These premises, unstated or perhaps unconscious, also operate to bar wildcats and slowdowns. Except for the normal strike that remains central to the act, other rights seem to be recognized only when the production process is not unduly harmed or where employees do not directly confront employer control over the production process.[19]

Even more than slowdowns, worker refusals to work when faced with health and safety risks directly challenge employer control over the quality of the work process. As will become even more clear in the next chapter, courts assume that the employer retains power over important managerial decisions involving the direction and scope of the operation. Thus, many judicial decisions assume that the law supports a hierarchical and autocratic structure of enterprise: employers, having purchased labor power, have a right to direct and control that power, and, concurrently, employees have no right to participate in the planning or operation of the production process,[20] at least beyond fairly clear statutory or contractual rights. Although this may reflect the form of hierarchical control generally used in modern industry, this situation is relatively recent in vintage and was in large part a response to the rapid growth of many firms after the Civil War. It was also motivated by a desire to control workers and to wrest control of the production process from skilled workers.[21]

Skilled industrial workers were often relatively autonomous in the nineteenth century, setting group production standards or creating their own work rules. Sometimes they even hired unskilled workers or subcontracted work to the lowest bidding employee. Often, they agreed to a certain volume of work per hour and, to some extent, set the manner in which the work would be done. Unions added a measure of deliberation and planning by creating explicit work rules, often referred to as "legislation." Worker cooperation and union legislation resulted from attempts to deal with "the chaos of an open labor market in an environment of unchecked industrialization and economic depression."[22] One employer response was the institution of the familiar pyramidical structure with its chain of command, which generally followed a military model. The model also encouraged expectations of loyalty and subservience.[23]

Initially, in the iron and steel industry, for example, the structure consisted of a number of small shops in one firm directed by an all-powerful supervisor.[24] As Richard Edwards notes, such control could not survive inherent contradictions. The widened base and markets of large firms and the greater complexity of organizing production raised the costs of disruptions at the same time that the labor movement was growing in size and substance.[25] The need to exercise greater control led to an expansion of the number of foremen[26] and, as a result, increased the perceived incidence of "arbitrariness, discipline, and harshness of the foreman's rule. Thus extension of control led directly to conditions on the shop floor that created a more effective challenge to control."[27] Close supervision, therefore, intensified the workers' reaction to it.

The "loyalty to a common enterprise" of which the Supreme Court has spoken could not grow out of a system where the very size of firms weakened personal associations and where firms emphasized repression and deskilling rather than incentives. Employers discovered that they needed systems to create positive incentives and to combat concerted, not just individual, resistance to discipline and control.[28] John Commons stated that "understanding the human element in industry is the acid test of the competency of capitalism today. Ignoring this great human problem and fumbling it add fuel to the fires of class conflict, and class conflict and production never go hand in hand."[29]

One result in the United States was the institution of "welfare capitalism" and the experiments with scientific management.[30] Welfare capitalism involved the creation of various nonjob benefits, consciously designed to increase production and morale and to weaken collective militancy, without in any way reorganizing workplace power relationships. The movement grew well into the 1920s, and some kind of "welfare" program was common in most firms, including such things as pension or sickness plans, safety programs, hospital and sanitary facilities, libraries, and education. Such programs, however, failed to end strikes and, for the most part, did not survive the Depression.[31]

Scientific management or "Taylorism," on the other hand, was directly responsible to management's perceived need to reform or reorganize workplace relations. Taylor's contributions were initially based upon employers' desires to speed up production and reduce "soldiering." Taylor's description of soldiering connoted laziness but his definition certainly also included the independent power of employees to determine for themselves the conditions under which they would work. Scientific management was not widely practiced, or at least if practiced, not generally implemented in conformity with Taylor's principles, and its legacy is still debated.[32]

One of Taylor's primary criticisms of management was that it lacked knowledge of the actual techniques of production. Such knowledge was critical, he believed, if management was to control production.[33] Thus Taylorism became another technique to attempt to wrest knowledge of the production process, and thus more control, from workers. Science, argued Taylor, could be used to settle questions of timing and pay, leading to industrial peace. Science, though, was clearly to be used to strengthen managerial prerogatives or control.[34] Functional autonomy of craftsmen was seriously threatened by these new management strategies. Taylor's time and motion studies "allowed management to learn, then to systematize the way the work itself was done." The standardization of methods "fundamentally disrupted the craftsmen's styles of work, their union rules and standard rates, and their mutualist ethic, as it transformed American industrial practice between 1900 and 1930."[35] The result was to place the worker at the lowest level of a highly stratified organization, leaving his "established routines of work, his cultural traditions of craftmanship, [and] his personal interrelations" under the authority of technicians.[36]

David Montgomery stresses that the appeal of scientific management must be seen as an attempt to "uproot those work practices which had been the taproot of whatever strength organized labor enjoyed in the late nineteenth century" rather than solely as a response to the increasing size of enterprise or new technology.[37] Moreover, there was a concerted attempt to discredit the older work practices, called "soldiering" by Taylor or "output restrictions" by others. Even progressives like Louis Brandeis and John Commons could state that management of the work processes was not a responsibility of labor. To Commons, who was certainly not a Taylorite, it was "immoral to hold up to this miscellaneous labor, as a class, the hope that it can ever manage industry."[38] Brandeis could praise scientific management for "reliev[ing] labor of responsibilities not its own."[39] Thus, the new order was seen as natural and inevitable, and prior forms of industrial organization were simply forgotten.

Despite Taylor's hope for decreasing conflict, Taylorism[40] was seen by employees and employers as a system for removing from workers the decisions over production and work speed or for excluding such decisions from the bargaining relation between employees and their foremen. This attempt to impose order could only conflict with the image of management that welfare capitalism tried to create.[41] The attempts to impose Taylorite measures, moreover, led to increased worker militancy and strikes at some establishments.

Other techniques of control, such as company unions,[42] the maintenance of a pool of unemployed workers, or the reliance on race, sex, or ethnic differences or discrimination to divide the work force also were often ineffective, although the legacy and impact of the attempts to divide the work force cannot be discounted. The greatest economic incentive was, of course, insecurity. No more serious encouragement exists for workers to "freely bargain with employers" than the threat of starvation. Wages varied widely and job tenure was not guaranteed.

The history of the post–World War II era is marked by the successful use of what Richard Edwards helpfully refers to as "technical" and "bureaucratic" control,[43] although such systems may have their roots in welfare capitalism of the 1920s and even in the civil service. Both of these systems move the "organization, coordination, and assignment of work tasks" from the immediate workplace and rest decision-making power in the structure of the firm itself. Power can be made fairly invisible when it is embedded in technical organization of work or in the firm's "social-organizational" structure. Technical control, commonly exemplified by the assembly line, involves designing machinery and the production process to maximize efficiency and minimize per-unit wage costs. The worker must adjust to machine time, but this development should not be seen as inevitable or somehow inherent in technology. Whether by design or not, machine time means that worker anger is directed at the speed of the line and not just at the action of a supervisor. Thus, work becomes more alienating. Work conflict now tends to be plantwide, a development that perhaps aided the rise of industrial unions in the 1930s.[44]

I certainly do not argue that technology necessarily or even usually is designed primarily to control the work process or to eliminate skilled labor, but I do mean to suggest that this has sometimes been the case and has often been overlooked.[45] "The history of inventions is not only that of inventors but that of collective experience, which gradually solves the problems set by collective needs."[46] But who defines the needs or goals, the rewards offered for certain solutions, and what resources are committed? The chairman of Western Union, for instance, testifying before a state labor-relations board in 1916, explained how technological displacement of skilled Morse operators became company policy and was related to labor-power considerations:

It was perfectly obvious to me when I first got a view of the telegraph business that we were too much involved with the man who knew the dot and dash— that was a trade which could not be rapidly learned; you couldn't go out and get a lot of intelligent people in to take their place[s], and I said to our people, we are on the wrong track; the hand-sending man, while he probably always will be needed to a certain extent, should not be the important factor in the transactions of the telegraph business.[47]

Bureaucratic control, developed primarily in the postwar period, was designed, at least in part, to compensate for the perceived failure of technical control, although such control is common to varying degrees in all industries. The "bureaucratic form" is so common that its existence is often taken for granted—it serves, for instance, as the backdrop for most contractual and arbitration disputes. Whereas technical control is embedded in the physical and technological aspects of production and is built into the design of machines and the industrial architecture of the plant, bureaucratic control is built into job categories, work rules, promotion procedures, discipline, wage scales, definitions of responsibilities, and the like. Bureaucratic control establishes the impersonal force of "company rules" or "company policy" as the basis for control.[48]

Modern grievance procedures, which normally involve successive appeal steps up the management ladder from foreman to manager to top management, recognize and reinforce a hierarchical structure. Such rules exist in unionized as well as unorganized firms, and they serve to institutionalize the hierarchical, decision-making power of management. Decisions, some discussed already and some to be discussed subsequently, seem to assume the inherent necessity for this form of industrial structure and its service as one of the bases upon which labor law is to be constructed.

I do not mean to imply that employee interests are not recognized or protected under federal labor law. The NLRA clearly has created a substantial zone of protection for employees wishing to join and participate in a union. I do mean to point out that statutory interests are often thwarted, or "balanced" out, in many areas of critical employee concern. The doctrines already discussed permit an employer to permanently replace employees who avail themselves of their Section 7 right to strike. Yet, some other types of "concerted activities" may lead to discharge even without the fact of replacement, although they ironically involve less disruption than a strike. Undefined zones of employer prerogatives exist, to be discussed and defined by the courts, which may often be superior to statutory interests despite the lack of express congressional support. Under the common law, courts imparted their own notions of proper industrial relationships limited only by perceived political and economic realities. The presence of the National Labor Relations Act, however, creates a different situation because the function of courts is not simply to weigh employee, employer, and public interests. Nevertheless, the valuation process has continued, and, almost unnoticed by scholars, many underlying assumptions do not seem to have radically altered. It is of less importance whether we assume that the Court's values are the same as Congress's. It is certainly difficult to determine this convergence, because Congress has been relatively silent on these matters. It is important, however, to note that an agenda exists whose dimensions are hidden but which certainly helps to decide concrete cases.

It is important that the impact of these cases falls mainly on employees, not unions, and employees who have relied and believed the promises made by the common wisdom and by the principles supposedly underlying the NLRA. Their interests may be terminated, without consideration, notice, and surely without bargaining, by a change in employer or other changes based on vague employer prerogatives. The stress on productivity applies even to cases that apparently do not involve core prerogatives. Nevertheless, decisions limit the kinds of pressure tactics that may be used and the extent of protection by the act, and even make the right to strike hollow in cases in which the employer finds permanent replacement a possible viable response. The emphasis upon managerial and capital prerogatives becomes even clearer in the material that follows.

PART TWO

COLLECTIVE BARGAINING AND

MANAGEMENT CONTROL

7

THE SCOPE OF MANDATORY BARGAINING:

SEEKING THE "CORE

OF MANAGERIAL PREROGATIVES"

Even where collective bargaining exists, the promise of industrial democracy has only been partially fulfilled, for neither the law nor the practice has accepted employees as full partners in the enterprise.[1]

The [Federal District] Court has spent many hours searching for a way to cut to the heart of the economic reality—that obsolescence and market forces demand the close of the Mahoning Valley plants, and yet the lives of 3500 workers and their families and the supporting Youngstown community cannot be dismissed as inconsequential. United States Steel should not be permitted to leave the Youngstown area devastated after drawing from the lifeblood of the community for 80 years.

Unfortunately, the mechanism to reach this ideal settlement, to recognize this new property right, is not now in existence in the code of laws of our nation.[2]

. . . [I]n establishing what issues must be submitted to the process of bargaining, Congress had no expectation that the elected union representative would become an equal partner in the running of the business enterprise in which the union's members are employed.[3]

THE MOST COMMONLY expressed goal of the Wagner Act was the achievement of industrial peace.[4] Thus the Senate Report on the act stressed the large number of strikes, the number of employees involved, and the estimated cost of these disputes. The report stressed that the act did not attempt to eliminate all causes of disputes nor the exercise of economic force because "disputes about wages, hours of work, and other working conditions should continue to be resolved by the play of competitive forces. . . ." But there was an attempt to eliminate disputes caused by the failure of employers to recognize unions and utilize the process of collective bargaining. It was thought possible to remove the provocation for a large proportion of bitter disputes by giving legal status to the procedures of collective bargaining and by setting up facilitating machinery.[5] Moreover, the very process of negotiation, which presumably led to the sharing of information and the creation of mutual respect, would lessen the incidence of economic warfare.

The goal was not new, nor was it necessarily abhorrent to all employers. The institution of collective bargaining, leading to a mutually respected trade agreement, had long been sought by certain employers who were seeking industrial order. During the Progressive period, for instance, a major source of economic unpredictability and instability involved the organization of production.[6] Attempts to control competition, especially in wage rates, led to interstate compacts in bituminous coal as early as 1885, although the agreements collapsed four years later, in part due to the absence of a strong mine union capable of keeping recalcitrant operators in line.[7]

Collective bargaining was positively viewed by some entrepreneurs. Thus, Marcus Hanna, reflecting one of the policies of the National Civic Federation, noted that the recognition of labor unions would introduce much needed stability into labor-management relations, defusing the perceived threat flowing from the current confrontation. Hanna wanted labor "Americanized in the best sense, and thoroughly educated to an understanding of its responsibilities, and in this way to make it the ally of the capitalist, rather than a foe with which to grapple."[8] The use of collective bargaining to secure a "depoliticalization" of industrial relations was widely recognized by many reformers, especially John Commons.[9]

The second cited major objective of the act was to encourage through collective bargaining the creation of equality of bargaining power which was a prerequisite to "quality and opportunity and freedom of contract."[10] The aim was to substitute the strength of collective action for the weakness of the individual employee. Entwined with the recognition of the inequality of bargaining power was the goal of placing money in the hands of employees, thereby stimulating economic activity. Thus, the Senate Report stressed the long-standing disparity between "production and consumption." This disparity resulted from a low level of wages that did not permit the masses of consumers to relieve the market of an ever-increasing flow of goods. Thus the Senate Report expressly referred to minimum wages and maximum hour legislation as a base, but not a substitute, for self-help in order to stabilize competitive conditions and create adequate consumer purchasing power throughout the nation. The actual scope of bargaining was never made clear. Moreover, it was perhaps obvious at the start that the encouragement of collective bargaining could not necessarily usher in a period of "equality of bargaining power."

Despite the broad goals and potentially wide-sweeping scope of the act, early judicial opinions, when deciding in favor of unions, generally stressed that the reach of the act was limited. Thus, as long ago as *NLRB* v. *Jones & Laughlin Steel*,[11] the Supreme Court stressed that although the act required bargaining, it did not require or "compel" agreement. Nor would the act interfere with "the normal exercise of the right of the employer to select its employees or to discharge them" as long as the employer's actions do not violate the statute.[12] The language used is defensive in tone and indicates, perhaps, the primary audience to which it is addressed. Do not fear, it seems to say, private ordering is still the order of the day except insofar as narrow incursions are required by the NLRA. The language suggests not the development of a new mode of legal thought, but, rather, the staying power of the views of the past in limiting the scope of change. The need to assuage hostile industrialists in 1937 may be understandable, but the continued use of such language suggests that something more is at stake than temporary stroking. Moreover, the fact that the Court tended to mask "the unavoidably ideological content of judicial action"[13] is merely a reflection of a common job tendency of judges, clearly recognized long ago by Oliver Wendell Holmes, Jr., for instance.[14]

The passage of the NLRA would seem to alter the assumptions of the past. Some historians believe that the New Deal "effected a veritable revolution in American Government"[15] and deem the Wagner Act "one of the most drastic legislative innovations of the decade."[16] Although most employers aggressively fought the bill, no one, says Leuchtenburg, "fully understands why such a radical law passed with so little opposition and by such overwhelming margins."[17] It is indeed quite possible that the Wagner Act was presented and passed at the most propitious time, following the Democratic victories in 1934 and coming on the heels of the Supreme Court's invalidation of the NIRA. The support belatedly given to the act by Roosevelt was caused by the destruction of the NIRA and the need for some labor legislation. Concurrently, the NIRA rejection by the Supreme Court may have fueled the belief that the act was unconstitutional, and, therefore, there was little cost in voting aye. The debate went rapidly, opposition in Congress was feeble, and even the Senate vote (63–12)

surprised Senator Wagner. Moreover, 1935 may have been the "apo-
gee of the New Deal as a progressive domestic reform movement."[18]

Yet, many of the judicial interpretations of the Wagner Act seem
inconsistent with this fairly commonly expressed perception of the
New Deal. Perhaps the act seems more radical than it was—even for
1935. One expressed goal, after all, was to contain radical labor elements and to institutionalize labor disputes within the confines of
the capitalistic order.[19] Thus, the views of the old National Civic
Federation and John Commons were reflected in the debates, although their weight should not, perhaps, be overestimated. It is also
true that neither the AFL nor the CIO, created only after the act's passage, challenged certain capitalistic norms.[20] Others have argued that
the New Deal, rather than breaking sharply with American traditions, created institutions which protected American capitalism
from major business cycles. In addition, like other legislation in the
1930s, the Wagner Act was partially supported because of its presumed Keynesian impact, that is, its hoped-for impact on the avoidance of depressionary wage spirals. Although labor law provided
"procedural restraints," Paul Conklin, for instance, argues that these
were "necessary for security and ordered growth."[21] The courts had
equated private property with the private right to manage the means
of production, and this equation seems to have carried over in the interpretation of the Wagner Act.

Assessments of the original purposes of legislation often appear
quite different from a tabulation of the act's consequences. For some
reason, legal writers seem peculiarly unable to predict the kinds of issues that will be raised by new legislation and, of course, the often
surprising tenor and direction of judicial interpretations. The text
that follows will reveal the extent to which certain goals, such as
those of industrial democracy and equality of bargaining power, are
routinely ignored by the courts. Instead, most pronounced in the bargaining area is the almost-never-stated goal of protecting inherent
managerial prerogatives *from* collective bargaining.

Two areas will be investigated in which the Court has presented its
values in stronger and clearer terms than elsewhere. The primary focus will be the extent to which the legal system regulates the bargaining agenda items included within the mandatory bargaining provisions of the act. Brief attention will be given to a seemingly different
but actually related pigeonhole, the regulation of employer responses
to concerted activities, which, I believe, is affected by similar no-

tions. Second, in the area of "successorship"—a term of the trade referring to capital transfers by sale or merger—the Board and courts
have stressed some basic economic values in startling clarity.

THE LEGAL CONTEXT

In the bargaining area courts have been fairly clear about certain underlying values, at least compared with the areas already discussed.
The key section in the Wagner Act, Section 8(5) [now Section 8(a)(5)]
made it an unfair labor practice for an employer to refuse to bargain
collectively with the authorized representative of the relevant group
of employees, subject to the provisions of Section 9(a). Section 9 of the
act deals with a variety of matters concerning the designation or se-
lection of unions as authorized representatives of employees and provides for NLRB-sponsored elections. Section 9(a) provides that the
union designated or selected by employees is to be the authorized representative "for the purposes of collective bargaining in respect to
rates of pay, wages, hours of employment, or other conditions of employment. . . ."[22] This phrase has long been read as limiting the scope
of an employer's obligation to bargain. That is, terms falling within
the scope of the obligation are deemed "mandatory"; those that do
not are referred to as "permissive." The dichotomy is significant, although the practical effect of these rules is unclear.

The doctrinal framework is easy to express. First, any party may insist upon a mandatory term, even to the point of creating a bargaining
impasse, and no party may legally refuse to discuss such a term. Permissive terms, on the other hand, may be discussed, but neither party
may insist upon such a term or demand that the other consider it.[23]
The most important rule, perhaps, is that which bars an employer's
unilateral change or imposition of a mandatory term without bargaining. A vague outer boundary exists beyond which union attempts
to enlarge the scope of bargaining intrudes into areas of "managerial
prerogatives," a phrase also employed elsewhere to restrict the scope
of the act.

I must add at the outset, heretical though it may be for a law professor to assert, that these basic rules do not necessarily affect bargaining. For instance, a relatively strong union or employer may find
some way to get the other side to discuss a permissive term. Whatever
the term's designation, a weak union, unable to exert pressure upon
an employer, may gain little power from having the Board determine

that the employer's refusal to discuss one of its terms violates Section 8(a)(5). Nevertheless, considerable legal, judicial, and professorial effort has been expended in the attempt to categorize particular items as permissive or mandatory or to delineate the boundaries between these categories. I will not add to this effort, but I do want to stress that the area contains more hints about submerged, and sometimes obvious, values.

Initially, the generally accepted notion that the phrase "wages, hours and other working conditions" is a phrase of limitation was hardly a necessary conclusion. The phrase may have been designed simply to state clearly those items whose inclusion was felt to be most necessary to best effectuate the bargaining duty.[24] The most obvious function of Section 9(a) was to adopt the principle of majority rule and exclusive representation, a principle that the predecessor agency, the National Labor Board, had accepted after considerable debate.[25]

Much of the early writing on the NLRA focused not on the terms *included* within the scope of mandatory bargaining but, rather, dealt with whether the section empowered the Board to determine that some terms were included at all! It is certainly a revealing fact that inquiry focused not on the scope of mandatory bargaining but on the power of the NLRB to define *any* terms as mandatory. Thus, Archibald Cox and John Dunlop, for instance, in an early and influential article, asserted that 9(a) was included "for the purpose of defining the area from which the union preferred by the minority should be excluded, *not* to define the subjects on which the employer and majority representative must bargain."[26]

The reference to minority unions is puzzling. Since minority unions have traditionally had no legally enforceable right to demand bargaining on anything, and employers are now legally compelled to bargain with the majority representative, there is no area from which minority unions have to be excluded. It is possible to read the section to obligate an employer to bargain with any and all "representatives" of its employees *for those employees,* but only to accord *exclusive* representation to a union if it secures the support of a majority of the bargaining unit. Such an approach is consistent with the literal language and the practice under the earlier Railway Labor Act. The Board, however, always read the statute to provide for representation only by majority unions.[27]

The main thrust of the Cox and Dunlop argument, however, was that the act was "concerned with *organization for bargaining*—not with the scope of ensuing negotiations nor with the procedures through which they are carried on." They argued that there was no evidence that the act either defined the subjects of mandatory collective bargaining or granted the NLRB the power to resolve the issue in disputed cases.

If, said the authors, an employer recognizes the union and engages in collective bargaining, he ought not to be held to violate 8(a)(5) for refusing to discuss issues such as pensions, merit increases, or subcontracting.[28] One problem, of course, is how we define "collective bargaining." Even Cox and Dunlop have trouble at this point—they say that "possibly an employer who refuses to discuss such a subject as wages, or hours of work, seniority, or the establishment of a grievance procedure could be said to be committing an unfair labor practice, for *tradition* teaches us that every union which has received *true* recognition has bargained for those subjects."[29] But this merely re-creates the same problem they want to avoid, because wages or hours of work, for instance, still would have to be defined. Moreover, "true recognition" merely begs the question—and "tradition" can teach us a variety of things. And what is the connection between what unions have traditionally bargained *for* and what an employer must bargain *about*? This approach would limit 8(a)(5) to practices existing prior to mandatory bargaining and the NLRA.

By 1940, the NLRB had assumed the power to determine what subjects were included in mandatory bargaining,[30] and Congress seems to have adopted this position in Section 8(d) of the Taft-Hartley amendments of 1947. The assumption, however, that the phrase was intended to have a limiting function is suggestive in itself. Congress may have wished to narrow its intrusion into what had previously been conceived as a zone of inherent managerial power, although this intention was not expressed. The phrase "other conditions of employment" in Section 9(a) could be read broadly, even if some limiting function for the phrase is acknowledged. Would there be areas of union interest that did not affect "conditions of employment"? There is little indication that these questions were well considered, or, for that matter, considered at all in 1935. There is little explicit evidence that Congress feared that the new obligation could compel bargaining in areas that should be left to unilateral managerial control, although employers could well have been concerned over such a possibility. Given the state of labor organization in the 1930s and the nonradical stance of most American unions, it is understandable that Congress would not have devoted much attention to this matter.[31]

The first National Labor Relations Board, created by executive order in 1934 and operating under the National Industrial Recovery Act, endorsed a broad reading of the duty to bargain, expanding interpretations from its predecessor, the National Labor Board.[32] Decisions made clear that employers must bargain in good faith, "match unacceptable proposals with counter proposals and . . . [must] exert every reasonable effort to reach an agreement binding it for an appropriate term."[33] The young Board repeatedly stressed the existence of an affirmative obligation on the employer's part, not simply a negative duty to avoid an intention to thwart any agreement.[34] In addition, employers were ordered to bargain over a wide range of matters that had an impact upon terms and conditions of employment, including changes in terms occasioned by plant relocation or "the introduction of a new line of products."[35] This history, as will be noted, was subsequently ignored by members of the Supreme Court.

When Senator Wagner submitted his second labor bill in 1935, it did not contain an explicit duty to bargain. It is incorrect to argue, however, that Section 8(5) [now Section 8(a)(5)] was merely an afterthought, for Senator Wagner made it clear that the duty, although difficult to state clearly, was nevertheless "implicit in the bill."[36] Witnesses, including members of the first NLRB, argued for the inclusion of an explicit statement of the duty to bargain.[37] No witnesses commented directly in opposition to the duty,[38] but this could be explained perhaps by the absence of an explicit bargaining obligation. The final bill was enacted with a mandatory duty to bargain, but there is little evidence on which to base any conclusions about the range of subjects included in the duty.[39]

Those legal decisions or articles which asserted that the Board had no authority to regulate the subjects of bargaining were not based upon a desire to widen the scope of mandatory bargaining.[40] Instead, this line of argument, found for instance in the influential articles by Cox and Dunlop,[41] was aimed at avoiding *any* regulation of subjects at all, a conclusion which means that either party can *avoid* bargaining over *any* matter by simply refusing to discuss it. This view obviously places an emphasis upon economic force and reflects the revival of notions of contractualism.[42] Cox and Dunlop argued that as long as collective bargaining occurs, "the substantive contents of the parties' agreements"[43] are of no public concern. Indeed, a stress on the nonregulation of outcomes of "free" collective bargaining means that unions through bargaining could waive the right to bargain about specific mandatory matters.[44] The fear of governmental intervention or impact was so strong that Cox and Dunlop, for instance, also argued that the obligation to avoid bad-faith bargaining should not include affirmative obligations to seek agreement because such a standard would ultimately lead to Board review of the substantive positions of the parties.[45]

Despite these concerns, most judicial and Board majorities have attempted to place restraints on the unlimited use of economic power. Such a view rejects the notion that 8(a)(5) provides only a narrow procedural requirement and seemingly comports with the congressional understanding that a vast disparity in bargaining power existed. To limit the use of economic power, the law has sought to map out areas in which mandatory bargaining is to occur. Thus, cases like *Borg-Warner*,[46] holding that parties may not insist upon nonmandatory items, choose elusive concepts of labor peace over the free use of economic power and assume that such doctrines will actually affect particular power relationships. The dissenter in *Borg-Warner*, Justice Harlan, argued that all legal matters were subject to bargaining and this implied the power to insist on any matter even to the point of creating a bargaining impasse. Thus, 8(a)(5) should only require an obligation to bargain in good faith. A third possible argument, that *all* proposed subjects were to be considered mandatory, was generally neither suggested nor discussed. Such an approach would give parties the right to insist that any matter be discussed but, in addition, would require an unwilling party to discuss *any* subject. Thus, this view of mandatory bargaining strikes closer to the heart of managerial prerogatives than any other.[47] Whether this view is harmful to goals of industrial peace is problematical, but the actual effect of *any* of the three possible approaches on peace is simply unknown.

Two points must be stressed. First, as already noted, a party needing Board assistance to compel bargaining over a particular matter is hardly in a position to achieve notable bargaining success. An employer, for instance, may be forced by legal doctrine to discuss subcontracting, but a union that needed the Board's aid to open the discussion in the first place might not noticeably be aided by the agency's intervention. The issue is at least ripe for empirical research.

The rational aspects of negotiation, although not to be ignored, are affected if not overshadowed by the use or threatened use of economic power.

Second, adopting a strategy that results in the *inclusion* of some subjects within mandatory bargaining in the name of labor peace has resulted in the *exclusion* of others. Yet, the *Borg-Warner* rule, that insistence upon a nonmandatory subject is a violation of 8(a)(5), has been strongly criticized because it interferes with "free" collective bargaining and is based on an inherently vague distinction.[48] A decision that a matter is not mandatory theoretically limits the extent to which the dispute can be resolved through collective bargaining and economic struggle. Moreover, it is conceivable that such determinations affect the content of those agreements ultimately reached, although it is difficult to secure evidence of such an effect.

In addition, because the bounds of mandatory bargaining are far from precise, a management that acts but guesses wrong will have to undo the disputed change. In *Fibreboard*,[49] which involved the subcontracting of maintenance work and the resulting destruction of the entire bargaining unit, the employer was forced to reinstate all its maintenance employees with a substantial back-pay award.

Whether the current approach to bargaining aids or hinders negotiation or industrial peace is far from clear. *Borg-Warner* may indeed limit the use of bargaining power by restricting the items upon which a party can insist. Whether this is an actual hindrance to bargaining is far from clear. Philip Ross, in defending *Borg-Warner*, has noted that the doctrine rarely is the basis of an unfair labor practice action.[50] But this may only mean that these disputes are resolved short of Board adjudication. One way to obtain a nonmandatory item, after all, is to surrender or concede on a mandatory issue.

Whatever the subsidiary rules, no guidelines exist to determine where the mandatory/permissive line should be drawn, either in the abstract or in any particular case. This should lead to the most serious objection to the dichotomy. My concern here is not that some subjects are included within the duty as mandatory items, a concern stressed by some scholars, but that some subjects are *excluded*. If excluded, a party can refuse to discuss the matter, thus placing a premium on the kind of economic force supposedly to be limited in the case of mandatory subjects. The only difference between the two areas is a legal determination that mandatory items are critical and that permissive matters are not. It is at this critical point that certain notions of "core" prerogatives arise, a fact virtually ignored in the early legal scholarship of the NLRA.

It is true that through economic pressure, mutual interest, or legal decisions, the phrase "wages, hours, and working conditions" has traditionally been read fairly broadly despite repeated judicial statements that the phrase is one of limitation. In addition, the phrase has not been restricted to matters historically included within collective bargaining at the time the NLRA was enacted.[51] Generally, courts analogize the disputed term to some matter clearly within the statutory phrase, such as wages or hours, or look for some clear effect upon such an interest. It is common in these cases for the court or agency to find the disputed matter mandatory, while carefully noting that not all matters affecting wages, for instance, are within the obligation and, furthermore, also noting that it is not required that the decision maker "mark the outer boundaries" of the phrase.[52]

It is interesting that restrictions on the scope of 8(a)(5) and 8(d) somewhat parallel those applied to Section 7. Thus, illegal proposals are not mandatory;[53] nor are those that are inconsistent with other obligations imposed by the act.[54] Other bargaining subjects are non-mandatory because they are illegal under other federal statutes.[55] Finally, some subjects are considered outside the scope of the act even though they are neither illegal nor violative of federal policy. Some are considered "peripheral," although it is not clear why unions would insist to impasse or file charges over an employer's refusal to bargain over peripheral items. Some are not at all peripheral to employee interests but are excluded from the obligation to bargain because of other policies or values. As under the common law, the reference to subjects as "peripheral" or of only "indirect" interest to employees masks the use of hidden judicial values.

The adoption of a "legal" as opposed to a "factual" definition of protected activities is similar in effect to the adoption of a restrictive view of mandatory terms of bargaining. Each approach creates a middle zone of ambiguity, having no clear or inherent boundaries, and serves to deflect investigation from major issues into the detailed, case-by-case slogging of traditional legal scholarship. Such a result was not necessarily intentional or planned, but it conforms to "balancing" methodology so common to modern legal thought. One could argue, however, that the appearance of evenhandedness and fairness masks the fact that the approach taken itself represents a value choice. Throughout this book I have argued that decisions are often based upon a hidden set of assumptions or values, but I do not wish to slight the recognition that the choice of approaches itself may reflect such assumptions, whether by intention or by effect.

The notion that a set of inherent managerial prerogatives exists suggests a timeless historical imperative. The language in NLRB and judicial opinions, not to mention arbitration opinions where the characteristic is most easily observable, often appeals to a "Genesis" view of labor-management relations: "In the beginning" there was management and some employees. Management directed the enterprise until limited by law and collective bargaining agreements. Management *still* possesses all power that has not been expressly or perhaps implicitly restricted by agreements. The power of an employer, then, is analogized to a state, having all powers not expressly restricted in the state's constitution. Moreover, management would prefer that these restrictions be narrowly interpreted and limited to the express terms of the written agreement.

Arbitral awards commonly refer to "reserved" or "residual" rights of management, even though arbitrators have found implicit restrictions in a wide variety of cases. The starting point for many arbitrators can be summed up in the following quotations:

It is axiomatic that an employer retains all managerial rights not expressly forbidden by statutory law in the absence of a collective bargaining agreement. When a collective bargaining agreement is entered into, these managerial rights are given up only to the extent evidenced in the agreement.[56]

It is a normal and well recognized principle in the interpretation of such agreements that the rights of management are limited and curtailed only to the degree to which it has yielded specified rights. [Even in the absence of a specific clause reserving managerial rights] . . . those rights are inherent and are nevertheless reserved and maintained by it and its decisions with respect to the operations of the business and the direction of the working forces may not be denied, rejected, or curtailed unless the same are in clear violation of the terms of the contract, or may be clearly implied, or are so clearly arbitrary or capricious as to reflect an intent to derogate the relationship.[57]

Initially, before unions came into the picture, all power and responsibility in all aspects of personnel management were vested in the company and its officials. . . . [T]he original power and authority of the company is modified only to the extent that it voluntarily and specifically relinquishes facets of its power and authority.[58]

The firmness of these historical statements is only overcome by

the extent of their historical inaccuracy. These common views tend
to ignore the fact that many industries, steel, for instance, began with
worker-controlled production processes, and they reflect only management's victory in taking control of the production processes in
these industries from skilled employees.[59] Moreover, behind the notion of reserved rights is the belief that these are prerogatives that
"management must have to successfully carry out its function of
managing the enterprise."[60] These notions then include the *assumption* that certain rights are necessarily vested exclusively in management or are based upon an economic *value judgment* about the necessary locus of certain power. In either case, the notion accepts as given
a state of affairs that has not existed at all times and whose development is not necessarily technologically or scientifically determined.
When viewed in this light, the almost commonplace observations
quoted above take on a quite different meaning.

Questions involving the regulation of the subject matter of collective bargaining did not arise for some years after the passage of the
Wagner Act. Cox and Dunlop believe that

older craft unions strong enough to present broader demands were content to
bargain about such traditional subjects as wages, hours of work, seniority and
union status. Others expanded the scope of their demands until they came
into conflict with management's reluctance to surrender its "prerogatives,"
and sharp controversies resulted over the proper functions of management
and union. But the issues were settled by negotiations resulting in an endless
variety of arrangements—with or without the resort to economic sanctions—
and there was little disposition to seek government intervention.[61]

Newly formed industrial unions, consolidating their position, had
little reason, motivation, or ability to push management beyond
more traditional areas. It may be, as Cox and Dunlop assert, that as
their strength grew, unions attempted to broaden the scope of joint
responsibility into areas "for which management had exclusive responsibility—not only pensions and merit increases but also the
scheduling of shifts, subcontracting, and technological change."[62]
Governmental action, especially under Section 8(a)(5), is no doubt
sought by unions lacking the clout to achieve their objectives
through the exercise of economic pressure. Yet, the Cox-Dunlop
stress on areas of exclusive managerial authority starts any analysis
with a thumb on the scale, and courts have relied on the same vague
benchmark. At the same time, courts have unaccountably ignored

decisions of the first NLRB in which the Board had no difficulty including matters such as plant location and even product lines within the regime of mandatory bargaining.

In the mass-production industries, *all* matters, whether wages, hours, or whatever, had been areas of exclusive managerial authority, because bargaining, except perhaps in a few, brief instances, had not previously occurred. Indeed, any limitation on employers' powers were seen as an infringement of managerial rights. As NLRB Chairman Madden said:

> When an employer was told that he could not discharge a workman because he had joined a union, a serious in-road was made upon a traditional and important component of his ownership. Employers, almost unanimously, did not welcome the change. I have never been able to see why they should welcome the change. I cannot remember instances when any other elements of our population have surrendered, with pleasure, powers and prerogatives that were traditionally theirs.[63]

The "limitation" notion suggests a core of managerial authority or responsibility that is to be free of governmental intervention, a notion that is either explicit or implicit in the cases. One could assume, then, that some matters will be held nonmandatory despite clear impact upon wages, hours, and working conditions. Moreover, unions, and to a lesser extent employers, will not be able to legally mandate bargaining over some matters vital to their interests.

THE "CORE" REVEALED

One of the most important decisions is the Supreme Court's opinion in *Fibreboard Paper Products* v. *NLRB*,[64] a decision noteworthy for the broad approach of the Warren Court and the cautionary, often-cited, and influential concurrence of Justice Stewart. The employer, noting the cost of maintenance work and its inability to reduce these expenses, announced that there was no need to bargain for a new agreement with the union representing the maintenance employees because it had decided to subcontract the work to an independent firm. The Court approved the Board's determination that the employer was required to bargain about the decision to subcontract the maintenance work as well as to bargain over the effects of such a decision upon employees. That is, although the employer would have to bargain over the impact of the subcontract upon employees in any event, the decision itself had to be subjected to negotiation because it was deemed to be a mandatory subject of bargaining. Thus, the employer's unilateral decision to subcontract maintenance work constituted a violation of Section 8(a)(5). In typical Warren Court fashion, the decision adopted a broad, policy-oriented approach to these issues but then narrowed its holding to the precise facts of the case. The Court's broad, inclusive approach to the scope of mandatory bargaining, despite its initial promise, seems to have had less effect on subsequent decisions than the cautioning phrases of Justice Stewart.

The Court majority first noted that subcontracting is "well within" the literal meaning of the phrase "terms and conditions of employment." The phrase seems "plainly" to cover the termination of employment present in *Fibreboard*. Second, the Court stressed that including "contracting out" within the scope of bargaining "seems well designed to effectuate the purposes of the National Labor Relations Act," which was designed to promote the peaceful resolution of disputes by "bringing a problem of vital concern" within the act's structure. The conclusion that contracting out was a matter of "vital concern" was "reinforced" by industrial practice, which demonstrated that subcontracting had often been a subject of collective bargaining. This experience presumably demonstrated that subcontracting was amenable to the bargaining process.

Finally, the "facts" of the case illustrated the "propriety of submitting the dispute to collective negotiation." At this point, the Court hinted at implicit limits to the scope of mandatory bargaining. It noted that the company's decision "did not alter the Company's basic operation. The maintenance work still had to be performed in the plant." In addition, "no capital investment was contemplated" because the company was merely replacing its employees with others. Therefore, the Court's decision would not "significantly abridge his freedom to manage the business."

The stress on the absence of "capital investment" and the lack of impact upon the employer's "freedom to manage" significantly limits the impact of the broad language preceding it. Moreover, the Court proceeded to hold that only the subcontracting involved in the case— "the replacement of employees in the existing bargaining unit with those of an independent contractor to do the same work under similar conditions of employment"—fell within 8(a)(5).

Predictably, decision makers in subsequent cases limited the possible scope of *Fibreboard* by stressing the presence of capital expenditures or the inappropriateness of mandatory bargaining because significant changes occurred in the enterprise. The Supreme Court's own narrow definition of its holding substantially limits its impact and the broad policy approach with which the decision begins. Why capital decisions, for instance, should fall outside of 8(a)(5) is not explained, nor does the Court explain why such a factor is relevant. One implication of the Court's language, made explicit by later decisions, is that decisions affecting income and capital should be treated differently.

Justice Stewart, concurring, faced these matters in perhaps typical fashion. He noted that the Court did not decide that "every managerial decision which necessarily terminates an individual's employment is subject to the duty to bargain." Thus, some decisions that clearly affect "conditions of employment" are excluded because of the nature of the managerial action.[65] Certain managerial decisions, Stewart stressed, may affect job security yet are not subjects of mandatory bargaining. He listed decisions concerning the volume and type of advertising, product design, the manner of financing and sales, but also noted that some of these decisions may have only an indirect or insubstantial effect upon job security and may be excluded on that ground alone. Unions may indeed have little interest in such matters. Stewart's notion that job impact is the linchpin of *Fibreboard*, on the other hand, although relied upon in subsequent decisions, is not necessarily supported by the majority's language.

The key portion of Stewart's concurrence involves employer decisions which may imperil or actually terminate employment yet, nevertheless, are not to be within the scope of mandatory bargaining. Here Stewart lists the decision to "invest in labor-saving machinery" or to "liquidate its assets and go out of business." These decisions, Stewart argues, "lie at the core of entrepreneurial control." The phrase tells us little more than that Justice Stewart knows a nonmandatory item when he sees one. Stewart's explanation is as follows: "Decisions concerning the commitment of investment capital and the basic scope of the enterprise are not in themselves primarily about conditions of employment, though the effect of the decision may be necessary to terminate employment." Thus, matters of capital and those "fundamental to the basic direction of a corporate enterprise" should be excluded.[66]

Stewart's stress on capital investment or on the scope or "basic direction of the enterprise" echoes the Court's own reasons for finding bargaining appropriate in *Fibreboard*, although the Court nowhere suggested that the presence of a capital change *necessarily* made the decision unsuitable for the bargaining process. Nevertheless, Stewart may accurately reflect implicit limitations in the Court's opinion, and other decision makers have so read the decision.[67]

It may often be true that certain capital decisions are not in themselves "primarily about conditions of employment," but the same could be said for the motivation behind some decisions involving work schedules, wages, and the speed of the production process which are concededly within the zone of mandatory bargaining. Generally, such decisions are motivated by concerns over efficiency, productivity, and cost effectiveness. Decisions to automate, merge, or terminate part of an enterprise may be "about" the same matters.

Moreover, although his attempt is unique, Stewart fails to explain other than in *ipse dixit* fashion why capital or "direction" decisions are not within the scope of bargaining. Unions may not have traditionally bargained about such matters, but the act is not to be frozen by practices extant in the 1930s. In addition, the legislative history does not inform us that this is so.

Indeed, a review of the legislative history of the 1947 Taft-Hartley Act supports a broad reading of the scope of bargaining. The House bill had attempted to limit mandatory terms to specified items relating very closely to wages and benefits, thus implicitly excluding other matters.[68] This attempt to specify the scope of bargaining was rejected in favor of the broader language now found in the act, designed to permit a more evolutionary process as well as to permit freer Board discretion.[69] The appropriate scope of bargaining, said the House Conference Report, "will inevitably depend upon the traditions of an industry, the social and political climate at any given time, the needs of employers and employees, and many related factors."[70] The statement is revealing because it clearly recognizes that the scope of bargaining depends initially upon power and, if federal adjudication is sought, upon "social and political" factors.

It is interesting, and I hope no longer surprising, that similar distinctions were made by common-law courts. Although even conservative courts like that of Massachusetts would recognize and refuse to enjoin a work assignment or jurisdictional dispute, courts in more liberal New York and elsewhere would enjoin the attempt to counteract the introduction or use of job-terminating machines as late as 1941.[71] Yet, job loss or work acquisition is involved in either case, and the employees' interest remains basically the same. The difference could be in the fact that one situation involves what may be deemed a more vital employer prerogative, that is, the making of a capital decision. Yet it is far from clear why decisions involving who gets the work should be distinguished from a decision to substitute machines for labor.

My students respond—"Well, that's capitalism." Perhaps so, but this explanation is not particularly illuminating. The early common-law decisions involving automation were often explained by the presumed advantage and public benefit of modernization and automation.[72] Justice Stewart may believe, as well, that the public benefits from exclusive managerial control over key capital decisions. Not all would agree that such control necessarily benefits the public or that such an assumption is silently embedded in the act.

What explains the feeling that there is a "core" of managerial prerogatives that lies outside the scope of mandatory bargaining despite impact upon wages, hours, and working conditions? Post-*Fibreboard* adjudication shows that the notion, although vague, does decide concrete cases. For example, the NLRB had held until recently that a decision to terminate a portion of a business enterprise is a mandatory term of bargaining.[73] Most appellate courts, however, have consistently refused to extend *Fibreboard* to situations involving the partial termination of an enterprise.[74]

The Board's position generally stresses the impact of managerial action upon employees: "We see no reason why employees should be denied the right to bargain about a decision [a partial termination of the business] directly affecting terms and conditions of employment which is of profound significance for them solely because that decision is also a significant one for management."[75]

The position of most appellate courts in partial termination cases is reflected in the following extract from the eighth circuit's opinion in *Adams Dairy*, where the dispute focused upon "a change in the capital structure of Adams Dairy which resulted in a partial liquidation and a recoup of capital investment. To require Adams to bargain about its decision would significantly abridge its freedom to manage its own affairs."[76]

Like the proverbial two ships passing in the night, the Board and courts do not seem to be talking to each other. The NLRB, at least, has attempted to reconcile to the extent possible the managerial interest involved with the obvious concern of employees. Surely a "partial termination" does not solely involve management's affairs; nevertheless, the eighth circuit tells us that such decisions are management's exclusive affair. This vague "managerial core" is operative in the doctrines mentioned in the first part of this volume, and its vagueness explains the steady stream of disputes and litigation searching for the boundaries of mandatory bargaining.

The legal issue is whether management must first notify the union and be willing to bargain about these critical decisions prior to acting.[77] In most cases, if there is no alternative, unions will reluctantly shift their concern to the "effects" of such decisions upon employees, a matter clearly within the duty to bargain. There is always the possibility, as the Court noted in *Fibreboard*, that a solution can be reached that eases the impact upon employees or that provides an alternative course of action.[78] Bargaining over "effects" only, of course, forces the union to accept management's decision and obviously weakens the union's bargaining range and power.

Bargaining over important decisions hardly means management is barred from acting, just as labeling a slowdown "protected" would not necessarily protect the jobs of the employees involved. Rather, it is textbook law that management can act *after* bargaining, usually after an impasse is reached, and good legal advice can usually guarantee that such a situation will occur, and fairly expeditiously as well. Moreover, if truly necessary, exceptions can be made if managerial decisions must be made with unusual dispatch. Thus, the impact of 8(a)(5) on these decisions has been grossly exaggerated by the courts. Yet, the symbolic significance must be great because judicial opinions are replete with "Sturm und Drang."

Consider *General Motors* v. *NLRB*,[79] in which General Motors converted a self-owned and operated retail outlet into an independently owned and operated franchise. As frequently occurs, the UAW was not informed of the change. Indeed, the firm misrepresented what was occurring to union stewards. Such deception is common in these cases despite the notion found in other cases that a "joint enterprise" exists. GM sold the outlet's personal property to Trucks of Texas, Inc., and subleased the premises. It also awarded Trucks a dealership franchise, but the sublease could be immediately terminated if Trucks's dealership was cancelled. Trucks advised former GM employees at the outlet that none would be retained, and the union sought NLRB assistance.

The NLRB designated the arrangement a "sale," a pigeonhole apparently created so that *Fibreboard* could be distinguished. The Board then relied upon Justice Stewart's "core" and other appellate court decisions, presumably the decisions that had overruled the Board on partial terminations, and rejected the charge. The District of Columbia Court of Appeals affirmed the Board decision because of the presence of a change in General Motors' operation. Judge Clark revealingly noted: "What UAW would have us do would turn over the management to it."[80] The statement is startling indeed. No doubt UAW's hopes of taking over General Motors' management functions were quashed.

Although the UAW termed the transaction a "classical contracting-out situation," a not unreasonable characterization, Judge Clark thought it sufficient to rebut the claim to state that the decision was "fundamental to the basic direction" of General Motors and, thus, was at the "core of entrepreneurial control." Presumably, this minor General Motors transaction was "fundamental" because the decision was part of GM's national policy of transferring its owned and operated retail outlets to independent dealerships.

The Board's analysis was fuller than Judge Clark's, but, as Justice Bazelon noted in dissent, it was based upon "broad, and purely speculative, assertions." The Board, Justice Bazelon properly noted, had held that no bargaining was required because the transaction was a "sale." The Board did not weigh the interests of GM in avoiding bargaining over its decision or its general policy, nor did the Board consider employee interests. The characterization of the transaction—as a "sale"—has little to do with the importance of the interests involved. The characterization of the transaction, however, seems to have everything to do with the resulting legal determination. Certain decisions or transactions, whether sales, mergers, or partial terminations, seem freighted with symbolic significance. How else can one determine what lies at the "core of managerial authority"? As the Board noted:

[D]ecisions such as this, in which a significant investment or withdrawal of capital will affect the scope and ultimate direction of the enterprise, are matters essentially financial and managerial in nature. They thus lie at the very core of entrepreneurial control, and are not the subjects Congress intended to encompass within "rates of pay, wages, hours of employment or other conditions of employment." Such managerial decisions oft times require secrecy as well as freedom to act quickly and decisively. They also involve subject areas as to which determinative financial and operational considerations are likely to be unfamiliar to the employees and their representatives.[81]

All decisions made initially by management could conceivably be deemed managerial in nature, yet this fact does not determine the scope of 8(a)(5). Management's desire for speed and secrecy may be also involved in many decisions that are concededly within the area of mandatory bargaining. Moreover, these "expenses" of bargaining do not necessarily increase because the transaction is labeled a "sale," a result based more on the form of the transaction (and legal advice) than its content.

The last sentence in the NLRB's statement quoted above suggests another partial rationale, that is, employees may be unfamiliar with certain types of "financial and operational considerations." The scope and complexity of current collective bargaining, as well as the foresight of many unions and union leaders, at least sheds doubt upon the proposition that unions are too ill-equipped to deal with such complex and weighty matters. Financial and capital considerations, after all, are a routine part of management's bargaining stance at bargaining sessions. True, most bargaining does not involve capital withdrawal or movement, but this is not to say that such matters are beyond the ken or interest of union representatives. Surely the employment effects of such decisions lie at the "core of *union* concern." The language of the Board means, rather, that unions can have no legally protected interest in such matters unless, of course, management voluntarily decides to share knowledge or decision making with the union.

It is true that managerial interests or decisions involve different levels of union expertise. As Robert J. Rabin has noted, where the employer is considering the introduction of labor-displacing machines, the union could argue for machines with less impact upon job opportunities, could stress the operational advantages of various types of machines, or could make work concessions that might make some machines preferable to others. Admittedly, the union may have "no special expertise that would enable it to suggest that as a technological matter one machine is preferable to another,"[82] but this is not invariably true. Management is often surprised by the technical and production lessons it learns from employees involved in the production process, and industrial relations literature contains many examples of productivity increases based upon the (often-belated) recognition of employee suggestions. Even if the matter is beyond union experience or knowledge, the result of mandatory bargaining is likely to be no more than a fairly expeditious series of bargaining sessions ending in the implementation of the company's decision.[83] Again, the realities of bargaining relations do not sustain the fears of the courts.

One implicit assumption seems to be that technological change (and perhaps all capital decisions) are predominantly scientific or technical matters and, as such, can be left to the experts. Yet, as many have noted, technology does not inextricably travel in one direction or call for a particular set of processes or consequences; variations are always possible depending upon the results and effects desired.[84]

It has been commonly assumed that technology is an independent variable which affects changes in social relations; it has its own immanent dynamic and unilinear path of development. Further, it is an irreducible first cause from which social effects automatically follow. . . . Social analysts have recently begun to acknowledge that the technology and the social changes it seems to bring about are in reality interdependent. . . . [T]echnology is not an autonomous force impinging upon human affairs from the "outside" but it is the product of a social process, a historically specific activity carried on by some people, and not others, for particular purposes. Technology thus does not develop in a unilinear fashion; there is always a range of possibilities or alternatives that are delimited over time—as some are selected and others denied—by the social choices of those with the power to choose, choices which reflect their intentions, ideology, social position, and relations with other people in society. In short, technology bears the social "imprint" of its authors. It follows that "social impacts" issue not so much from the technology of production as from the social choices that technology embodies.[85]

The practical effect of vague rules or even case-by-case adjudication in this area lies in the area of remedies. If employers are motivated to act and not bargain, little can be done when a year or two later the employer has been found remiss in failing to bargain. Equipment may have been sold or moved, and the enterprise, or a part of it, may have been closed.[86] The result is a lack of effective remedies which, given the vagueness of the "core" concept, does not encourage respect for law or aid in prediction.

The concern over the predictability of legal results can, of course, be resolved by excluding matters from the scope of bargaining. In a decision in June 1981, the Supreme Court basically adopted the Stewart concurrence in *Fibreboard*. In *First National Maintenance Corpora-*

tion v. *NLRB*,[87] seven members of the Court expressed great concern for managerial exclusivity, convenience, and predictability. Briefly, the employer provided housekeeping and maintenance services to customers, and the dispute arose when the employer refused to bargain with a newly certified union over its decision to terminate its service agreement with a nursing home. The employer apparently felt the agreement was not economically beneficial, while the nursing home expressed dissatisfaction with the employer's lack of efficiency. The factual situation may limit the scope of the decision, but I wish to focus upon the policies reflected in Justice Blackmun's decision.

Blackmun acknowledged that a partial closing has an obvious impact upon employment and that Congress stated in 1947 that the scope of bargaining "should be left in the first instance to employers and trade unions, and in the second place, to any administrative agency skilled in the field and competent to devote the necessary time to a study of industrial practices and traditions in each industry or area of the country, subject to the review by the courts."[88] "Nonetheless," Blackmun confidently stated, "Congress had no expectation that the elected union representative would become an equal partner in the running of the business enterprise in which the union's members are employed."[89] While "equal partnership" was hardly the union's goal, the statement shows the extent to which the Court has simply removed the policy of encouraging industrial democracy and worker participation from the act.

Although there are numerous suggestions that the decision should be viewed as narrow, the relationship of Blackmun's expressed concerns to the views previously discussed should be clear. Broadening bargaining, under existing law, would not create a "partnership," because under existing law the employer can institute a change after an impasse is reached. Union participation would certainly be consistent with the notion of a "common enterprise" relied upon by the Court to create *employee* obligations of deference and loyalty.

Blackmun phrased the issue raised by the employer's argument that it need not bargain at all in revealing terms—whether a decision to terminate "should be considered part of petitioner's retained freedom to manage its affairs unrelated to employment."[90] Explicitly, then, he adopted the position that there is an inherent body of exclusively managerial functions. In functional terms, the policies cited by Blackmun as implicit in the statutory concept of bargaining tend in the other direction. Blackmun recognized that the union's concern ("a matter of central and pressing concern to the union") is obviously legitimate and that the function of bargaining is to resolve disputes and thereby encourage industrial peace: bargaining "will result in decisions that are better for both management and labor and for society as a whole." Because the union only represented First National's employees at the nursing home, the employer's termination of its contract with the home effectively ended the union's representational status. In this sense, the situation precisely parallels *Fibreboard*, where the union represented only the maintenance employees. Nevertheless, Blackmun concluded, "management must be free from the constraints of the bargaining process to the extent essential for the running of a profitable business." Apparently, the decision whether to bargain over "managerial decisions" will be left to management, for there was no evidence that bargaining would somehow threaten the continued viability of the enterprise.

Although Blackmun purported to create a balancing test[91] and to focus upon the amenability of the dispute to resolution via the bargaining process, the dissenting Justice Brennan correctly noted that the test used considers only the interests of management. Moreover, the majority's feeling that the dispute is not resolvable through negotiation is based only upon speculation.[92] Indeed, the appellate court had reached the opposite conclusion. Blackmun stressed the "need for speed, flexibility and secrecy," the need for confidentiality, and the need to avoid "futile" bargaining because the union would otherwise have a weapon for delay that could "thwart management's intentions in a manner unrelated to any feasible solution the union might propose." It is depressing to note that *none* of these interests was implicated in this case, nor did Blackmun even argue that secrecy or the other concerns cited justify the refusal to bargain in *this* situation. If the result is based upon a balancing of interests, it is surely an odd approach. Only one side of the balance is considered, and the managerial interests *conceivably* involved do not even have to actually be present.

Decisions such as *First National Maintenance* are viewed as inevitable by those who view collective bargaining as a system that institutionalizes workplace conflict and legitimizes employer prerogatives by propounding a myth of joint union-employer law making.[93] Indeed, collective bargaining and the security of the trade agreement were seen by numerous employers as long ago as the early part of this century as necessary for long-term managerial planning and for reducing workplace militancy.[94] This critique carries many insights, but it can be easily overstated. To the extent that labor relations and collective bargaining exist in a world of unequal influence and bargaining power, most systems of accommodation would begin unequally. More important, collective bargaining was desired by many unions as the only realistically perceived method of creating worker input into workplace decision making. As this investigation suggests, collective bargaining under the NLRA need not come laden with the premises courts have created, assumptions that recognize and even protect managerial independence and prerogatives. The traditional writing of legal, economic, or industrial scholars tends to eloquently describe workplace democracy and industrial self-governance, concurrently overlooking the realities of actual workplace life and the legal doctrines discussed in this volume.

Even in theory, unions can become partners in workplace planning and decision making only with equal power. Although the law creates protections for unions, it makes no attempt to equalize bargaining power, and indeed the Court has slapped down the Board when it attempted to consider relative bargaining power in reaching a decision. Unions that are not strong enough to close down an employer by striking are limited in the pressure devices they can employ. Secondary boycott provisions of Taft-Hartley, for instance, restrict weapons often felt necessary for unions, especially for those which are not in a position to close down the workplace by a strike. To a union that is weak vis-à-vis a particular employer, the duty of an employer to bargain is, thus, less significant than it may first appear. And even if some rough equality exists, the law itself permits employers to refuse to discuss important matters of capital movement or shifts in managerial direction.[95] Because nonmandatory items need not be discussed, economic force cannot be exerted to compel negotiation of such matters. The bankruptcy in theory can be seen by attempting to derive from the writings which particular matters are to be left to exclusive managerial control and which fall within the area of joint determination, a question arising not only during negotiations but also during the life of a collective agreement.

8

VALUATION IN OTHER GUISES: EMPLOYER

RESPONSES TO COLLECTIVE ACTION

THE CONCEPT THAT THE NLRA shall not intrude in areas of "managerial prerogative" arises explicitly in another, nonbargaining area whose themes are quite closely related to the scope of bargaining. The focus of this area is employer responses or countermeasures to protected employee activity. The complexity of this area, reflected by the volume of relevant law review commentary, mandates a fairly cursory summary here. This area involves Section 8(a)(3) and deals with employer actions that "by discrimination in regard to hire or tenure of employment or any term or condition of employment . . . encourage[s] or discourage[s] membership in a labor organization."[1] The purpose of the section, as generally explained, is to insulate employee job interests or opportunities from choices about membership or nonmembership in a union, or the level of participation in a union.

Most of these cases focus upon the propriety of a discharge, arguably discriminating against employees for exercising statutory rights. Generally, the inquiry focuses upon the reason for the employer's action, that is, looks at whether the discharge was based upon anti-union animus or upon legitimate business considerations. These cases primarily raise questions of fact rather than law. Difficult problems arise because a wide range of employer action, other than discharge or other forms of discipline, may discourage union membership, participation, or adherence to contract demands. Many of these cases tend to arise in bargaining situations and, thus, are intimately related to the foregoing discussion. Cases reaching the Supreme Court have involved the offer of superseniority to strike replacements;[2] an employer's lockout designed to avoid a possible strike at a more financially damaging date;[3] a total or partial termination of an enterprise;[4] and the structuring of fringe benefits so as to favor non-strikers over strikers.[5]

All these cases involve employer actions that could conceivably "discourage" union membership or collective activity. Despite impact upon protected employee interests, the Court has often required proof of antiunion animus, either to "discriminate" or to "discourage" membership. Sometimes it has permitted intent to be inferred either from the inherently discouraging effects of the employer's actions or from the significant foreseeable impact of the employer's actions upon union interests. And in *Erie Resistor*, discussed earlier, it permitted an explicit balancing of interests, the result of which was an employer violation despite the absence of proof of antiunion animus.

The Court's frustrating fluctuations under 8(a)(3) have been documented many times,[6] and I do not wish to review the Court's meandering ways. It is important to stress, however, that notions of managerial prerogatives have played a significant role. First, if a Section 8(a)(3) inquiry requires a search for intent, then analysis under that section will differ from that under the generic violation, Section 8(a)(1). Although a finding of antiunion animus would always lead to an 8(a)(1) violation, such intent is not generally required to find a violation since a determination under that section generally involves only a balancing of interests. The intent requirement, when mandated in an 8(a)(3) situation, usually masks the same kind of balancing of interests or of weapons.[7] An intent requirement serves to shift certain risks to employees just as does the adoption of an "objective" test in health and safety work stoppages. Thus, given the difficulty of proving antiunion animus, the adoption of such a requirement will force unions and employees to bear the costs of "discouraging" impact where antiunion animus exists but cannot be proved. And should no animus actually exist, the intent requirement places the protection of employer freedom above harm to employee interests. On the other hand, the adoption of an "impact" rather than a motivation standard will protect employee interests while prohibiting employer actions which the courts may not prefer to regulate.

Julius Getman has said that 8(a)(3), for instance, involves "an attempt to achieve a compromise between the employee's interest in freely choosing whether or not to engage in union activity and the employer's interest in running his business as he sees fit."[8] As in all the areas thus far discussed, employee interests are based upon the statute. The employer's interests, on the other hand, are not statutorily expressed, and the typical reference is to employer prerogatives to run "his business." Yet, a "balancing" approach gives these interests equal significance.

Linguistically, 8(a)(1) is the generic unfair labor practice which covers the field, protecting against interferences with Section 7 rights. The more detailed violations are narrower, yet also involve interferences with rights encompassed by Section 7. Thus, any violation of 8(a)(3) or 8(a)(5), for instance, also involves a violation of the broader Section 8(a)(1). Thus far, there is little problem. But the Supreme Court has suggested that some situations must be adjudicated *only* under 8(a)(3) and not the broader 8(a)(1). Such a position creates a separation between these two provisions and suggests, obviously, that 8(a)(3) involves a different and no doubt narrower area of employer prohibition. This notion is directly contrary to clear statements in the legislative history about the role of 8(a)(1) and the purpose of the narrower unfair labor practices, one of those few situations in which a lawyer can make such a bold statement.[9]

Nevertheless, this distinction has been employed, not unsurprisingly, in cases of "managerial prerogatives." The notion first appeared in a discharge case, *NLRB* v. *Burnup & Sims*,[10] in which 8(a)(1) was used to support a violation. The Court found no need to reach the 8(a)(3) motivational issue. Justice Douglas mysteriously explained that Section 8(a)(3) was not applicable because "[w]e are not in the area of management prerogatives."[11] No one had previously suggested that the presence or absence of such prerogatives was relevant to the application of either 8(a)(1) or (3), and the statement was left unexplained.

The hint became operative in the celebrated *Darlington Mfg. Co.*[12] decision. *Darlington* is noteworthy for two reasons. First, the Court held that in cases reflecting the exercise of "managerial prerogatives," a violation of the NLRA can only be found under the narrower unfair labor practice section, 8(a)(3). Thus, the balancing of interests approach generally followed under 8(a)(1) is to be avoided when certain crucial management interests are at stake, irrespective of (and perhaps because of) the impact upon employees. Second, the Court's sensitivity to managerial prerogatives led it to adopt a bizarre analysis, creating unique standard pursuant to its 8(a)(3) inquiry.

The employer, to put the matter simply, closed the Darlington mill in order to take reprisal against employees who had just voted to be represented by the Textile Workers Union. The issue of antiunion motivation was not in doubt, and no test of inference, impact, or balancing was required. The fourth circuit, however, reversed the Board's finding that the closing violated 8(a)(1) and (3) on the ground that an employer may close all or part of its business *whatever* the motive.[13]

The Supreme Court approved the notion that an employer might with impunity close an entire business but provided some restriction for an antiunion, partial closing. Justice Harlan began by stating that 8(a)(1) and its balancing of interests approach could not apply in a case of total closure. The reason was that decisions to end a business are "so peculiarly a matter of management prerogative that they would never constitute violations of 8(a)(1), whether or not they involved sound business judgment, unless they also violated 8(a)(3)." Thus, just as under the bargaining obligation of 8(a)(5), certain managerial decisions are so crucial that they must be free of any governmental regulation. Why a decision to close motivated by antiunion intent needs legal immunity was not explained. As in a *Mackay* situation, employees pay the ultimate penalty for exercising rights guaranteed under the act.

Technically, the case did not involve the "right to close" at all. The NLRB had treated the issue as a partial closing of one of many mills controlled by Deering Milliken. Significantly, the NLRB did not order the employer to reopen; rather, it ordered back pay for all Darlington workers until they obtained substantially equivalent employment or were placed upon preferential hiring lists at other plants controlled by Darlington's employer group, Deering Milliken. The first part of the order would counter any blacklist operating at other South Carolina mills, but the employer could have easily satisfied the alternative requirement. The "preferential hiring" remedy is not burdensome to the employer; unfortunately, it also provides little solace to the affected employees. Nevertheless, the remedy meant the issue was not whether the employer had the right to close but, rather, whether it had the right to close to punish employees and be *free* of any financial obligation for the affected employees.

The opinion first treats the situation as if it were a total closing of an employer's operation. The Court found the possibility that a total closing could result in compensation to affected employees "startling." The Court's "rationale" was explained and criticized by Clyde Summers:

The rationale of the Court in *Darlington Mills* is nearly as startling as its conclusion. To the argument that the employer's closing his plant was similar to a discriminatory lockout or a runaway shop, the Court answered that, "One of the purposes of the . . . Act is to prohibit the discriminatory use of economic weapons to obtain future benefits." The discriminatory lockout and runaway shop discourage collective employee activities in the future. "But a complete liquidation of a business," said the Court, "yields no such future benefit for the employer." We had always supposed that the purpose of the statute was affirmatively to protect employees in the exercise of their rights, not merely to preclude employers from profiting from destruction of those rights. Indeed, the dominant remedial principle, particularly in Section 8(a)(3) violations, has always been to make the injured employees whole and not merely to deprive the employer of his ill-gotten gains.[14]

The Court permitted the application of 8(a)(3) only in cases in which an employer closes a *part* of an operation, for in such cases there would be the possibility of future employer benefit. Even in this situation, the Court was unwilling to rely upon the finding of anti-union motivation made by the Board and unquestioned by the fourth circuit. Instead, and perhaps only for this type of case, it created a *new* 8(a)(3) test: the Board must prove that (1) the closing was "motivated by a purpose to chill unionism in any of the remaining plants of the single employer" and (2) "the employer may reasonably have foreseen that such closing will likely have that effect." Summers's comment on this part of the decision forcefully attacks the Court's premises.

The Court's phrasing of the required findings is puzzling, but the core of the requirement is plain. It is not enough that Deering Milliken discharged part of its employees because they voted for the union. It is not enough that such discharge had the effect of intimidating the remaining employees. There must be an express finding that the motivation for discharging some is to intimidate the others. The Board may have little difficulty in making the necessary findings in this case, but only because of the employer's lack of finesse. If a multiplant employer closes his only unionized plant but vigorously asserts to his other employees that the closure was solely for economic reasons, proof of the necessary purpose to intimidate the remaining employees may be extremely difficult. Indeed, such motivation may in fact be absent, for it is enough for the employer that he has escaped collective bargaining in the only plant where the employees chose to unionize. Similarly, if a runaway employer reopens in a non-union area under a new name, concealing from his new employees that he is a fugitive from collective bargaining, proof of either the purpose or the effect of intimidating his new employees will be impossible. He is content to be rid of the union for the time being, and if his new employees organize, he can make another quiet escape. This scarcely guarantees to employees the right to bargain through representatives of their own choosing.[15]

An employer, then, violates the act only if the closing of a part of an enterprise is motivated by a desire to frighten employees at other plants who may be watching. Retaliation directed at the Darlington employees—the only group to organize—is simply irrelevant. The entire decision is startlingly clear in its total disregard for the interests of the employees who have become unemployed due to their support or a union. Again, Summers:

> The mischief in the Court's reasoning is that it ignores the rights of those who have been discriminatorily discharged. The essence of the Court's logic is that discharge for supporting the union is not itself an unfair labor practice, that it is no wrong as to the ones discharged, and that the law is not concerned with their injury. Discrimination against them is an evil only when it intimidates others; any remedy given them is only to make others feel secure. This is to see in the execution of hostages nothing more than an intimidation of the living; it is to make murder a crime only when the killer's purpose is to instill fear.[16]

In a later case involving 8(a)(3), the most recent excursion into this tangled web, the Court held that proof of motive could be dispensed with in cases where the employer's "conduct was 'inherently destructive' of important employee rights."[17] The NLRB could find a violation in this type of case even though the employer presented evidence that its action was motivated by legitimate business considerations. In other words, in "heavy impact" cases, a balancing process could be applied. This decision, *NLRB v. Great Dane Trailers*, surely highlights the bizarre nature of *Darlington*, which presented a situation that could hardly be *more* destructive of employee rights. Indeed, there was no dispute in *Darlington* about the employer's antiunion intent.[18]

Since *Great Dane, Darlington* stands as an anomaly, perhaps to be applied only in situations involving a total or partial termination. Other employer decisions, perhaps, are also "so peculiarly matters of managerial prerogative" that, no matter how destructive the impact upon employee statutory rights, violations can only occur if discriminatory motivation is present. *Darlington* involved discrimination, antiunion motive, and clear impact upon protected rights.[19] Yet, the managerial decision involved was considered so vital that the Board could not be trusted to regulate it either under a balancing test or even pursuant to normal 8(a)(3) doctrine. Simply put, ceasing business, even for antiunion reasons, supercedes the statutory rights of employees affected. It is generally acknowledged that the decision, like most 8(a)(3) cases, is the result of a "weighing of competing interests with the search for motivation being merely a 'fictive formality.' "[20] A weighing process it might conceivably be, but surely one affected with an underlying set of assumptions and values. No amount of employee interest is apparently sufficient to outweigh certain employer interests. The thrust of this study is to indicate that decisions like *Darlington Mills* can no longer be considered aberrations from the common wisdom, cases of judicial temporary insanity. Rather, the case is perhaps the more shocking example of the continuation of judicial policy making. As in *First National Maintenance*, the Court has indicated that there exists a body of inherent managerial interests, an assumption that not only was reflected in common-law decision making prior to 1935 but that also underlies NLRA adjudication.

As perceptive observers like Summers acknowledge, *Darlington* is "inherently incredible" and "the results do not square with the words and purposes of the statute." Beside expressing outrage, how can one intelligently respond to such a decision? One response is simply to recognize that the Court's tortured logic is the result of fitting a preordained conclusion into what on the surface looks like a traditional legal mode of exposition. The Court's holding is indeed inconsistent with the language and policies of the act, but it is surely explainable in light of the hidden values courts wish to sustain.

9

AS THE LAST TWO chapters have shown, the belief that inherent managerial prerogatives are embedded in the act operates both to restrict the scope of mandatory bargaining and to broaden the range of permissible employer responses to the assertion of statutory rights. The legal burden in these cases is to explain when core managerial interests are at stake. Such a task is difficult if not impossible, perhaps explaining why assertion normally substitutes for analysis.

It may be true, as Justice Stewart suggests in *Fibreboard*, that modern technological developments have placed strains on collective bargaining, and bargaining over certain matters is qualitatively different from dealing with customary matters such as wages and hours. Dealing with the effects of automation and unemployment can hardly be thought of as a modern problem for unions. Yet, Justice Stewart concluded that modern problems might eventually induce Congress to give unions "a far heavier hand in controlling what until now have been considered the prerogatives of private business management. That path would mark a sharp departure from the traditional principles of a free enterprise economy."[1]

Justice Stewart's language has an ageless ring, carrying into the present views that date from the nineteenth century. Justice Stewart's notion, that union participation in particular areas would mark a "sharp departure from the traditional principles of a free enterprise economy,"[2] is more of a political or economic statement than a legal one. The content of these "free" enterprise notions would require a separate study to analyze, but it should not be necessary to expend great energy to recognize the general weakness of its basic assumptions.

Throughout American history, the question has rarely been one of whether government should regulate or interfere at all in industry or commerce; rather, the question generally was how and when the government should act. Historic battles over road and canal building, the "sectional" controversies, or conflicts over tariffs and government land and resource policy, are only a few of the areas of governmental involvement in the economy.[3] Moreover, the supply of labor and the contours of the employment relation have been regulated since colonial days. It may be true that government has primarily been involved as a business partner rather than as a regulator, and as a partner sharing only in the risks but not the profits of enterprise.

More fundamentally, however, the language of the nineteenth century sounds hollow given corporate structure and power today.

The clichés of private enterprise survive but serve primarily to disguise the essentially public character of the great corporation, including its private exercise of what is, in fact, a public power. Such a corporation fixes its prices; it controls its costs; it persuades its consumers; it organizes its supply of raw materials; it has powerful leverage in the Community; its needs are *pro tarito*, sound public policy. . . .[4]

The notion of "free enterprise" as used by Stewart and others serves to justify unequal bargaining power, perhaps on the ground that this inequality is required for efficiency, productivity, and profitability. Without effective governmental regulation, however, the bargaining cases remove any effective private, countervailing force to oligarchic enterprises. The result is to justify noncompetitive, nonaccountable enterprise in the name of competition and social value despite a statute designed, in part at least, to respond to unequal bargaining power.

The notion of private property that is used in other areas of labor law to restrict the scope of statutory provisions is rarely used in the bargaining area. The distinction made between capital decisions and other kinds of economic matters may ultimately stem from notions of private property. Perceptions of free enterprise, or managerial autonomy, on the other hand, more neatly fit the bargaining area. Property notions have more usually been employed where analogies to common-law trespass and property law are easily made. Thus, property "rights" are used, for instance, to regulate union solicitation and distribution by employees on company premises and to generally foreclose any rights to respond to employer captive audience speeches. Increasingly in recent years, "property" has become a critical obstacle to unions, and perhaps the most serious tactical problem is that the Court's recent notions of property are highly vague and abstract. The precise right need not be explained, nor is there any obligation to explain how the right is invaded. A particularized, detailed focus might suggest a balancing of interests, which, for now, seems to go too far for a majority on the Court.[5] Thus far, the Court has talked about managerial prerogatives not as adjuncts to property rights but as more akin to contractual rights. But for the fact that these cases arise under a statute, the language is very similar to constitutional decisions of an early day upholding inherent rights of capital.

Whether Stewart believes management *should* possess certain unencumbered prerogatives is, as he would admit, different from the question of what Congress intended. Unfortunately, Congress told us little. The rejection of the House bill in 1947 which restricted bargaining to listed topics hardly means, as Stewart suggests, that Congress in the Taft-Hartley Act sought "to define a limited class of bargainable issues."[6] There was indeed such an effort, at least in the House, but it failed. It is also not clear to what extent Congress rejected this limited approach, although the Conference report suggests that the scope of bargaining should be left to the parties and, if necessary, to the Board.[7] As Harry Wellington notes, "The guidelines . . . will not be found by close attention to bits and pieces of particular legislative history. The guidelines rather must be found in the larger purposes and goals of the statute and the relationship of the duty to bargain to those goals."[8]

To employers, of course, the basic concern is a desire to avoid bargaining at all over certain matters. The need to move quickly and in secrecy may sometimes be present, but the cases rarely reflect these imperatives, as *First National Maintenance* demonstrates. Bargaining may result in a compromise of the employer's decision or position, but the real concern may be the fact of bargaining with a union at all, a fact bearing great symbolic content. After all, some kind of bargaining on important decisions often occurs *within* management, and speed of implementation seems to become important only after management reaches a firm decision. Perhaps the most striking aspect of Justice Stewart's statement in *Fibreboard* is the fear that unions would have a "far heavier hand in controlling" previously recognized prerogatives. Surely, the Justice is aware that mandatory bargaining does not create a duty to agree nor a duty to concede shared control. Moreover, since employers can act *after* beginning should an impasse occur, a not unplannable circumstance, the implication is that these cases are not about functional concerns at all but, rather, are basically attempts to draw status lines.

Would a broad reading of the subjects of bargaining sharply depart from "free enterprise" principles? A more appropriate question might focus upon the extent to which such principles are implicitly enshrined in the interstices of the NLRA. The determination of the appropriate subjects of collective bargaining and the definition of the spheres of company policy formation which are a sole concern to management is often thought to be one of the burning problems of industrial relations. The *Washington Post* editorialized on January 10, 1946, that "the question how far employees should have a voice in dictating to management is at present one of the hottest issues before the country."[9] Although the threat of "dictation" is often expressed, the language in which the problem is customarily presented by management is in terms of "the invasion by unions of managerial functions" or "the encroachment by labor on managerial prerogatives," and this language echoes in judicial opinions. Management is often convinced that unions are seeking such inroads and that the attempt holds grave dangers for our economy and, thus, it must be halted.[10] The allusions are military: unions seek to invade an area long held (and properly so) by management.

MANAGERIAL FEARS IN THE POSTWAR PERIOD

Managerial fear of union incursion became most pronounced in the 1940s, although similar fear had been expressed for almost a century. The immediate postwar concern of management was caused by actions and policies of unions during the war that went beyond mere "business" or "bread-and-butter" unionism. Some unions in the early days of the war urged the creation of joint labor and management councils to run industries. Going further, the CIO urged a national planning effort that would make labor "a co-equal with management, with the government acting as an arbitor of these two relatively independent groups in a free society."[11] By 1930s standards unions after the war engaged in aggressive collective bargaining. The bargaining agreements of the 1930s were not extensive documents owing to the relatively weak and defensive posture of unions. The agreements in newly organized industries dealt primarily with recognition. The first UAW–General Motors agreement, for instance, could be printed on one page. Yet, the "intrusions" of postwar bar-

gaining seem tame in the 1980s because the union's primary challenges were directed to personnel actions, especially to an insistence
upon seniority and the limiting of managerial discretion in relation to
matters such as promotion and layoff. Yet unions were also concerned with job content, technological change, seasonal demand, the
opening of new plants, and financial policies that bore on wage determination. It was the union's responsibility to regulate the employer
"at every point where his action affects the welfare of the men."[12]
Such policies chilled managers who had been raised in an era of virtually unlimited power.

By 1946, collective bargaining developments had left business executives with "anxiety . . . about the future; uncertainty as to where
the process will end; a fear that it will eventually culminate in such
stringent impairment of management's freedom that it will not be
able to do its job satisfactorily."[13] Clearly troublesome was Walter
Reuther's demand in August 1945, for a 30 percent wage increase
without a concurrent rise in the cost of General Motors' products.
Reuther had also called for GM to "open the books," so the union
could ascertain the company's ability to pay higher wages at existing
prices. A General Motors representative saw the demands as "an
opening wedge whereby the unions hope to pry their way into the
whole field of management. It leads surely to the day when union
bosses, under the threat of strike, will seek to tell us what we can
make, when we can make it."[14] The statement is certainly ironic
in light of the breadth of bargaining in the auto industry in the
1980s, when auto makers sought concessions from the United Auto
Workers Union.

The expressed concerns of management in the postwar period
reveal that they recognized that there was no intellectual way to
separate the interests and desires of unions from some "core" of managerial prerogatives. Efforts to define or limit the scope of bargaining
failed both at the President's National Labor-Management Conference in 1945[15] and during the deliberations that led to the Taft-Hartley Act in 1947. At the conference, for instance, unions refused to
specify any functions that were exclusively managerial. The industry
members could only "conclude, therefore, that the labor members
are convinced that the field of collective bargaining will, in all proba-
bility, continue to expand into the field of management. The only
possible end of such a philosophy would be joint management of enterprise."[16] Moreover, the issue was discussed in the deliberations

that led to the Taft-Hartley Act, but no restriction on the scope of bargaining emerged despite the efforts of House members to attempt to specify those items that lay at the "core" of managerial prerogatives.

Justice Stewart's position is similar to the 1948 statement of Charles E. Wilson, then president of General Motors:

If we consider the ultimate result of this tendency to stretch collective bargaining to comprehend any subject that a union leader may desire to bargain on, we come out with the union leaders really running the economy of the country; but with no legal or public responsibility and with no private employment except as they may permit. . . . Under these conditions, the freedom of management to function properly without interference in making its every-day decisions will be gradually restricted. The Union leaders—particularly where they have industry-wide power—will have the deciding vote in all managerial decisions, or at least, will exercise a veto power that will stop progress. . . . Competition will be stifled and progress in the improvement of industrial processes which reduce the cost and price of the goods produced by industry will be halted. . . . Only by defining and restricting collective bargaining to its proper sphere can we hope to save what we have come to know as our American system and keep it from evolving into an alien form, imported from East of the Rhine.[17]

Mr. Wilson was then referring to a UAW demand that General Motors bargain over pensions. Wilson could consider pensions "the prerogatives of private business management" in 1948, but pension bargaining is common today and has been so since the 1940s. Presumably Justice Stewart would *exclude* from his understanding of the "traditional principles of a free enterprise economy" those traditional principles that history has discarded.

Mr. Wilson's picture of the evolution of the American system "into an alien form imported from East of the Rhine," may simply be the kind of rhetoric that brings polite forms of "right on" at certain kinds of meetings.[18] Generally, American unions do not seek codetermination or control over managerial decisions, although some unions advocated such policies during wartime. Indeed, few unions in the world are as committed to the "free enterprise economy" as American unions. If unions have not demonstrated interest in certain areas of business decision making, it may not be due to a belief that these matters should be of sole concern to management but, rather, because unions may not have yet perceived any connection between such areas and their own interests or, if they have, may have felt powerless to seek participation. Union efforts to "invade" managerial prerogatives after World War II, for instance, were defeated in large part by employer resistance.[19]

Perceptions, institutions, and economic conditions change, and views about what is of direct interest to employees will change. But we should not assume that the presumed "invasion" of managerial preserve is a new phenomena. Just as strikes against replacement by machines have a long tradition, so have some unions long been concerned about areas Justice Stewart would easily characterize as outside of mandatory bargaining. Mine workers, for instance, have been concerned over the price of coal since at least 1869, having become aware of a relationship between fluctuations in coal prices and wages.[20]

It is simply wrong, moreover, to assert that union concern over technological change and subsequent unemployment are somehow new historical phenomena. The pace of machine substitution for labor was often amazing, rapid, and widespread in the latter half of the nineteenth century, and the matter did not pass unnoticed by employees or their unions.[21]

American workers have long faced the threat of replacement by machines. After the Civil War, for instance, machines and the increasingly minute division of labor threatened skilled workers with the destruction of their "capital." In addition, it was thought that machinery would lead to overproduction and the threat of unemployment. Indeed, whole crafts were wiped out, the value of skilled workers' education and skill was ruined or at least diminished, and their wage value in the employment market was often greatly reduced. The human cost of this kind of "technological change" is often overlooked, but the anguish is not soon erased from memory. The introduction of machines was not the only threat faced, for the increasing tendency to divide tasks and to use unskilled workers ("green hands") was also seen as threats to skilled labor.

Responses varied, but workers and unions generally saw machinery, as the rest of the public did, as inevitable and possibly beneficial. The traditional response of skilled workers was to attempt to control the supply of labor in a trade. To this end, unions sought control over the training and certification of skilled employees, through apprenticeship programs or local legislation such as building codes. Union devices to protect skills and to overcome the increased supply of labor also included attempts to shorten the work day, to limit immigration, to pass children and womens' legislation in order to bar or limit their employment, to draft work rules, or to achieve bargains with employers.[22]

Skill, after all, was the workers' major weapon for controlling supply in a preindustrial economy, and unions and workers sought to adapt the same "principles and tactics it had developed in a preindustrial situation to the changes produced by industrialization."[23] Many crafts had been weakened by division of labor by 1860. "Mechanization only intensified the substitution of semiskilled and unskilled workers for craftsmen."[24] New techniques and machines reduced skilled levels and thus, it was argued, increased the numbers of persons who could perform the work. After a period of initial optimism about machines, many labor spokesmen decided that although machines might well be inevitable they were not necessarily beneficial. The decision not to attack the introduction of machines was based more on a perception of the futility of such an attack than on a recognition of some sacrosanct body of managerial prerogatives.[25]

Although disputes and some litigation resulted over job displacement by machines in the nineteenth century, most of the disputes involved now-conventional issues of wages and union recognition. Attempts to bargain over these matters were restricted by a variety of legal devices. New issues have seemingly arisen today, but this should come as no rude surprise. Indeed the seeming newness of issues of automation, subcontracting, or plant removal should not hide the fact that issues of job security have long been a staple part of collective bargaining or, at least, labor-management relations. Collective bargaining should indeed be a "flexible, dynamic institution,"[26] but basic problems have not really been altered.

Are workers and their unions too unsophisticated to deal with these matters? The record suggests that unions have become quite sophisticated about "managerial" decisions, a sophistication recognized by Neil Chamberlain in 1948, although many managers do disparage the competence and intelligence of union leaders in relation to business operations. There is a seemingly superior fund of knowledge stemming from management's monopoly of operating positions, a monopoly that arguably permits the occupants of the position a range of knowledge and experience often unknown to a union leader.[27]

THEORIES OF MANAGEMENT AND THE SCOPE OF BARGAINING

The judicial reluctance to part with implicit boundaries to mandatory bargaining is rarely explained. Justice Stewart in *Fibreboard* or Blackmun in *First National Maintenance* tells us more than is usually found, but these statements are more of a description than an analysis. It might be useful to look more closely at management's fears, for those fears may be reflected by judges. Neil Chamberlain has compiled a variety of concerns supporting managerial resistance to shared authority.[28] One fear is that union penetration threatens business organization itself by destroying unified final authority. This view explains management's opposition to collective bargaining as being based primarily on their conception of management and its responsibilities. American business is subject to many uncertainties. "Leadership is necessary to assess the uncertainties, to adjust to change, and to create change. The creation of change, through the continuous discovery of new markets and the introduction of new products and more efficient methods of production, has long been thought to be an essential and perhaps the key factor in the successful operation of the dynamic American economy."[29]

In large part the reaction of employers to unions, and to government involvement as well, is caused by their perception of risk. Many factors can upset even a successful enterprise. A sudden shift in demand or a sudden fall in prices can turn prospective profits into sizable losses. A new invention can dissolve special advantages that a firm has long enjoyed. Business, therefore, feels the need to be able to respond to new conditions quickly, a state requiring foresight but also flexibility. Thus unions are seen as a serious threat to reduce necessary freedom to make decisions.

Managers believe that they have the responsibility for directing an enterprise in such a way that the "collective result of their individual decisions determines the direction of the economic system." Its decisions are crucial for the success of individual enterprises and the whole economic system. One result is a reluctance to share authority with other institutions such as government or labor.[30] It is interesting to note that these objectives are rarely explained in functional terms but are usually stated as absolute verities.[31]

This view perceives the union as challenging the "single line of authority" upon which the corporate system is based. "Authority" is certainly a vague concept, and the objection ignores the amount of internal and external influence, bargaining, or regulation, which already constrains "authority," as well as those undisputed areas of mandatory bargaining.

A second fear stems from a perception that unions challenge the discharge of management's legal responsibility, stemming from its acceptance of authority with the corresponding obligation to exercise it according to the interests of those conferring that authority. This no doubt is the source of the "private responsibility" reference in Charles Wilson's earlier quoted statement. Because of its legally imposed responsibility to stockholders, management must resist granting unions a share in managerial determinations because union interests do not coincide with those of the owners.[32] The view also has a traditional ring, and statements are often made sufficiently vague so that the responsibility could be understood to be a public or social obligation rather than a private, economic concern. In rejecting the UAW's offer to arbitrate differences during the negotiation of the UAW-GM 1945–46 contract, GM stated: "Stripped of its deception, the union proposed that General Motors relinquish its rights to manage the business. This was not an offer of arbitration but a demand for abdication." The officers of GM would be forced to "surrender their functions and responsibilities to outsiders including a representative of the union."[33] The vigor with which this view is held and expressed is only exceeded by its ability to beg the issue. The question, indeed, is focused upon the legal obligations of management.

As Chamberlain notes, when management states that unions have no *right* to "invade" its area of prerogatives, it is really saying unions *should not*.[34] By imposing a duty to bargain collectively, the NLRA recognizes a legal claim to the interests of a corporation by a party other than the stockholders. A union cannot compel the exercise of a managerial duty, but it does have the privilege of refusing to work except upon its own terms. The extent of union penetration will ultimately stem from union power rather than from the NLRB, for the act requires bargaining and not concession. The nature of the resulting sharing is not expressed or regulated by the NLRA, except to the extent that the mandatory/permissive line grants the right to refuse to even bargain about certain subjects.

It is ironic that despite the emphasis on individual bargaining, employees have generally been treated "collectively" by their employers since the latter half of the nineteenth century. This was especially true as the size of enterprises expanded. Moreover, given the emphasis of managerial prerogatives since 1935, it is interesting to note that management has long been concerned about various aspects of their employees' lives. During the period of welfare capitalism, for instance, employers concerned themselves with the schooling, housing, recreation, and religion of their employees and engaged in various social work efforts as well.[35]

These areas of concern extended well beyond the more normal realms of production and wage scales. Yet, although altruistic reasons were sometimes given for welfare activity, it was generally seen as a good, sound business investment. Young people and immigrants had to be acculturated and socialized to the rhythms of the factory.[36] Welfare activities, it was hoped, would encourage good sober work habits, prevent sickness and injury, and thus maintain a dependable and loyal work force. The "central purpose of welfare capitalism [was] avoidance of trade unionism."[37] Clearly, some viewed welfare activities as a method of heading off worker efforts for greater industrial democracy, especially after World War I. "With labor crying for democracy, capital must go part way or face revolution."[38]

A third managerial concern is that the union challenge to managerial authority is a threat to efficiency as well as authority. Again, this view does not aid in drawing lines. It does reflect the notion that law should be employed to restrict efforts by unions to interfere with economic efficiency as defined, of course, by the perceived needs of capital. In addition, it suggests the extent to which employee concerns are seen as *incidental* to the function of the enterprise. Thus, Justice Stewart's concerns are reflected in a manager's complaints about the costs of "divert[ing] management and men from their *real jobs* of production to straighten out difficulties between the management and the union. You would be surprised at the amount of money we have paid to union men and management just to straighten out these difficulties *with no relevancy of such payments to the operation of our productive machinery.*"[39] One response is that the NLRA has broadened the notion of what is of internal concern to an enterprise, just as a host of other federal statutes have broadened obligations to employees, stockholders, consumers, and the general public.

A fourth objection, a lack of union responsibility, will seem familiar to those who were members of college faculties in the late 1960s. Union proposals, it is said, may have long-term effects on the company, creating effects well after the particular union official has left the scene. Moreover, it is argued, management, not the union, will be blamed for retrenchment or bankruptcy.[40] These views are similar to the notion that management has a single and exclusive responsibility to stockholders. Moreover, such views are obviously based upon status assumptions, concluding that employees are only interested in their pay check whereas management must take into consideration broader issues of economic and social policy. I do not mean to underestimate the depth of conviction underlying these beliefs, but it is also true that most groups, when faced with demands for participation in what was formerly an exclusive preserve, suddenly find that their being in complete control is socially necessary or economically wise.

There are other fears, and some need little response. Union leaders are looked upon as inadequate to share responsibility. Moreover, union motives are often questioned. Behind union penetration, one manager states, lies "a lust for power and a movement towards some form of socialism." More commonly expressed is the fear of the possible end result of union penetration. Management understandably is concerned over its perceived loss of authority, the lack of precise legal guidelines, and uncertainty of the future. Until clear lines are established, management is "in the position of an army retreating and regrouping." Hence, it must resist all incursions, if only to buy time. In addition to the sometimes expressed fear of ultimate revolution is the concern that labor should not impede the "free action as owner . . . of private property." Of course, union action also is perceived as threatening the personal goals of the managers, their security, recognition and sense of worth, and their self expression.[41]

This is not to say that all management shares the same fears of union "penetration." Many understand that American unions desire to possess the freedom to criticize management rather than to codetermine all managerial policies. If responsibility or ability is the basic concern, the concern applies equally well to those areas of admitted joint responsibility.[42]

Chamberlain's view, supported by some managers, is that there is no feasible way to separate matters of joint responsibility and those of exclusive managerial authority.[43] If line drawing is impossible across the industrial spectrum, as well as for any period of time for one enterprise, what does this suggest about the appropriate legal response to these issues? Obviously, attempts to define the management function do not seem to help in resolving the dispute. Neil Chamberlain has perhaps most clearly and thoroughly attempted to rationalize the management function.[44] Some of the theories of managerial function he presents are merely descriptive, and most reflect the fears discussed above. Thus, one traditional approach defines the managerial function as the locus of decision making. Such a theory might argue for limiting the scope of bargaining so as not to undermine the basic purposes of management, but such theories tell us nothing about how and where lines are to be drawn when management is clearly compelled to bargain about some issues. Moreover, absolute power is unreal given the internal and external, governmental and private, constraints on managerial desires.

Similarly, to define management as those "accorded a legal basis for exercising the decision-making authority" is simply to refocus on management's legal power and obligations. Union leaders may possess a different constituency and responsibility than managers, but this difference in fact does not necessarily point to any conclusion, as Chamberlain himself notes. The same could be said for any theory focusing upon the managerial ownership or control over property. The "ownership" of property may provide power to use that property, but it does not exclude attempts by others to urge different uses.

Except for authoritarian relationships . . . , people can be managed and directed only with their consent. While property rights carry with them a power of disposition of goods, they do not carry an equal power to use those goods *if* the cooperation of others is necessary to that use. . . . [T]here is nothing in the law to stop the union from demanding as the price of the cooperation of its members a voice in some matter previously independently determined by management.[45]

Chamberlain seems indifferent to the assumed costs to managerial independence. "Potentially," he notes, "no area should be excluded."

Chamberlain recognizes that many participate in decision making and that one could define management in process terms.[46] Chamberlain's own theory stresses that management involves a series of bargains with interested parties within and without the corporation. The essential management function, he believes, involves the subsequent coordination of these various bargains. He sees the decision-making process as a "multi-lateral bargaining process" where the bargaining results are the corporate decisions. Management is not the process. It is, rather, defined by its authority to coordinate various bargains.

Whatever might be said for the insights in Chamberlain's "coordination process,"[47] it is perfectly consistent with a broad definition of bargaining. Yet this theory may provide a hint of the problem. Since management engages in a variety of "bargains" with stockholders, suppliers, dealers, shippers, consumers, and the government, only it, the argument might go, has the broadness of vision to adequately deal with certain problems.[48] Bargaining does involve unions in a form of participation concerning various decisions, but unions do not seek to coordinate the agreement reached with all other arrangements made by management. True, such an argument misreads the actual effect of a broad reading of 8(a)(5) and, indeed, tells us nothing about where to stop this fearsome incursion into protected territory once the invasion has begun. But the critical point is not the vagueness of the feeling or its patent weakness as an analytical tool. What is significant is the fact that this feeling seems to be alive and presumably well (and often found) in decisions of the Supreme Court.

Judicial decisions reveal the legal conception of the narrow role unions are to play. This narrow view is clearly seen in the concluding section of this paper dealing with successorship situations. Karl Klare, I believe, is quite correct in arguing that judicial decisions treat "workers as sellers of labor power and as consumers of commodities, but not as producers," and this "hindered them from achieving an alternate perspective in which worker self-activity, the process by which workers produce value by embodying their labor power in things, services, and relationships, would be recognized as the basis of all production in, and reproduction of, society."[49] The decisions, moreover, encourage unions "to accept the social order as given and to seek to defend and better the lot of their members only within its ground rules."[50] This limited view of "legitimate union activity stood in every sense as a barrier to the possibility that labor would participate in bringing about fundamental social change."[51] Of course, this narrow role for employees was reinforced by powerful norms in society outside the legal system as well as by the self-perception of unions themselves.

THEORIES OF THE LABOR MOVEMENT: THE WISCONSIN SCHOOL

The view that the duty to bargain should be narrowly defined could be supported, although it has not expressly been, by the theories of the Wisconsin School. The most influential school of labor theory is associated with John R. Commons and Selig Perlman. The views of

Commons and Perlman in labor economics, theory, and history have been highly influential, and serious criticism of their position seems a fairly recent phenomenon.[52]

In Common's view, a rapid expansion of markets after the Civil War changed the market for labor as well as for goods. This led to a division of functions which left the labor function separated from that of merchant and manufacturer. This is a determinist view, which assumes that economic events occur outside of human will, purpose, or intention. Moreover, it overlooks the extent to which worker and owner battled over control of the work process.[53] Instead, the theory assumes that a natural division occurred, caused by natural forces.

Much of the theory of the Wisconsin School rests on the supposition that American industry is basically competitive. Shoe workers, Commons asserted, unionized as a response to "the menace of competition" arising from expanding competitive markets for shoes.[54] Competitive pressures separated the interests of workers and owners, leading to union attempts to organize. In conjunction with Selig Perlman's stress on the "job consciousness" motivation of workers, the theory tended to focus on the "psychological, market, and legal capabilities of groups of workers to organize and bargain rather than on the structural, technological, and political capabilities of employers to prevent unionization and frustrate bargaining."[55] Thus, failure to successfully organize could be attributable to a lack of class consciousness of workers rather than to the superior political and economic power of employers.

In addition, the theory holds that the individual worker was forced to defend the interests of his craft. The purpose of unions, therefore, was to "establish 'rights' on the job, . . . by incorporating, in the trade agreement, regulations applying to overtime, to the 'equal turn,' to priority and seniority in employment, to apprenticeship, to the introduction and utilization of machinery, and so forth." Collective action would be the "safest way to assure this group control over opportunity."[56]

Thus, workers' concerns were thought to be job related, and narrowly so, because workers saw their opportunities as limited. Restrictive horizons were caused by the changes in market conditions which made it unlikely that workers could become or regain positions as autonomous economic units. Instead of seeking change, workers sought to make their lot as workers in a particular craft or trade secure.[57] This view and the corresponding narrow outlook of the American Federation of Labor was shaped by a shift from the notion of expansive opportunities to a "more pessimistic trade union psychology, built upon the premise that the wage-earner is faced by a scarcity of opportunity."[58]

Before we go further, it is worth our noting that this assigned perception of scarcity is not only inconsistent with Fourth of July oratory down to the present, but it is also inadequate to explain the outlook of the AFL. Indeed, others believe that the psychological effect of the frontier, the possibility of becoming an entrepreneur, or language and ethnic diversity was primarily responsible for the handicaps of early efforts of union organization. In any event, many workers in the latter half of the nineteenth century may well have believed that opportunities for occupational mobility were limited, but this does not explain why their unions had to follow an AFL-like line. And, indeed, not all unions did. The Perlman view focuses upon the AFL and the craft unions and conveniently overlooks more socially minded or revolutionary unions. "Winners' history" tends to ignore organizations such as the Knights of Labor and Industrial Workers of the World. As David Montgomery has noted, Perlman's focus upon wage and job consciousness "accomplished the feat of fitting collectivist mentalities into the image of an individualistic national consensus so smoothly that it has been faithfully trotted out as 'the answer' by subsequent generations of textbook writers. . . ."[59] The conservative job-centered approach to collective bargaining is not necessarily explained by a perception of scarcity of opportunity.

More to the point, perhaps, is Perlman's second argument that worker, and hence union, perceptions are based upon an awareness that workers are inherently unable to deal with the economic sphere. "The typical manualist is aware of his lack of native capacity for availing himself of economic opportunities as they lie amidst the complex and ever-shifting situations of modern business." This view cannot explain the job-conscious focus of the craft unions which, after all, are *unions* and not associations dedicated to helping their members become entrepreneurs. Moreover, it denigrates the capacity and intelligence of workers. Entrepreneurs, those "captains of industry," after all, were apparently not affected by this concern. They were risk takers. Thus, Perlman can argue that "a scarcity consciousness has always been typical of the manual worker, in direct contrast to the consciousness of abundance of opportunity," which stimulates the self-conscious businessman.[60]

Perlman wrote in the 1920s and, thus, had no opportunity to consider the Depression and the emergence of the CIO, whose broad social objectives and rejection of voluntarism distinguished it from the AFL. The CIO certainly did not arise during a period of widening perceptions of opportunity and mobility.

Perlman's *Theory* needs to be reassessed, and perhaps discarded, on historical and empirical grounds alone, even though all must concede that the job-centered philosophy still operates strongly in the labor movement. Again, to say that job-centered unionism is adopted because it is deemed to be the most effective strategy is miles away from stating that workers are inherently incapable of any other approach. One might assume that the workers' situation is caused by scarcity consciousness, exploitation, psychological maladjustment, or alienation. Such assumptions might aid in understanding and explaining the desire for unions, but it would hardly explain their goals and aspirations.[61]

The primary relevance of the Perlman-Commons school at this point is that it insists that workers and their unions are concerned about narrow job interests. If this is so, then it can be assumed that some matters, which may nevertheless have an impact upon jobs, are not appropriate matters of union (or worker) concern. Because worker interest is focused "only" and narrowly upon the job, other matters are beyond the scope of legitimate union concern. The neatness of the Commons' view is that it assures us that unions want it to remain this way. Thus, despite the annoying data provided by a union's position in a particular case, the courts can protect managerial prerogatives while believing that they are responding to the traditions of the labor movement.

10

THE INTEREST IN THE MOBILITY

OF CAPITAL: THE EXPLICIT USE

OF UNDERLYING PREMISES

THE INTEREST IN contractualism would suggest that once a collective agreement is signed, it should be legally enforceable. Nearly all collective agreements are structured so that questions of interpretation and enforcement are directed to grievance and arbitration procedures set out in the agreement. Arbitration awards may be challenged in court, although the chance of success is very limited, or legal question may arise about the range of issues subject to arbitration. These contractual issues, if brought to court, arise under Section 301 of the NLRA, empowering federal courts to enforce collective agreements. A breach of contract is not necessarily an unfair labor practice, and thus the NLRB may not be involved in the dispute.

The NLRB and the courts, however, may be alternative dispute-resolution systems, for instance, when a labor-management dispute can be characterized in contractual or unfair labor practice terms. Thus, a refusal to bargain or to arbitrate in certain situations may be characterized either as a breach of the collective agreement or as a failure to bargain in good faith. One such situation often exists when one employer replaces another by merger or sale. Employees of the predecessor company may seek to enforce the collective bargaining agreement against the new, or successor, firm or, alternatively, may seek merely to continue its representational status and attempt to reach a new collective agreement. The new employer, of course, will not be a party, or signatory, to the predecessor's agreement, and it will generally claim it has no contractual obligations under this contract. The obligation to bargain is more complex, and the new employer will seek initially to set its own wages and working conditions even if it must bargain at some time with the union that was already on the scene.

The common mode of legal thought would note that conflicting interests exist in these situations. The most relevant to this investigation are the new employer's desire to make a significant capital change free of contractual bargaining obligations and the union's desire to maintain its representational status and protect the contractual and security interests of its members. Even though an agreement had been reached therefore, a change in the identity of the employer raises the possibility that interests in capital mobility will be given significant weight. Doctrines exist, however, to limit notions of contractualism or capital freedom, and they are referred to as the "law of successorship." The values implicit in this area of the law is the focus of this chapter.

The successorship area is highly topical, as well as relevant, and clearly reflects the valuation of capital mobility over statutory concerns. It deals primarily with the contractual and bargaining obligations of employers who take over the business of another, primarily by merger or sale. Given the incidence of mergers and the currently high rate of business failures, serious legal questions arise when a new employer, the "successor," takes over from another. The basis for even treating these situations in a separate doctrinal category, as problems of "successorship," is that economic interests of employees and the concern for labor stability should sometimes overbalance a policy of narrow contractualism or unregulated managerial freedom. In addition, the doctrine (actually doctrines) seeks to strike some accommodation between protecting accrued representational and contract rights of employees, and perhaps the avoidance of labor unrest, on one hand, and, on the other hand, the interest generally expressed as a property right to freely transfer assets and rearrange businesses. The doctrinal development suggests that successorship is not to be treated as an abstract concept. Thus a successor employer may be bound under federal law to arbitrate grievances under the predecessor's labor contract[1] and may in certain situations be liable for the predecessor's unfair labor practices.[2] Yet, the successor employer is not required by Section 8(a)(5) to abide by the predecessor's collective agreement or even to bargain with the predecessor's union about initial terms and condition of employment, even if the union represents a majority of the new work force.[3]

In 1964 the Court held in *John Wiley & Sons*, its first foray into this complex area, that a successor employer could be compelled to submit to arbitration issues involving which contractual obligations of the predecessor, if any, survived the sale and, thus, may be binding on the successor.[4] The action to compel arbitration was brought under

NLRA Section 301, a provision creating federal jurisdiction over actions "for violations of contracts between an employer and a labor organization." Traditional rules of contract, said the Court, were not to be determinative in the development of federal law under Section 301. The holding, based on federal and not state law,[5] was that "the disappearance by merger of a corporate employer which has entered into a collective bargaining agreement with a union does not automatically terminate all rights of the employees covered by the agreement, and that, in appropriate circumstances, present here, the successor employer may be required to arbitrate with the union under the agreement."[6]

Because the Court had held that an arbitration clause may survive a merger, even when asserted against an employer who was not a party to the agreement, it is conceivable that the arbitrator could find that substantive portions of the agreement survive as well. Thus the new employer may find itself bound to economic obligations to which it in no sense voluntarily or consciously consented. Some commentators, not without reason, believed that the predecessor's agreement necessarily survived the change of employers, for the survival of the arbitration clause alone would otherwise be difficult to explain.[7] The force of this argument led the Board in 1970 to reverse its prior position and hold that a new employer (if it met the standards as a "successor") must generally abide by the predecessor's agreement.[8] (The problem of determining when a new employer is a successor is interesting but irrelevant for purposes of this discussion.) Thus, the new employer must bargain with the predecessor union under Section 8(a)(5). At the time, then, parallel obligations existed under Section 301 and under 8(a)(5).

Although complexity existed in defining when a new employer was technically a "successor" for arbitration or bargaining purposes, the *Wiley* decision, decided in the same year as *Fibreboard*, seemed to say that critical capital decisions were not free from the equally valid concerns of affected employees: "The objectives of national labor policy, reflected in established principles of federal law, require that the rightful prerogative of owners independently to arrange their businesses and even eliminate themselves as employers be balanced by some protection to the employees from a sudden change in the employment relationship."[9]

The recognition of employee interests in these kinds of situations is particularly important because most of an employee's working conditions under the American labor system, such as employment rights, wages, and benefits, are set by private negotiation rather than by federal law.[10] A transfer of ownership may not only end the job security functions of a grievance clause but also may end contractual benefits and the seniority system by which they have been earned. The many purposes served by a collective agreement, it could be argued, should be as worthy of recognition as the effectuation of easy capital movement.

The noble judicial sentiments expressed in *Wiley* about the need to protect employees from sudden changes ironically come one year before *Darlington*, where, of course, no protection was afforded to employees out of work due to a "sudden change" in the employment relationship. *Wiley*, unlike *Darlington*, could be justified by the "preference of national labor policy for arbitration," a preference created in large part by the Court itself.[11] The policy in favor of arbitration, viewed as a substitute for industrial unrest or strikes rather than litigation, would be weakened should a "change in the corporate structure or ownership of a business enterprise" automatically terminate a previously established duty to arbitrate. Despite the asserted interest in protecting employee expectations, it is noteworthy that the Court rested its decision largely upon protecting the integrity of arbitration and the avoidance of industrial warfare. In this sense, the Court's use of industrial policy in *Wiley*, rather than more traditional, consensual notions stemming from the law of contracts, should not be seen as a substantial variation from the assumptions described in this volume.

It must be emphasized that *Wiley* only meant that the question of survival of all or part of a collective agreement could in certain cases be sent to a private, neutral arbitrator. The arbitrator might decide that the agreement did not survive the merger. Moreover, this kind of issue is far from the question of permissible employee participation in the crucial decision to sell or merge under Section 8(a)(5). Under *Wiley* an arbitrator determines the scope of the understanding between the parties, and the question arises under Section 301 because the union seeks to "enforce" its arbitration clause in court. On the other hand, an action under NLRA Section 8(a)(5), brought initially before the NLRB, could involve the legitimacy of a unilateral managerial decision to merge made without prior notice to the union and bargaining.

Nevertheless, putting the policy in favor of arbitration aside, the employee interests cited by the Supreme Court in *Wiley* to support the result seemingly applies to other areas, many of which have already been discussed. Thus, the Court correctly noted in *Wiley* that employees do not usually participate in decisions leading to a change in corporate ownership or any change in corporate structure. Employee interests, the Court recognized, will rarely be considered in these negotiations although employees may be vitally affected. It would seem to follow that an employer contemplating a merger or sale should be obliged to bargain over such a decision. Perhaps, as the Court stresses, the *Wiley* result would ease corporate transitions and lessen industrial tension.

Surely the same argument could also be made, for example, about partial terminations challenged under 8(a)(3). The Court, however, especially after *Darlington*, has been less concerned about the impact on employees of changes in corporate structure where statutory, as opposed to contractual, rights are at stake. Presumably, the Court seems to believe that in contract enforcement cases such as *Wiley* the issue involves the extent to which already bargained-for rights are affected by managerial decisions. A generous, proarbitration policy may not significantly interfere with managerial prerogatives, for the arbitrator will only decide to what extent contract provisions survive the change in employers. As this study has attempted to show, judicial decisions tend to reflect a fear that liberal readings of the statute will unduly interfere with important prerogatives of owners. Thus, even though the employers could avoid NLRB scrutiny by bargaining with the predecessor union prior to a change, the law of 8(a)(5) may not parallel that of the arbitration area. Yet, arbitration, as the Court itself often reminds us, is "part and parcel of the collective bargaining process," and it is conceptually difficult to separate the obligation to arbitrate from the obligation to bargain. Arbitration, after all, is encouraged not as an end in itself but as a device for the peaceful resolution of disputes. These disputes can arise at other times as well, and it would be strange if the Court should favor the "peace interest" when arbitration is involved, but not when bargaining itself is the issue.[12]

As the tone of these comments suggests, the concern for employees expressed in *Wiley* has been seriously undercut in recent cases based upon the themes reflected in earlier sections. In *NLRB v. Burns International Security Services, Inc.*,[13] the Court faced a change of employers in the 8(a)(5) context. Burns succeeded Wackenhut, via competitive bidding, as the provider of plant protection services at a facility of Lockheed Corporation. Burns retained a majority of the former Wackenhut employees, and these employees constituted a majority of Burns's complement of employees at the facility. Nevertheless, Burns refused to honor the predecessor's agreement or to recognize and bargain with the union that had represented the Wackenhut employees.

The Union decided not to arbitrate the survival of the arbitration clause as in *Wiley*, but to allege instead a violation of the duty to bargain under 8(a)(5) of the NLRA. The Supreme Court held that this made all the difference. The Court did hold that Burns had the obligation to bargain with the union, but only because Burns had hired enough former Wackenhut employees to constitute a majority of its work force. This duty did not carry with it the obligation to abide by the terms of the predecessor's collective bargaining agreement. The Court distinguished *Wiley* on a variety of grounds, stressing that the NLRA encourages parties to set contract terms themselves without government interference. Although a contract was surely imposed on John Wiley under normal contractual principles, those "contract continuity" policies were expressed in a Section 301 case involving the strong federal policy favoring arbitration, whereas *Burns* involved only the obligation to bargain under another section of the NLRA. Because federal law governs both situations, albeit in different forums, the distinction is difficult to fathom. This especially is so because, if the union in *Burns* had sought arbitration under the Wackenhut contract rather than NLRB assistance, it seemingly would have been granted, pursuant to *Wiley*.[14]

The basic concerns of the Court in *Burns* were expressed with startling clarity. The Court was unwilling to "burden" the successor employer (or the union) with a previously existing contract that might be either uneconomic or inequitable in the new setting, a problem that did not seem to bother the predecessor union.

"A potential employer," said the Court, "might be willing to take over a moribund business only if he can make changes in corporate structure, composition of the labor force, work location, task assignment, and nature of supervision. Saddling such an employer with the terms and conditions of employment contained in the old collective-bargaining contract may make these changes impossible and may discourage and inhibit the transfer of capital."[15]

Moreover, the Court noted with apparent irony that, if the contract did survive, the prior Wackenhut employees might possess contractual job security that would bar Burns from replacing the old Wackenhut guards. Surely this was one of the *primary* concerns of the Wackenhut employees. The Court turned the interest in labor peace on its head, arguing that "saddling" the new employer or the union with the old contract might actually lead to strife because the contractual terms might not correspond to "economic power realities."

The Court's views are highly revealing. Although there has been a considerable amount of scholarly attention given to this area,[16] it is only significant here to note that the "benefits" to employees of contractual survival noted in *Wiley* have become "problems" to employers in *Burns*.[17] The Court in *Burns* focused almost exclusively on the burdens contract survival would impose on the successor employer and the need to accord complete freedom of capital movement. As "problems" the Court notes that Burns, if it was bound by the Wackenhut contract, could discharge employees only pursuant to the terms of the agreement, and Burns would also be compelled to abide by the contractual terms and accrued rights of employees.[18] This is a likely result of contract survival, but they are serious "problems" *only* if the goal is to permit the new employer full freedom to organize the enterprise as it sees fit. As Charles Morris and William Gaus perceptively note, such "results are 'benefits' in the double sense that they protect the employees of a business that is continuing under a new owner, and that they provide for the private resolution of potential labor disputes."[19]

These "problems" which could inhibit the "free flow of capital" reveal the shift from *Wiley*, where the Court sought some limited accommodation between the "rightful prerogatives of owners independently to rearrange their business" and the correspondingly weighty interests of employees to be protected "from a sudden change in the employment relationship."[20] The significant role served by the collective agreement in the arbitration area is narrowed in *Burns* so that the agreement serves as only an economic bargain, a bargain that should recognize the new "economic power realities." Yet the economic terms of a contract are not the sole or even the most important function of an agreement that also sets up a dispute resolution system, a measure of job security, and provides for the accumulation of a wide range of job benefits. The shift in policy is unmistakable, and despite the Court's attempts to distinguish *Wiley, Burns* suggests the dubious current status of *Wiley*.[21]

When a collective bargaining agreement is signed, the employer gains the value of planning certainty because wages and working conditions are contractually set for a specific period. Indeed, this interest in predictability seems to underlie the judicial hostility to certain kinds of collective action during the term of the agreement. The agreement has obvious importance to employees as well. The contract reflects an investment by employees in the operation, for they agree to live under the regime of the contract and usually waive the right to strike at any time. In a real sense, the agreement is part of the value of the business. Arguably, this value is part of the purchase price when the business is purchased by a successor. This conclusion would also be consistent with notions about the presumed "cooperative" nature of the enterprise which the Court has used to limit the scope of employee action in the protected conduct area. Yet, the Court in *Burns* shows little interest in prior employee investment in the enterprise. Such a view is seemingly consistent with implicit judicial assumptions and values in the areas of labor law already discussed.

It may be possible to maintain a semblance of concern for employee interest by restricting *Burns* to the 8(a)(5) context, thus permitting *Wiley* to continue to govern in arbitration situations. In the bargaining or 8(a)(5) context, the Court had previously stressed its concern that the NLRA should not interfere with private collective bargaining and warned the NLRB to steer clear of contract making.[22] Whereas the Board's function is to "oversee and referee the process of collective bargaining, leaving the results of the contest to the bargaining strengths of the parties,"[23] Section 301, on the other hand, is designed to enforce compliance with agreements. Yet, ironically, the Court has been quite willing under Section 301 to encourage arbitral integrity and the arbitral process irrespective or in spite of the intentions of the parties. The famous arbitration "trilogy" of the early 1960s makes it difficult for a party to avoid compulsory arbitration or to get effective review of an arbitration award. Moreover, a union promise not to strike, a "no-strike" clause, will be *implied* coextensive with an arbitration clause, and so strikes over matters that could be arbitrated can be enjoined or result in a monetary judgment for breach of contract despite the absence of an explicit no-strike clause.[24] *Wiley* itself reflects the victory of federal policy over the contract expectations of the successor employer. The inconsistency between *Burns* and *Wiley* lies less in the holdings than in the statements of underlying policy.

The current vigor of *Wiley* was further undercut in a recent case which raised the very issue present in *Wiley*, that is, the duty of a successor employer to arbitrate under Section 301 pursuant to a predecessor's collective agreement. In *Howard Johnson Co. v. Detroit Local Joint Executive Board*,[25] the Court refused to order arbitration. Although *Wiley* was again distinguished, the Court substantially undercut the continued viability of the decision by applying the principles of *Burns*. First, the Court unconvincingly noted that Howard Johnson had acquired the business (by purchase and a rental of property) from a company that continued to exist after the transfer, rather than via a complete merger, as in *Wiley*. More significant, the Court held that the duty to arbitrate would not be imposed unless there was a "continuity in identity" in the business enterprise, which included a "substantial continuity in the identity of the work force. . . ."[26] No continuity exists and hence no obligation to arbitrate arises, unless the new employer hires a new work force, a majority of which are predecessor employees. To make the noose even tighter, the new employer is permitted upon the takeover to hire anyone it wishes, limited only by the 8(a)(1) and (3) restrictions against discrimination. Thus, the makeup of the work force is within the new employer's discretion, and the employees' interest in security rests upon the manner in which that discretion is exercised.

Even if a duty to bargain does continue despite the change in employer, the earlier *Burns* decision had made it clear that the new employer may in most instances freely set initial terms and conditions of employment upon takeover without bargaining because these were deemed to be *new* terms rather than unilateral *changes* of existing terms. An employer's unilateral change in a working condition normally violates 8(a)(5), but the Court in *Burns* had expressed considerable difficulty in understanding how a successor employer could have "changed" any term. As is generally true in critical cases, the Court substituted assertion for rationale: "[A] successor employer is ordinarily free to set initial terms on which it will hire the employees of a predecessor."[27] Not only can the new employer freely set new terms, but bargaining need not begin until the successor has hired, if it decides to do so, the employees of the predecessor in sufficient numbers to constitute a majority of its work force. Thus, the successor employer has a wider range of freedom than other employers, despite the existing restrictions on the scope of 8(a)(5) already discussed. Given any employer's rights to act independently on "core" managerial decisions, why this extra freedom from contract adherence or *even bargaining* is necessary in light of its impact upon employee interests is difficult to understand.[28]

A new employer, even if a "successor" in the abstract, has the power to avoid *Wiley's* duty to arbitrate or the duty to bargain as long as it carefully, but without discrimination, chooses its new work force. It has no obligation to hire or prefer the predecessor employees; indeed, it has legally inspired incentives not to do so. (Of course, as in the case of an employer's right to replace economic strikers, the incentive to replace or refuse to hire can only be exploited by certain employers in particular circumstances.) In addition, even though the duty to bargain may still exist, the new employer can initially set new terms and conditions of employment without bargaining. With care and good legal advice, then, a new employer can avoid the concerns expressed in *Wiley* about the value of arbitral resolution of disputes and the protection of employees facing a change in the enterprise. The previously existing contract rights of employees can be lost as can their right to be represented by a union. Indeed, their very jobs depend upon employer discretion to hire them. The full freedom of capital mobility from the interests of employee concerns is complete.

Many commentators had argued, correctly it now appears, that *Wiley* and *Burns* could not rationally be reconciled, despite the Court's protestations.[29] Morris and Gaus argue, with some pessimism, that the cases can be reconciled by reading *Burns* as a limitation on the NLRB rather than as a determination that the underlying policies of *Wiley* are of doubtful value. Although this forces us to ignore the capital "problems" language of *Burns,* it is true that meaningful distinctions exist between the NLRA and Section 301. The contract covered by Section 301 exists independently of NLRA considerations such as the majority status of the union.[30] Moreover, the future unknown decision by an arbitrator is not the same as a Board determination that successors are bound to the entire agreement.[31] The *Wiley* path, through arbitration, permits an arbitrator to discard those provisions made unworkable by the new conditions. Ironically, parties are generally less interested in the survival of an arbitration clause, a clause only having viability if there is a valid agreement, than with other portions of an agreement. Thus, for example, an agreement providing for seniority normally relates seniority to the acquisition of a wide variety of contract benefits. Parties generally do not intend that this acquisition process should end simply because a particular contract terminates. Nevertheless, if contract making via federal law is to be avoided, it would seem to be no less unforgivable because it is perpetrated by a private arbitrator than by the NLRB. And *Wiley* may limit "capital" freedom too, although not so much as the vanquished argument in *Burns* might have done.

If the cases do coexist, a contract does not survive a merger or sale for 8(a)(5) purposes but may nevertheless survive for Section 301 purposes. It is hard to see how or why a contract is binding under one provision but not under another. Morris and Gaus support their belief that accommodation is required because *Burns* seems an "apparent departure . . . from the mainstream. . . ."[32] Yet, the values expressed in *Burns*, at least after the preceding discussion, can hardly be deemed surprising, and *Howard Johnson* certainly threatens the continued viability of *Wiley*. The seeming inconsistency of *Burns* and *Wiley* was noted by the Court itself in *Howard Johnson*, foretelling the ultimate demise of *Wiley*. The Court applied the policy of *Burns* in a Section 301 case because, the Court stated, federal law under 301 had to be consistent with NLRA principles. Otherwise, a successor's rights would depend upon the forum chosen.[33] This would be the precise result if *Wiley* and *Burns* should coexist. The Court based its decision in *Howard Johnson* on the successor's necessary freedom to hire its own work force and on a policy in favor of free reorganization of businesses. Thus, for this Supreme Court at least, it is likely that the protection of managerial freedom will receive greater attention than even the encouragement of arbitration as a peace-enhancing mechanism. As in *First National Maintenance*, the Court is likely to exclude matters from the regime of bargaining or from the bargaining process rather than follow the more integrative, cooperative approach generally followed.

The area of successorship is excruciatingly complex, and many complexities have been omitted from this discussion. It should be clear, however, that these cases represent more than the historical shift from the more liberal Warren Court to the far less liberal Burger Court. The policies of *Burns* is understandably seen as an aberration, but so is *Darlington Mills* and, of course, *Mackay*. When most of the major decisions are seen as aberrant, something more is indicated than merely insufficient research or thought. Instead, it is time to face the inability of the received wisdom to predict or justify the decisions and directly confront the values upon which these doctrines are based.

11

CONCLUSION: THE EMPLOYMENT RELATION

AND THE PREMISES OF LABOR LAW

ALTHOUGH DECISIONS IN labor law are not usually written in status or contractual terms, many of the decisions involve the construing and constructing of status or contractual relationships. The employment relationship is viewed by courts through a set of assumptions, involving status and class views, and the NLRA is treated as if it overlaps, but barely alters, this presumed relationship. Indeed, the statute is often used to enforce those aspects of the contractual relationship that courts create.

Thus, for instance, it is misleading to focus on the process in the traditional way, that is, on whether concerted activity, otherwise protected, falls outside of statutory protection because of employee acts of disloyalty. There is no legislative history, under the Wagner Act at least, to suggest that Section 7 is limited and, even more clearly, nothing that gives any indication where a line is to be drawn. Although the courts obviously do refer to the issue in these terms, the legal formulation masks a quite different process. Logically, the courts seem to have initially presumed that a particular kind of loyalty obligation exists. To find that certain actions are unprotected because they violate these obligations is to say that the act assumes the maintenance of these contractual or status obligations even when they seem inconsistent with the thrust or literal language of the act.

It is the NLRB and the courts, of course, who define the scope and content of the employment relation. The substantive rights and obligations, except those created by collective agreements, are not generally left to private law making. Indeed, contracts of employment are rarely written nor are they usually fleshed out orally. The statutory context hides, I believe, the process by which decisions are reached. Under the common law, the reliance on contractualism was obviously clearer even though these courts also masked value judgments.

A number of recent Supreme Court decisions strikingly reaffirm the contract and status assumptions discussed throughout this study. I wish to conclude with two recent decisions from vastly different areas which highlight the ideas expressed throughout this volume. One recent decision relies upon the notion that a worker's lot is to sell labor for a livelihood, rather than to make an investment in the enterprise. In *Teamsters* v. *Daniel*[1] the Court held that noncontributory pension schemes were not "securities" within the meaning of the Securities Acts. Although the holding may be correct, the language of the opinion reveals the Court's view of the employment relation. The Court rejected the argument that the employee "invests" in the pension fund by allowing a portion of his or her compensation to be deferred as a pension benefit and by contributing labor in return for these payments. The employee, says the Court,

surrenders his labor as a whole, and in return receives a compensation package that is substantially devoid of aspects resembling a security. His decision to accept and retain continued employment may have only an attentuated relationship, if any, to perceived investment possibilities of a future pension. Looking at the economic realities, it seems clear that an employee is selling his labor primarily to obtain a livelihood, not making an investment.[2]

What seems clear to the Court may not seem so clear to employees to whom a pension is a critically important job benefit. It is doubtful that the "purported investment is a relatively insignificant part of an employee's indivisible compensation package."[3] The Court, by finding it impossible to segregate an employee's investment from his noninvestment interests, overlooks the possibility that the *entire* compensation package is a return for the employees' "investment" of labor. The notion that an employee's interest is limited to a pay check is painfully ironic given the Court's stress in other circumstances on the "common enterprise." At base, then, the Court assumes that employees sell their labor in return for a livelihood, and even if, arguably, part of this exchange could be deemed an investment interest, such an investment cannot be separated from other more predominant noninvestment interests, such as wages. Aside from pensions, then, the Court assumes that workers do not invest anything in an enterprise. Their labor is purchased like other commodities; it may be treated as a commodity and the labor power purchased is not an investment by the employee in the enterprise. Decisions like *Barlow's*, holding that warrantless OSHA inspections are unconstitutional, and implicitly rejecting any property or statutory interest in employees' safety interests, or other cases where enterprises are referred to as "his property" or "his business," simply follow from this assumption.

Moreover, the definition of "employee" itself indicates a particular status assumption. Recently, in *NLRB* v. *Bell Aerospace*,[4] the Court held that managerial employees, a group never clearly defined and probably undefinable, could not be considered "employees" under the NLRA and, thus, secured no rights under the act. The act grants rights only to "employees." Managerial employees were "employees," but the Court nevertheless felt that Congress intended to exclude them from statutory coverage. This conclusion was reached even though Congress had an opportunity to discuss and act on the issue in 1947 but failed to do so. Indeed, Taft-Hartley expressly excluded some employees, notably supervisors, a group that falls within the vague "managerial" category.

Bell Aerospace represents an attempt to mask or avoid the recognition that a clear confrontation exists between owners, on one hand, and workers, on the other. To blur the confrontation, a vaguely defined group was created, composed of those who are neither traditional blue-collar workers nor owners. At most, perhaps, these "managerial employees" may act as a surrogate for owners. Again, a category having neither clear nor inherent boundaries is created. The use of such a category deflects investigation from major issues to the detailed, case-by-case investigation of traditional law work, revealing, as the cases will no doubt reveal, no intellectually respectable way to define the category or to distinguish it from statutorily *included* professional employees or from statutorily excluded foremen.[5]

The majority quotes approvingly from Justice Douglas's dissent in *NLRB* v. *Packard*,[6] which held, prior to being legislatively reversed by Congress in Taft-Hartley, that foremen could constitute an appropriate unit under the act:

The present decision . . . tends to obliterate the line between management and labor. It lends the sanctions of federal law to unionization at all levels of the industrial hierarchy. It tends to emphasize that the basic opposing forces in industry are not management and labor but the operating group on the one hand and the stockholder and bondholder group on the other. The industrial problem as so defined comes down to a contest over a fair division of the gross receipts of industry between these two groups. The struggle for control or power between management and labor becomes secondary to a growing unity in their common demands on ownership.[7]

In other words, Justice Douglas, and the current Court, believed that to consider foremen or managerial employees as "employees" under the act would lead to a perception that the crucial battle is between workers and owners. This would mean that the basic conflict between these two groups is one over profits or maybe "gross receipts." Yet, this is the very perception of the struggle, between "employers and employed," that Holmes recognized as competition in 1896. "One of the eternal conflicts out of which life is made up is that between the effort of every man to get the most he can for his services, and that of society, disguised under the name of capital, to get his services for the least possible return."[8]

The battle to Holmes is between "capital" and "labor." The existence of "management," as distinct from owners, was not as clearly perceived when Holmes was writing. By 1947 Justice Douglas can refer to the basic conflict as being between "management and labor," thereby permitting him to castigate any decision even suggesting that a different zone of combat exists. If the workers and the management are the opposing forces, "of course" it becomes necessary to separate the two combatants for purposes of possible unionization, "[f]or if foremen are 'employees,' " said Douglas, so are "all who are on the payroll of the company, including the president; all who are commonly referred to as management, with the exception of the directors."[9]

Douglas's attack comes during the very period that writers are noting the developing distinction between owners and management and schools of management or business are attempting to explain their unique attributes. But managerial skills, like those of engineers (as David Noble has so clearly revealed),[10] exist to carry out the financial goals of the owners. To define the battle as *exclusively* between management and labor is to legally recognize management as the "flak catchers"[11] of owners and to blur the essential conflict of interest recognized by the original Wagner Act itself. One more concerned about immediate practical effects would recognize that the decision may exclude from the ambit of the act one of the fastest growing categories of workers or, at least, make white-collar organization more difficult just at the time that the union's traditional blue-collar base is shrinking.

Recent embellishments on the *Bell Aerospace* theme also demonstrate the limited status to be accorded employees, at least those employees entitled to NLRA protection. The Court held that faculty members at Yeshiva University and at similar institutions are "managerial employees" because they make recommendations "in every case of faculty hiring, tenure, sabbaticals, termination and promotion."[12] In addition, faculty "effectively determine curriculum, grading system, admissions and matriculation standards, academic calendars and course schedules."[13]

The initial question is why this catalogue of rights or powers, assuming they are meaningful at most private colleges and universities, should have anything to do with unionization or coverage under the statute. Professors, I suspect, are rarely moved to join unions because they have been denied the right to prepare calendars or to alter grading systems. Hiring and tenure decisions are more important, but such matters are generally not the issues over which unionization usually occurs. Universities may have originated as communities of scholars,[14] or so we are wont to believe, but few function this way in relation to traditional trade-union concerns such as salary levels and job tenure, especially in an era of contraction and retrenchment.

It is true that the scope of academic governance at many institutions is quite different from the Court's conception of bargaining that excludes "managerial" matters. Should particular factors make collective bargaining unworkable or unfeasible, an argument based upon statutory policies could be made.[15] Thus, it is possible that arguments based upon employer structure or employee function, such as access to employment or confidential data, could be legitimately used to deny coverage under a statute designed to encourage collective bargaining.[16] It is also possible to argue that managers could not possibly carry out their job tasks if they were in unions; for instance, managers, being infected with the principles of unionism, will cease to be coldly efficient profit maximizers. Managers would cease to exclusively represent managerial or ownership views and, instead, would stress community interests over striving, initiative, or risk taking.[17] The Court, however, does not suggest that Yeshiva's faculty (or Bell Aerospace's buyers) have functions that make effective bargaining unlikely. Certainly the evidence of faculty bargaining makes it difficult to argue that bargaining on a college or university level is unworkable. Instead, the Court merely finds certain workers are not entitled to statutory protection because they perform *functions* that the Court deems "managerial."[18]

While trying to distinguish academe from the factory, the Court reveals its view of the factory. In the Court's view, statutory "employees" have no legitimate right to make managerial decisions or even to be involved in determining such issues. If employees seek such involvement, they exceed the bounds of mandatory bargaining in the act as the prior section has shown. Thus, they would be engaging in unprotected activity in attempting to force bargaining over such issues, and the employer would have no statutory obligation to negotiate. If, on the other hand, the employer grants or workers secure substantial involvement over such matters, then they become managers and are deprived of the act's protections.

In a strange sense, the benefits of the act are conditioned on a distinction between certain kinds of job functions that, in turn, is premised on a determination that certain functions are inherently managerial and others are not. Those categories exist primarily in the minds of the judges. The professoriate at Yeshiva are deprived of the act's protections because of the relatively democratic nature of academe, a model the Court is unwilling to countenance as conceivable in any other setting under the NLRA. In addition, the categories assume a status system in the plant. As the Court has stated, managerial employees are "much higher in the managerial structure" than those explicitly mentioned by Congress.[19]

Employees covered by the act are presumably those who have some conflict of interest with management because the Court finds no conflict between managerial employees, or the professors of Yeshiva, and employers. Yet, employees are required to act in ways that will benefit the employer, eschewing various kinds of effective collective action because the workplace is a "cooperative" enterprise. Thus, if an employee is faced with a work order that seems inconsistent with the agreement, the employee must use the grievance process rather than engage in self-help for the benefit of the enterprise. Moreover, employees are required to act in certain ways to benefit the production process as well as to support an employer's desire for rational, long-term planning. Employers, however, are permitted to act irrespective of prior employee investment. The preeminent value seems to be the need of capital to move freely, even though when an enterprise partially or totally terminates operations or is merged or sold, valuable interests of the employees may be completely lost.

As the text has sought to demonstrate, the NLRA has obviously affected employer hegemony to some extent, but it has not significantly weakened this authority. Indeed, assumptions about inherent employer authority are used to interpret, that is, to narrow, the thrust and language of the act.

Nor has collective bargaining been a completely satisfactory response to exclusive managerial power even though its benefits cannot be ignored. Beyond the economic benefits unionized employees have gained through collective bargaining, agreements establish rules that protect employees from arbitrary managerial power. Such rules protect against arbitrary actions that adversely affect job opportunities and also provide for rational allocations of benefits. The process serves two functions that the supporters of the Wagner Act intended, that is, collective bargaining serves a "cooptative, integrating role that of necessity invites and legitimates certain forms of industrial conflict and overt expression of workers' power" as well as serving a "disciplinary, conflict-suppressing role."[20] Collective bargaining has little relationship to the modern conception of industrial democracy for it accepts as a basic premise the authoritarian and bureaucratic nature of enterprise.[21]

Alfred Chandler argued that the influence of families and financiers tended to grow weaker in the management of modern enterprises, while the influence of workers, through unions, grew. Yet union influence "directly affected only one set of management decisions—those made by middle managers related to wages, hiring, firing, and conditions of work. Such decisions had only an indirect impact on the central ones that coordinated current flows and allocated resources for the future."[22] Unions, perhaps because of their relative lack of power, may have avoided reaching the core of managerial sensitivity. Modern labor law has helped to institutionalize this reluctance into legal dogma.

It may thus be correct to view collective bargaining as serving to legitimate employer power: "[C]ollective bargaining could be held as providing legitimation for a system characterized by extreme division of function, mobility of resources, and free contract."[23] Collective bargaining and arbitration also reinstitute and reinforce the status notions found in decisions of common-law courts. Arbitrators and the Board, for instance, require that employees show respect, in actions and words, to supervisors. Perhaps empirical evidence might show that insulting or obscene language is rarely directed to employees by supervisors, although no such studies are ever cited. On the other hand, supervisors, given their power, may have no need to insult employees. Similarly, employees are almost always discharged or suspended prior to a grievance hearing irrespective of proof of any possible threat to production, coworkers, or property. The effects of such a power upon employees should not be discounted. Finally, the right to discipline, along with the right to manage is normally expressed in the collective agreement as Charles Spencer has noted:

Collective bargaining has accomplished very little in altering the fundamental assumptions, attitudes and attachments of corporate employers concerning discipline in the workplace. The right to discipline its employees has been broadly conceded as an inalienable right of management, implicit in ownership of capital, a basic property of the productive process, a timeless relationship between worker and boss, and is solidly validated in most union contracts, in classical language stating that "the Company retains the exclusive rights to manage the business and the plants and to direct the working forces . . . including the right to hire, suspend or discharge for proper cause. . . ." The quotes are from the Steelworkers Union contract, but it is substantially the same in most union contracts, and though it sounds innocent enough, it is under this contractual right that employees are given time off, sometimes up to a year, or are discharged from employment, without benefit of the rights citizens enjoy under the due process of our legal system.[24]

As the legal doctrines discussed show, collective bargaining may substitute the weakness of one for the power of the many, but the result is not a contract of employment. Unless modified by the agreement, many of the old master-servant notions are still embedded in the relationship. Indeed, collective bargaining itself partakes of a status system. The collective agreement is not a contract of employment, but it does set the terms and conditions for all employees presently employed or subsequently hired. Workers obtain these rights by their membership in a group.[25] Tannenbaum has observed that the "industrialism that destroyed a society of status has now recreated it."[26] Yet it is not clear that contract ever served to substantially alter status assumptions.

The notion of contract stresses the voluntary exchange of freely bargained promises, appealing to values of individualism, while simultaneously completely ignoring the economic reality of the "bargain." "The worker has to sell his labour power to live whereas the employer is not similarly constrained to buy labour."[27] The asymmetry of the relation goes even further. While the employee receives a defined rate for the job, the employer receives a potential whose ultimate development is largely for it to determine. The employer's side of the bargain is, therefore, essentially open ended. While employers impose rules of great specificity which reduces employee discretion to minimal levels, employers possess maximum discretion in making decisions concerning the goals and methods of production and the behavior and rewards of all participants. This asymmetry has been maintained by economic and state power.

The state, through statute, and employees themselves, via bargaining, may lessen employer discretion, but these attempts may ultimately "renew the legitimation."[28] Over forty years after the passage of the Wagner Act, the common-law notion of inherent worker obligations operates and often limits the seeming implications of federal labor law. No doctrine more readily reveals this conclusion than *Mackay*—workers may legally strike, but they may nevertheless be permanently replaced. The doctrine obviously mocks the protection of the right to strike, but it does continue the notion that workers have no property interest in their job. Similarly, employers' right to bargain over job content or critical investment decisions is limited by notions of inherent managerial prerogatives.[29] Outside of those directly job-related matters falling within the area of mandatory bargaining, employers are as free to act as they were prior to 1935. Obviously, the vast majority of employees, unrepresented by unions or excluded from statutory coverage, are even less able to have a voice over managerial changes that critically affect their work and their jobs.

Moreover, the inherent obligations and responsibilities of the parties have not markedly been altered by labor legislation. Workers, "in service," have obligations of loyalty to their employer. They may not, for instance, disparage the employer's product even though such action occurs in the context of a labor dispute. Indeed, judicial statements suggest that the labor laws were designed to *strengthen* bonds of loyalty. Except where limited by statute, courts have been reluctant to impose anything close to corresponding responsibilities upon employers. Mergers, transfer of operations, terminations, for instance, often occur without forewarning, and indeed, employees and unions are often misled about the nature of the situation. Nevertheless, such failures to respect the integrity of workers in the common enterprise do not affect the legal decisions reached.

Thus, just as the nineteenth-century notion of contract was infused with older master-servant doctrines, a similar conclusion can be reached concerning modern American labor law. Although I do not mean to disparage the accomplishments and value of collective bargaining as a device for limiting otherwise arbitrary or at least exclusive exercise of managerial power, the institution does not seem to have altered basic legal assumptions about the workers' place in the employment relationship.

NOTES

INTRODUCTION

1   J. Atleson, "Threats to Health and Safety: Employee Self-Help Under the NLRA," 59 Minn. L. Rev. 647 (1975): Atleson, "Disciplinary Discharges, Arbitration, and NLRB Deference," 20 Buffalo L. Rev. 355 (1971).

2   J. Atleson, "Work Group Behavior & Wildcat Strikes: The Causes and Functions of Industrial Civil Disobedience," 34 Ohio St. L. J. 750 (1973).

3   The argument raised here is not unique to the field of labor law. Richard Parker has recently noted that there is good reason to question "a rationalist analysis of the practices of constitutional argument." Legal academics, in constitutional law as in other areas, continually point out the failure of courts to rationally justify outcomes. When continual failure is demonstrated, he asks, "might it not be [that] the standards do not capture all that the enterprise is about?" Parker, *Political Vision in Constitutional Argument*," p. 45 (unpublished manuscript).

4   The analysis of American labor law could be seen as part of the emerging literature of demystification, the unmasking of the hidden value structures underlying particular and outwardly value-free legal doctrines or modes of thought in order to reveal the social functions of law. Such an analysis would conclude that if the normal rhetoric of legal discourse does not explain the legal decisions, but the cases can be explained by another set of values and assumptions, then the *social function* of the legal process is to obscure and to make contingent political and social choices seem inevitable or natural. See, *e.g.*, K. Klare, "Judicial Deradicalization of the Wagner Act and the Origins of Modern Legal Consciousness, 1937–1941," 62 Minn. L. Rev. 265 (1978); D. Kennedy, "Toward an Historical Understanding of Legal Consciousness," 3 Research in Law & Sociology 3 (1980).

Although this book can fit into this literature, my goal is not to deal with the social functions of law or legal thought. I wish to unmask or decode labor law, but ultimate conclusions about the function of law are left to the reader.

5   In 1947 Congress amended the act to bar some conduct that would otherwise fall within Section 7. Secondary pressure and work-assignment strikes, for instance, were made unfair labor practices. It seems clear that economic harm to employers was the primary harm sought to be alleviated, although there was concern that minority unions were employing these weapons to achieve recognition. See, *e.g.*, R. W. Fleming, "Title VII: The Taft-Hartley Amendments," 54 Nw. L. Rev. 666, 681 (1960). Organizational picketing was restricted by Section 8(b)(7) in 1959. Provisos in 8(b)(7) and 8(b)(4), however, recognized that constitutional elements of speech were involved in union pressure devices.

6   Gateway Coal v. UMW, 414 U.S. 368 (1974).

7   J. Atleson, "Threats to Health & Safety," *supra* note 1.

8   Textile Workers of America v. Darlington Mills, 380 U.S. 263 (1965).

9   C. Summers, "Industrial Democracy," 28 Clev. St. L. Rev. 29, 41 (1979).

10 The Supreme Court's love affair with arbitration ultimately led to more restric-
    tions upon strikes. Strikes in breach of contractual no-strike clauses could result
    in monetary damages and, recently, court injunctions, despite the Norris-La-
    Guardia Act. Even a strike not in violation of an express no-strike clause could be
    enjoined or subject to damages if the strike was "over" a matter subject to an arbi-
    tration clause.
        The interest involved here was said to be the protection of contractual arrange-
    ments, but the latter cases make clear that the enforcement of promises was not
    the real moving force. Rather, the Court was concerned with the protection of the
    grievance process as a private dispute resolution device. Two basic aims, the pro-
    tection of the employer-union system for dispute resolution and the protection of
    the employer's economic interest, run through much of the law and especially the
    areas that will be subsequently discussed.

11 Explicit statutory prohibitions on employers and unions often turn on objectives
    or means employed rather than on effects. To the extent that motivation or object
    is critical, the act often comes close to penalizing bad thoughts rather than bad ac-
    tions. In certain areas, problems with subjective requirements have led to tests
    stressing the impact of the employer's actions upon employee interests rather
    than intentions. See, *e.g.*, NLRB v. Great Dane Trailers Inc., 388 U.S. 26 (1967);
    NLRB v. Gissel Packing Co., Inc., 395 U.S. 575 (1969).

12 Like the "means-ends" test, of which this distinction is a part, courts are free to
    decide what is one's self-interest and what is not. See also, Local 189, Amalga-
    mated Meat Cutters v. Jewel Tea, 381 U.S. 676 (1965).

13 P. Selznick, *Law, Society & Industrial Justice* at 54 (Russell Sage 1969) [herein-
    after cited as *Selznick*].

14 "As exchange relations became ever more numerous and pervasive, more geo-
    graphically wide ranging, and more based on specific and structurally differenti-
    ated functions and services, the more attenuated became the relevance and indeed
    the practicability of diffuse long-term reciprocation. The personal relations, tradi-
    tional bonds, and community ties which could underpin purely local face-to-face
    transactions could not bear the weight of spatially dispersed markets, the emer-
    gence of intermediaries, and the increasing rationalization of economic activities
    in the direction of monetary measurement and acquisition. Relations became in-
    creasingly marked by specific short-term reciprocation—by economic as against
    social exchange." A. Fox, *Beyond Contract: Work, Power & Trust Relations* at
    160 (Faber & Faber 1974) [hereinafter cited as *Fox*].

15 Clayton Act, Section 6, 38 Stat. 730, *as amended* 15 U.S.C.A., Section 12 et seq.
    But see D. Brody, *Steelworkers in America: The Nonunion Era* at 27–49 (Harper
    Torchbooks 1960).

16 *Fox* at 166.

17 As early as the 1820s, middle-class opinion in England saw no incompatability be-
    tween the principle of equality before the law and the deliberately discriminatory
    labor codes such as the British Master & Servant Code of 1823, which punished

the workers by prison for breaches of contract, yet imposed at most only modest fines upon employers. *Fox* at 189.

18   Quoted in *Fox* at 182.

19   E. Pessen, *Most Uncommon Jacksonians* at 121 (SUNY Press 1967).

20   See, *e.g.*, Dawley & Faber, "Working-Class Culture & Politics in the Industrial Revolution: Sources of Loyalty and Rebellion," 8 Journal of Social History 466–80 (1975).

21   E. J. Hobsbawm, *The Age of Revolution, 1789–1848* (Mentor 1962).

22   K. Polanyi, *The Great Transformation* at 163 (Beacon 1944).

23   *Selznick* at 136; *Fox* at 183–84. As Alvin Gouldner noted, the contract only binds the worker to a "diffuse promise of obedience." The expectations and understanding of both parties are vague and unclear; even if one sees the contractual relationship as possessing status elements, the ambiguity of contract remains. John R. Commons, for instance, argued that a worker accepts a position of subordination when accepting a job because "what he sells when he sells his labour is his *willingness* to use his faculties to a purpose that has been pointed out to him. He sells his promise to obey commands." J. R. Commons, *The Legal Foundations of Capitalism* at 284 (Macmillan 1932).

But, as Gouldner asks, "which commands has the worker promised to obey. Are these commands limited to the *production* of goods and services only? Under the terms of the contract, may an employer legitimately issue a command unnecessary for production? *Who* decides this anyhow, worker or employer?" A. W. Gouldner, *Wildcat Strike* at 162–63 (Antioch Press 1954).

The notion of the labor contract does not answer these critical questions which focus upon authority relations and work behavior. Legitimacy of authority tends to take the form of general principles, but *acts* of authority are always specific. Thus, it is clear that work obligations are in practice indeterminate. R. Hyman and I. Brough, *Social Values and Industrial Relations* at 23–24 (Basil Blackwell 1975).

Marx's distinction between "labor" and "labor power" deals with the same problem. Marx stated that a worker sells only his "labor power," that is, his ability to work, but he does not sell a given amount of labor or real output. Tensions arise when the employer attempts to transform "labor power" into "labor" because no bargain was made concerning the actual amount of work to be done. See Gouldner, 162–65.

24   See O. Kahn-Freund, "Blackstone's Neglected Child: The Contract of Employment," 93 Law Quarterly Review 508 (1977); G. De N. Clark, "Unfair Dismissal and Reinstatement," 32 Modern Law Review 532 (1969).

25   *Selznick* at 123.

26   J. Schouler, *A Treatise on the Law of Domestic Relations, Embracing Husband and Wife, Parent and Child, Guardian and Ward, Infancy, and Master and Servant* (5th ed. 1895); I. Brown, *Elements of the Law of Domestic Relations and of Employer and Employed* (2d ed. 1890).

27   *Fox* at 185.

28   "The early authorities clearly sustain the principles of the text that the master may moderately correct his servant for negligence or misbehavior. . . . But this power does not grow out of the contract of hiring and its lawfullness has been de-

nied by a writer of eminent authority as not being consonant with the spirit and genius of contract." T. Reeve, *The Law of Baron & Femme, of Parent and Child, Guardian and Ward, Master and Servant* at 374 (1846 ed.).

29   See *Fox* at 209.

30   This discussion is based upon *Fox* at 187–88.

31   Quoted in *Fox* at 188.

32   E. J. Hobsbawm stresses that workers "liked to work, and their expectations were remarkably modest." E. J. Hobsbawm, *The Age of Capital, 1848–1875* at 244 (Mentor 1979). Workers came from an environment where hard work was a mark of a person's worth. Craft workers were moved by craft knowledge and pride, and while they might balk at some orders, craft norms set standards for performance. See also D. Montgomery, *Workers' Control in America* (Cambridge U. Press 1979).

   The workers' noncapitalistic approach to work benefited employers more than workers. Employers were motivated to buy in the cheapest markets and sell in the dearest. The sellers of labor, though, generally did not ask the highest wage the market would bear nor did they offer in return the minimum quantity of work they could get away with.

33   From this situation, Marx developed his theory of exploitation and social class.

34   *Selznick* at 135.

35   R. Morris, *Government and Labor in Early America* at 390–513 (Harper Torchbooks 1946).

36   E. Genovese, *Roll, Jordan, Roll: The World the Slaves Made* at 25–49 (Pantheon 1974).

37   *Fox* at 188–89.

38   See, *e.g.*, J. Feinman, "The Development of the Employment at Will Rule," 20 Am. J. Legal History 118 (1976); C. Summers, "Individual Protection against Unjust Dismissal: Time for a Statute," 62 Vir. L. Rev. 481, 484–91 (1976); L. Blades, "Employment at Will v. Individual Freedom: On Limiting the Abusive Exercise of Employer Power," 67 Colum. L. Rev. 1404 (1967); C. Peck, "Unjust Discharges from Employment: A Necessary Change in the Law," 40 Ohio St. L. J. 1 (1979); R. Weyand, "Present Status of Individual Employee Rights," NYU 22d Ann. Conf. on Labor 171 (1970).

39   A number of recent decisions have used tort or contract principles, and sometimes a combination, to protect against abusive or bad-faith discharges or to imply a warranty of good faith. See. *e.g.*, Monge v. Beebe Rubber Co., 114 N.H. 130, 316 A. 2d 549 (1974); Fortune v. National Cash Register Co., 373 Mass. 96, 364 N.E. 2d 1251 (1977).

40   See decisions cited in Summers, *supra* note 38, at 488–89.

41   Compare decisions denying recovery in actions of quantum meruit for wages to employees who leave their employment prior to the end of their term with the quite different results in building contract cases. See Stark v. Parker, 2 Pick 267 (Mass. 1824) and Haywood v. Leonard, 7 Pick 181 (Mass. 1828).

1   THE RIGHT TO STRIKE

1   NLRB v. Mackay Radio & Telegraph Co., 304 U.S. 333 (1938).

2   Section 7 of the NLRA provides that "Employees shall have the right to self-organization, to form, join or assist labor organizations, to bargain collectively through
representatives of their own choosing, and to engage in other concerted activities
for the purpose of collective bargaining or other mutual aid or protection. . . ." 28
U.S.C. Section 157(1970).

3   It is unclear whether some tacit understanding had been reached between the
union and the employer about the fate of the eleven employees. The eleven were
not invited to the union meeting to save "embarassment" although some apparently appeared. A two-thirds vote was decided upon, and the motion to return to
work passed, 22–6 with 8 employees declining to vote.

4   NLRB v. Mackay Radio & Telegraph, 1 NLRB 216 (1936).

5   Section 8(1), now 8(a)(1), makes it an unfair labor practice for an employer to "interfere with, restrain, or coerce employees" in the exercise of the rights guaranteed in Section 7.

6   1 NLRB at 201 (1936).

7   NLRB v. Mackay Radio & Telegraph, 87 F.2d 611 (9th Cir. 1937).

8   NLRB v. Mackay Radio & Telegraph, 92 F.2d 761 (9th Cir. 1937).

9   304 U.S. at 345.

10   *Ibid.*

11   *Id.* at 345–46. The Court cited NLRB v. Bell Oil & Gas, 91 F.2d 509 (1937), a decision that appears irrelevant.

12   NLRB v. Mackay Radio & Telegraph, 1 NLRB 201, 216 (1936).

13   NLRB v. Mackay Radio & Telegraph, Record on Appeal, NLRB Reply Brief, 15–16.
    The NLRB's predecessor, the NLB, had held that strikers remained employees
while on strike and were entitled to displace their replacements whenever the
Board found the strike had been caused by the employer's violation of Section 7(a).
Perhaps this means that the displacement could not exist if they were merely eco-
nomic strikers. See A. Roth and Company, 1 NLB 75 (1934) and Joseph F. Corcoran
Shoe Co., 1 NLB 78 (1934).

14   At present, strikers who are replaced and, thus, "not entitled to reinstatement"
are eligible to vote in representation elections in any election within 12 months of
the commencement of the strike. NLRA Section 9 (c)(3). Replacements, as employees, may also vote. At the time of *Mackay*, strikers could vote but replacements could *not* then vote. In re American Oil, 7 NLRB 210 (1938). The stability of
the employer-replacement relationship was deemed "notably tenuous." In re
Satorious Co., 10 NLRB 493, 494–95 (1939). Should an election be held, and the
union win, the employer must deal with a union representing strikers whom it refuses to reinstate and replacements the union wishes were not present.

15   See, *e.g.*, J. Atleson, *et al.*, *Collective Bargaining in Private Employment* at 17
(BNA 1978).

16   It is interesting to note that *Mackay* may not have seemed at all startling in 1938.
A number of the legal articles written at the time merely state the holding. Leonard B. Boudin, writing in 1940, however, sympathetically sets out the rights of
strikers and criticized the *Mackay* dictum. Boudin, "Rights of Strikers," 35 Ill. L.

Rev. 817 (1940). Boudin explains the dictum as being based upon a belief that the hiring of replacements is a justifiable employer response to a strike. That notion must have assumed that the act's framers did not contemplate that the right to strike would be unimpeded by the employer's right to hire replacements. *Id.* at 830. See also, Note, 51 Harv. L. Rev. 533 (1938), arguing that *Mackay* was inconsistent with the provisions of the NLRA.

Boudin acknowledged that "of course" employers may hire replacements, and he only challenged the notion that strikebreakers can be retained over the reinstatement requests of strikers. The strikers, he noted, are still employees, a position made clear under NLRA Section 2(3). Boudin's arguments are based less on policy and more on implicit antiunion motivation and the effects of replacements upon the right to strike. Why should the employer prefer inexperienced workers? Loyalty to strikebreakers is criticized, since such loyalty has not induced employers to honor promises of permanent employment when strong unions have negotiated the reinstatement of strikers and the displacement of replacements. Boudin argues that the only significant difference between the two groups of employees is that one group participated in a strike, a factor whose use would seem to constitute discrimination within the act as well as interference with the right to strike.

17 See, *e.g.*, the legal method used in Republic Aviation Co. v. NLRB, 324 U.S. 793 (1945). The approach makes it possible to find a violation in cases like *Republic Aviation*, where the employer barred union solicitation during nonworking time, despite the absence of objective proof that the employer's action actually interfered with union organization. At the same time, the approach makes it possible to find no violation, as in *Mackay*, despite obvious "interference."

18 NLRB v. Mackay Radio & Telegraph, 304 U.S. 333, 345 (1938).

19 Local 761, IUE v. NLRB, 366 U.S. 667 (1961).

20 See generally, H. Gillespie, "The Mackay Doctrine and the Myth of Business Necessity," 50 Texas L. Rev. 782 (1972).

21 NLRB v. Erie Resistor, 373 U.S. 221 (1963).

22 *Id.* at 231.

23 The result of *Mackay* could be the total replacement of a striking work force and the possible termination of the union's status. Future cohesion, of course, would not become a concern in this situation.

24 See J. Getman, "The Protection of Economic Pressure by Section 7 of the National Labor Relations Act," 115 U. Pa. L. Rev. 1195, 1204–5 (1967) [hereinafter cited as *Getman*].

25 G. Schatzki, "Some Observations and Suggestions Concerning a Misnomer—'Protected' Concerted Activities," 47 Texas L. Rev. 378, 383 (1969) [hereinafter cited as *Schatzki*]. The mechanism by which the act of replacement removes the union can be easily explained. The employer may cease to bargain with the union when it has objective evidence that the union no longer represents a majority of employees. The evidence needs to be "objective," but the evidence need only be sufficient to support a "good faith doubt" of majority status. See, *e.g.*, NLRB v. Gulfmont Hotel Co., 362 F.2d 588 (5th Cir. 1966). See generally, R. Gorman, *Basic Text on Labor Law* at 108–16 (West Pub. 1976). The replacement of a majority of the employees through the hiring of permanent replacements, of course, undermines the normal continued presumption of majority support. NLRB v. Titan Metal Mfg.

Co., 135 NLRB 196 (1962). The employer's withdrawal from bargaining places the burden on the union to seek a NLRB determination that it still represents a majority of the employers. The normal route is for the union to charge a violation of 8(a)(5). See Gorman, *id.*

The employer or employees may also file for a Board-sponsored election. During the first 12 months of the strike, the total work force is assumed to include the replaced economic strikers. NLRB v. Guenther & Son, 427 F.2d 983 (5th Cir. 1970). Thus, permanently replaced economic strikers may vote in such an election for a period of 12 months after the commencement of the strike but so may the replacements. 29 U.S.C. §159(1)(1970). Since the replacements may also vote, a replacement is permanent if the employer so designates the employee. Pacific Tile & Porcelain Co., 137 NLRB 1358, 1360 (1962). The union obviously risks decertification during this period, especially if replacements outnumber strikers. After this 12-month period, decertification of the union is even more likely because the replaced strikers may no longer vote. See Note, "Right of Economic Strikers to Vote in NLRB Elections," 12 Syracuse L. Rev. 218 (1960); Gillespie, *supra* note 20, at 786–87. The advantage thus given employers exacerbates the already emotional atmosphere caused by the hiring of replacements.

I have omitted a discussion of election procedures, but Section 9 provides instructive insights into the values which often outweigh the supposedly weighty interest in employee free choice. No election can be held, for instance, if a valid election has been held within the previous 12 months. NLRA, §9(c)(3). The section does protect employee will as once expressed, but the section bars an election even though employees chose "no union" in the election and even though a new union seeks representational status. See Section 8(b)(7)(B), which also bars recognitional picketing in this situation. Support for incumbent unions as well as the interest in stability and employer planning underlies "contract bar" rules, which bar election petitions for three years during the life of a collective agreement. Some of these rules clearly protect unions, at least incumbent unions, primarily from employer attempts to undercut the status of the union. Not coincidently, employers are also protected from a change of representative, the disturbance of a new election campaign and election, and the possibility of having to negotiate a new agreement. Surely at least one function of some of these rules is to assist the employer's interest in long-range planning. Some of these rules can also be justified on the ground of NLRB convenience, efficiency, and the need to maintain the integrity of NLRB-sponsored elections.

26   Erie Resistor Corp. v. NLRB, 373 U.S. 221 (1963).

27   NLRB v. Great Dane Trailers, Inc., 388 U.S. 221 (1967).

28   Some feel the distinction is important. Thus, Archibald Cox can say that a union might be reluctant to engage in a strike "which, if lost, would subject the employees to reprisals because it was not a protected activity, even though the same union would favor the strike if the only risk attendant upon its loss were that some of the employees' jobs might be filled by strike-breakers." Cox, "The Right to Engage in Concerted Activities," 26 Ind. L. J. 319 (1951). Basically, Cox is saying the fear of reprisals (discharges, etc.) is substantially greater than the fear of permanent replacement.

29   Many 8(a)(5) refusal-to-bargain cases, for instance, are fought to protect the status

of replaced strikers rather than for the often minimal vindicatory value of a cease-and-desist order.

30   Ironically, some legal restrictions may create obstacles to the use of *Mackay*. The United States Employment Service cannot refer persons to enterprises involved in labor disputes, and some states have adopted similar restrictions. Gillespie, *supra* note 20, at 782, 789.

31   Giddings & Lewis, Inc. v. NLRB, 110 LRRM 2121, 2123 (7th Cir. 1982). The incoherency of post-*Mackay* doctrinal development is neatly demonstrated by this recent case. The employer hired permanent replacements for a substantial number of employees. When the strike ended, the employer established a preferential hiring list of strikers who had been permanently replaced. As employees quit or left employment, the employer hired from this list. Two years later only 176 of the original 700 employees on the hiring list remained. The employer issued a handbook containing new rules to be followed in the case of a layoff. In cases of recall to work, the permanent replacements and reinstated strikers would be recalled on the basis of seniority. But the crucial question focused upon the order of recall and the effect on the remaining unreinstated strikers. The problem was that replacements and reinstated strikers would not lose their positions upon recall to more senior, unreinstated strikers. Thus a layoff would not "activate a striker's right to reinstatement."

Under the act unreinstated strikers remain employees. A recall of a junior employee instead of a more senior, unreinstated striker would seem literally to discriminate against strikers or interfere with the right to strike. Such logic, of course, does not follow from *Mackay*, but later cases have held that employers may not offer superseniority to obtain replacements *(Erie Resistor)*, must reinstate strikers when poststrike production reaches normal levels *(Fleetwood Trailers)*, and must reinstate strikers as their replacements leave *(Laidlaw Corp.)*.

There are two possible problems, however, in applying these precedents to *Giddings & Lewis*. First, the extra or "super" seniority is given to replacements *and* reinstated strikers so the discrimination does not affect *all* who struck but only those who were unfortunate enough not to be reinstated at the point the layoff occurs. Second, the situation involves a layoff rather than a departure of replacements. The second point would not seem critical, and the court stresses the first. The case is significant because of its treatment of the employer's interest and misreading of *Erie Resistor*.

The court, although mentioning the lack of discrimination against strikers as a group, seemingly rested its holding on the employer's need to obtain strike replacements. The seventh circuit held that the employer was merely *assuring* replacements of the permanent status to which they were entitled! Any other result, said the court, would "eviscerate the *Mackay* rule" because employers would be able to guarantee replacements employment only until a layoff occurred. "Such replacements could hardly be called 'permanent.' "

The employer's interest, however, is acquiring replacements, not actually guaranteeing them employment thereafter. *Mackay* stressed the employer's right to seek and acquire replacements, not its need to guarantee permanent status at some later time. "Permanency," moreover, is a myth in any event. *Nothing* guar-

antees these replacements a job or protects them from employer discharge, change
of heart, or displacement through collective bargaining. The employer's desire to
keep the replacements literally discriminates against unreinstated strikers, and
this desire is quite different from the basis of *Mackay, i.e.,* the "right" to keep
production going *during* a strike. The court turns the right to seek and acquire
replacements into the right to grant permanent preference to replacements as
against unreinstated strikers in layoff situations.

Another way to accomplish what the court feels employers are legitimately entitled to obtain is to grant superseniority at the time replacements are hired. After
all, the *Mackay* rule was based on maintaining production during a strike, not
maintaining replacements at some later time. Although the employer's interest is
identical, the Supreme Court in *Erie Resistor* held that superseniority may not be
offered *despite* a good-faith belief in its necessity in order to obtain replacements.
The seventh circuit avoids this serious problem by simply misreading *Erie Resistor*, stating that it bars discrimination against strikers when they *return* to
work. That is, the concern in *Erie Resistor* was that returning strikers would find
themselves in relatively inferior seniority positions because of the superseniority
granted to strike replacements. In *Giddings & Lewis*, however, the seventh circuit says reinstated strikers are "treated no differently than replacements. . . ."
That is true but beside the point. These groups receive protection that *unreinstated* strikers do not receive, and *that* is the issue. Admittedly, *Erie Resistor* did
stress the possible long-term effects on collective action because a cleavage between strike replacements and reinstated strikers existed in the work force due to
a grant of superseniority, but it also relied upon the damaging effect of the *mere
offer* of superseniority on the strike itself. The grant of seniority protection, said
the Supreme Court, "necessarily operates to the detriment of those who participated in the strike as compared to nonstrikers." The Supreme Court clearly held
that the grant of superseniority was discriminatory, and this included its effect
upon those strikers who did *not* accept the offer.

Thus, in essence, the seventh circuit permits a grant of superseniority to replacements (and reinstated strikers) that could not lawfully be granted at the time
of hiring. The interest supporting the seventh circuit's holding, the interest
in continued production during the strike, is the same interest held insufficient
in *Erie Resistor*. Moreover, as noted, the court increases the scope of *Mackay* so
that the right to hire replacements now includes guaranteeing permanency to
replacements long after they are hired, a situation not involved in *Mackay*, while
it ignores the fact that permanent status is solely within the discretion of the
employer.

32   Once the balance is made, there seems to be no need to consider the facts or situa-
     tion existing in any particular case. Thus, the seventh circuit interpreted *Mackay*
     to eliminate any need for a case-by-case application of any balancing test even
     while contradictorily conceding that subsequent cases such as *Erie Resistor* and
     Fleetwood read *Mackay* as "employing a balancing test. . . ." Giddings & Lewis,
     Inc. v. NLRB, 110 LRRM 2121, 2123 (7th Cir. 1982).
33   Vegalahn v. Guntner, 167 Mass. 92, 44 N.E. 1077 (1896).
34   C. Perry, A. Kramer, & T. Schneider, *Operating During Strikes*, Wharton School,

Univ. of Pa., Labor Relations & Public Policy Series 23 (1982).

35 American Ship Building v. NLRB, 380 U.S. 300, 317 (1965).

36 *Id.* at 317.

37 NLRB v. Insurance Agents' International Union, 361 U.S. 477 (1960).

38 B. Janes, "The Illusion of Permanency for *Mackay* Doctrine Replacement Workers," 54 Texas L. Rev. 126 (1975).

39 29 U.S.C. Sections 158(a)(3) and (b)(2).

40 See Janes, *supra* n. 38, at 126–27.

41 One writer found only two cases brought by replacements who were laid off under state law. Both courts denied the claims on the ground that "permanent" employment was indefinite. The legal doctrine of promissory estoppel was rejected, as was the claim that accepting a job under strike conditions operated as additional consideration. See *id.* at 148–49; Bixby v. Wilson & Co., 196 F. Supp. 889 (N.D. Iowa 1961); Albers v. Wilson & Co., 184 F. Supp. 812 (D. Minn. 1960).

42 See Hot Shoppes, Inc., 146 NLRB 802 (1964).

43 See NLRB v. Lightner Publishing Co., 113 F.2d 621, 625–26 (7th Cir. 1940); G.C. Conn. Ltd. v. NLRB, 108 F.2d 390, 401 (7th Cir. 1939); Jacob Hunkele, 7 NLRB 1276, 1288–89 (1938), *modified*, 20 NLRB 123 (1940).

44 See Covington Furniture Mfg. Co., 212 NLRB 214 (1974). See NLRB v. Fleetwood Trailer Co., 389 U.S. 375 (1967).

45 A common situation involves a union's claim that the employer has bargained in bad faith in violation of 8(a)(5). The usual remedy, a cease-and-desist order, will not alter the union's weaker bargaining power, but the issue may be fought if a strike resulted and replacements were hired.

46 It is also true that permanent replacement does not necessarily remove the status of "employee" from a replaced striker. When a strike has occurred, production generally remains low for some time after the termination of the strike. The Court has held that a striker's right to reinstatement is not affected by the availability of jobs on the day the employee seeks reinstatement. Such employees remain employees and are entitled to reinstatement when full production resumes. NLRB v. Fleetwood Trailer, 389 U.S. 375 (1967). It is possible to read the decision as granting a preferential right to future job openings despite the fact that the striker's job was abolished or the striker was replaced. If strikers are replaced, they remain "employees" even though they may have no right to reinstatement when they initially seek it. For some undetermined period of time, their "employee" status entitles them to reinstatement upon the departure of the replacements. The right is conditional on the employees' not having acquired "regular and substantially equivalent employment" or is actually lost if the employer can demonstrate "legitimate and substantial business justifications" for the refusal to reinstate. "Employees on strike were not strangers to employers. . . . [T]hat *striking employees* is a name that denotes a status is only the latest judicial recognition of a commonly known fact. And this fact existed long prior to the Congress's declaration in the Wagner Act defining employees." Laidlaw Corp. v. NLRB, 414 F.2d 99, 103 (7th Cir. 1969).

47 Operating Committee for Economic Development, *The Public Interest in National Labor Policy* at 88 (1961).

48 *Schatzki.* See also, Comment, "Replacement of Workers During Strikes," 75 Yale L. J. 630 (1966).

49 See *Getman* at 1204, n. 43.

50 Senator Wagner's first Labor Relations Bill protected the status of strikers and explicitly denied employee status to employee replacements. This bill, which was not adopted, would have given strikers the right to return to their jobs even if "permanent" replacements had been hired. It would, therefore, have permitted employers to hire, at most, only temporary replacements. Legislative History of the National Labor Relations Act, 71935 at 2 (G.P.O. 1949). As Gillespie has noted, this provision received no debate or vote. Thus, the enacted statute's scheme on the issue cannot be interpreted as congressional opposition to the notion of permanent replacement. Gillespie, *supra* note 20, at 790, n. 56.

51 See, *e.g.*, Gillespie, *supra* note 20, at 787; *Schatzki* at 385; *Getman* at 1204.

52 See Adair v. US, 208 U.S. 161 (1908); Union Pacific Ry. v. Ruef, 120 Fed. 102 (C.C.D. Neb. 1902). See Note, 24 Va. L. Rev. 661 (1938).

53 Marshall v. Barlow's, Inc., 436 U.S. 307 (1978). The Court's *Barlow* holding that OSHA inspectors require a warrant prior to an investigation may be constitutionally correct, but the decision completely ignores OSHA's intent to protect employees and denies any property right of the employees.

  Compare the treatment given by the Court to Congress's attempt to make it illegal for common carriers to discriminate on the basis of union membership. Adair v. US, 208 U.S. 161 (1908). The Erdman Act was treated as an invasion of both personal liberty and property under the Fifth Amendment. Assuming an equality of bargaining power, the Court held the act interfered with the right to make contracts for the "purchase of labor of others." *Id.* at 172; see also Lockner v. N.Y., 198 U.S. 45 (1905). It was unconstitutional in *Adair* to coerce an employer to "accept or retain the personal services of another . . ." Adair v. US, 208 U.S. 161, 174. Of course, it was equally wrong to compel an employee to "perform personal services."

54 Plant v. Woods, 176 Mass. 492, 57 N.E. 1011 (Mass. 1900).

55 State courts, such as that of Massachusetts, would permit the infliction of economic harm if it could be justified as competition. Workers, however, were not thought to compete with their employers; rather, they were engaged in a joint productive endeavor. Thus, even a garden-variety strike for higher wages could not be justified as competition, the only recognized justification for the infliction of economic harm. Nevertheless, "[t]he Massachusetts judges knew that strikes for wages and other direct benefits—in brief, all collect bargaining strikes—had to be made lawful as a matter of political expedience." C. Gregory, *Labor and the Law* at 73 (Norton & Co., 2d rev. ed. 1961).

56 Walker v. Cronin, 107 Mass. 555, 564 (1871).

57 Apparently, pressure by unionists against nonunionists was not generally seen as competition. Yet, normal labor-management struggles were not seen as competition either. The reference to competitors, therefore, means employees have no protection against the superior economic power of the employer, often masquerading as market forces.

58 Vegelahn v. Guntner, 167 Mass. 92, 44 N.E. 1077 (1896).

2   THE WAGNER ACT AND THE NEW DEAL

1   Every decision by the Board in its early years was considered important and not only to the particular union or employer involved. The perceived "prolabor" bias of the Board, it is argued, was largely due to institutional reasons that were "quite independent of the philosophies of the individuals appointed to the Board." M. Edelman, "New Deal Sensitivity to Labor Interests" at 159, 171, in *Labor & The New Deal*, M. Derber & E. Young, eds. (U. of Wis. Press 1961). Because there were no union unfair labor practices, and the Board could not put employers in a stronger position than they already occupied, all decisions "either favored union growth or permitted the status quo to continue." Edelman at 171. Edelman also notes the "intimate relation between the security and status of the Board's staff and the interest in guaranteeing the right to organize and bargain collectively." Moreover, Board actions publicized a variety of employer practices considered irresponsible or abhorrent. Such decisions encouraged Board sensitivity to employee concerns and strengthened the view that unions were necessary for the protection of employees.

2   Thornhill v. Alabama, 310 U.S. 88 (1940).

3   U.S. v. Hutcheson, 312 U.S. 219 (1941).

4   Apex Hosiery Co. v. Leader, 310 U.S. 469 (1940).

5   See P. Irons, *The New Deal Lawyers* at 302 (Princeton 1982).

6   I. Bernstein, *The New Deal Collective Bargaining Policy* at 26 (U. of Calif. Press 1950). Advisers like Frances Perkins & Rexford Tugwell had little faith that unions could serve as instruments of advancement. *Id. at* 26–27.

7   *Id.* at 131. Bernstein believes that the New Deal did move from recovery to reform, and ironically, the Court was partly responsible. "By raising a constitutional bar against moderate change the court influenced Roosevelt to seek more far-reaching solutions." The most far-reaching New Deal reform measures followed the *Schechter* decision, which overturned the NIRA. Bernstein is not completely convincing on this point. See also, B. Rausch, *The History of the New Deal, 1933–1938* (Creative Age Press 1944).

8   Bernstein, *supra* note 6, at 131.

9   48 U.S. Stat. 198 (1933).

10   Bernstein, *supra* note 6. Peter Irons states that 7(a) was a concession to labor leaders, who were then backing Hugo Black's thirty-hour bill, a bill opposed by the administration. Irons, *supra* note 5, at 203.

11   Similar policy had been declared in the Railway Labor Act of 1926 (44 U.S. Stat. 577) and in amendments to the Bankruptcy Acts, March 3, 1933 (47 U.S. Stat. 1467).

12   48 U.S. Stat. 213 (1933).

13   The creation of company unions may have unintentionally paved the way for independent unions by helping to break down the fear of unionism that companies had long created. For a fictional episode, see Thomas Bell, *Out of this Furnace* at 288–98 (Liberty Book Club 1950).

14   Bernstein, *supra* note 6, at 131.

15   See generally, A. Bernheim & D. Van Doren, eds., *Labor & the Government* (McGraw-Hill 1935); P. Irons, *supra* note 5, at 204. In 1932 the National Industrial

Conference Board reported that more than 60 percent of surveyed company unions were founded after the enactment of the NRA. In 1935, the Bureau of Labor Statistics said two-thirds of these unions were created in the NRA period. Indeed, company unions grew more rapidly than trade-union membership in this period.

16 Hugh Johnson, administrator of the NRA, announced within days after his appointment that the NRA would not "compel the organization either of industry or labor" and that codes dealing with wages and working conditions would be approved even if the terms were not the result of collective bargaining. Subsequently, Johnson spoke favorably of the open shop and weakened concepts of exclusive representation by permitting employers to make agreements with individual employees.

17 For an excellent discussion of the operation of the NLB, see J. Gross, *The Making of the National Labor Relations Board: A Study in Economics, Politics & Law* at 7–40 (SUNY Press 1974) [hereinafter cited as *Gross*]. See also, P. Ross, *The Government as a Source of Union Power* at 57–71 (Brown U. Press 1965).

18 H. Millis & E. C. Brown, *From the Wagner Act to Taft-Hartley* at 22–23 (U. of Chicago Press 1950) [hereinafter cited as *Millis*].

19 See *Gross* at 33.

20 *Millis* at 23.

21 Bernstein, *supra* note 6, at 58–62.

22 See U.S. Senate Comm. on Education and Labor, Hearings, To Create a National Labor Board, 73d Cong., 2d Sess., March 14–April 9, 1934, parts 1–3.

23 *Gross* at 64–72.

24 For a description of these strikes, see I. Bernstein, *The Turbulent Years* at 217–317 (Houghton Mifflin 1970).

25 For its text and the executive order establishing the NLRB, see Decisions of the National Labor Relations Board, July 9, 1934–December 1934, at v–vi (Washington 1935).

26 For a discussion of the work of the boards, see Bernheim & Van Doren, *supra* note 15.

27 See, generally, Bernstein, *supra* note 6, at 77–83.

28 The frustration of the NLRB was caused by the Justice Department's insistence that the case referred to it by the Board for prosecution should be "fully and completely prepared in all legal details." Gross provides a clear description of how this process worked. *Gross* at 126–27. This condition could not be satisfied because the Board had no power to order the production of witnesses or documents. If a regional board scheduled a hearing on a complaint, for instance, the employer might refuse to appear. Because there was no method of forcing the employer's attendance, the Board would be forced to proceed without hearing the employer's side of the case. The regional board would then issue findings of fact and a decision. If the employer refused to comply, as was common, the record was forwarded to the National Labor Relations Board for further action. The Board would prepare tentative findings of fact based on the findings of the regional board and would send a notice to the employer that a hearing would be held at which it could show cause why the tentative findings of fact should not be made final. The employer would again refuse to attend, and the Board's findings of fact would become final. Should the Justice Department bring the case to court, the employer, now forced

to appear, might produce facts throwing a different light on the controversy. The Department of Justice, therefore, would be reluctant to direct a district attorney to proceed with the case without facts that the Board could not supply.

29 See *Gross* at 70.

30 *Millis* at 25. One of the noteworthy decisions of the first NLRB was its decision to dispense with mediation and, instead, act only as an adjudicator of disputes. See *Gross* at 77. This decision, Gross believes, represents a fundamental shift in the locus of decision-making authority: "The NLB and the old NLRB, in particular, accelerated a transition, a fundamental and historical significant change, that would shift the control of decision-making authority from the employers and unions in dispute (where the NLB's original commission to seek a settlement acceptable to the parties placed the power) to a national labor board that would issue decisions on the merits of individual cases and would, in the process, develop a "case law" of the labor-management relations. This gradual shift in the locus of decision-making power, from the parties to the National Labor Board, had other profound and lasting effects on the formulation and administration of labor policies. The rejection of mediation, partisan representation, and voluntarism meant that American labor policy would henceforth be developed by law and litigation through legislative enactment, the growth of a body of NLRB case precedent, and the application of administrative law. The great and lasting significance of the work of the NLB and the old NLRB is found in their assertion of the first principles of the national labor policy and the preparations for establishing administrative processes and legal methods in the emerging field of industrial relations . . ." (*Gross* at 2–3).

31 Workers, generally unorganized, caused the largest incidence of strikes since the First World War. During the first three months of the NRA, days lost to strikes quadrupled over the level of the prior six months. Irons, *supra* note 5, at 205.

32 The Wagner Act's design was the result of lessons learned from prior experience with legislation, the boards, and Resolution 44. Emphasis was placed on the resolution of statutory rights rather than the adjustment of differences. The new agency would be independent of the Department of Labor to separate it completely from mediation. Exclusive jurisdiction of the NLRB would avoid prior problems of inconsistent interpretations of overlapping agencies. General enabling legislation was employed to broaden administrative discretion and flexibility, and procedures were carefully based upon precedents of other agencies that had been judicially approved. See Bernstein, *supra* note 6, at 88–89.

33 Fleming, "Significance of the Wagner Act" at 128, in *Labor and the New Deal*, Derber & Young, eds. [hereinafter cited as *Fleming*]. Roosevelt believed that strikes would retard recovery and was concerned that a powerful labor movement would have interests that might not be consonant with the broader designs of the New Deal. Arthur M. Schlesinger, Jr., *The Coming of the New Deal* at 110–18, 136–46, 401–3 (Houghton Mifflin 1958).

34 See R. Moley, *After Seven Years* at 304 (Harper and Bros. 1939).

35 Irons, *supra* note 5, at 231.

36 49 Stat. 449 (1935).

37 Senator Wagner, 79 Cong. Rec. 7570 (1935).

38 Cited in M. Derber, *The American Idea of Industrial Democracy, 1865–1965* at 321 (U. of Illinois Press 1970).

39 *Id.* at 135.

40 American unions have an ambivalent attitude toward governmental intervention in union-management relations. Despite the AFL's rejection of voluntarism in the 1930s and the concurrent embrace of New Deal legislation, they have been wary of governmental intervention. The rubric for such concern is the constant trumpeting of "free collective bargaining," raised whenever governmental actions seek to alter existing relationships that seem favorable or, at least, more favorable than the results of governmental intervention.

The AFL's concept of "voluntarism" was echoed by other groups who feared that governmental assistance could become state oppression. Many in the ACLU, for instance, were discomfited by federal support for workers' rights because they believed that the use of state power generally led to a denial of rights, and especially so in the case of workers. The ACLU Board thus initially opposed the NLRA. Cletus Daniel, *The ACLU and the Wagner Act*, Cornell Studies in Industrial and Labor Relations no. 20 (1980); J. Auerbach, "The Depression Decade" at 76–78, in *The Pulse of Freedom: American Liberties, 1920–1970*, Alan Reitman, ed. (Norton & Co. 1975).

41 There were, however, many statements to the effect that neither the NIRA nor the NLRA created any new rights or principles in regard to labor. Section 7(a) of the National Industrial Recovery Act closely tracked the language ultimately to become Section 7 of the Wagner Act. There was nothing new, it was argued, about the basic ideas contained in Section 7(a). The principal draftsman, Donald Richberg, said that the substance of the paragraph came from his familiarity with the Railway Labor Act of 1926, the Norris-LaGuardia Act of 1932, and the 1933 amendments to the Federal Bankruptcy Act. See D. Richberg, *The Rainbow*, chap. 3 (Doubleday Books 1936).

Moreover, the legislative history of the Wagner Act also includes a number of statements to the effect that the principles of the act were not perceived to be new. Thus, Senator Wagner stated: "The National Labor Relations Bill which I now propose is novel neither in philosophy nor in content. It creates no new substantive rights. It merely provides that employees, if they desire to do so, shall be free to organize for their mutual protection of benefit. Quite aside from section 7(a), this principle has been embodied in the Norris-LaGuardia Act, in amendments to the Railway Labor Act passed last year, and in a long train of other enactments of Congress." 1 Legis. Hist. of NLRA at 1312 (1948).

42 See D. Montgomery, *Workers' Control in America* at 161 (Cambridge U. Press 1979).

43 The rise of unionism in the 1930s can be attributed only partially to the Wagner Act. Unskilled employees were anxious to organize for some years prior to 1935, as the spirit of organization after the passage of the NIRA demonstrates. The Depression altered the views of employees and weakened the resistance of the employers. Militant action such as sitdowns stem from worker dissatisfaction and not simply from tactical decisions by union leaders. Economic difficulties forced employers to abandon many of the benefits of welfare capitalism which were de-

signed to weaken employee attraction to unionism. Resistance to unions was costly both when business was poor as well as when it was improving. D. Brody, "The Emergence of Mass Production Unionism" at 247–49, in *Change and Continuity in Twentieth-Century America*, Braemen, Bremner, Walters, eds. (Ohio State U. Press 1964). Finally, the employers could no longer count upon government assistance. Thus, the surprise decision of U.S. Steel to recognize SWOC in 1937 and the breakthrough at General Motors occurred some weeks *before* the constitutionality of the Wagner Act was established.

In neither the case of U.S. Steel nor that of General Motors could the unions involved have availed themselves of the procedures of the NLRA. As Lee Pressman, counsel for SWOC, admitted: "We could not have won an election for collective bargaining on the basis of our own membership or the results of the organizing campaign to date." Saul Alinsky, *John L. Lewis* at 149 (Putnam 1949). Similarly, the UAW had only organized a minority of workers at General Motors. Moreover, neither company granted *exclusive* representation, the form of recognition specified in the NLRA.

The initial success of the CIO was seriously threatened by a faltering economy in 1938, declining membership in some unions, and internal dissension. The CIO was finally solidified by World War II, which dramatically raised employment, weakened the resistance of employers to collective bargaining, and caused a substantial expansion of the federal role in labor-management relations. Brody, "The Emergence of Mass-Production Unionism" at 258–61.

Nor did strikes cause the *passage* of the Wagner Act. Strikes were increasing in 1934, but the result was Public Resolution 44, a decidedly mild response seemingly motivated in large part by a desire to deflect Wagner's efforts for an effective regulatory scheme. The first National Labor Relations Board created by P.R. 44 had no greater power than the discarded National Labor Board. Nevertheless, as Skocpol notes, strikes fell off in mid-1934 and were *declining* when the NLRA was passed in 1935. The elections of 1934, however, had created an overwhelmingly liberal Congress, and the elections were no doubt a major factor in the NLRA's ease of passage. T. Skocpol, "Political Response to the Capitalist Guises: Neo-Marxist Theories of the State and the Case of the New Deal," 10, no. 2 Politics & Society (1980) [hereinafter cited as *Skocpol*]. Yet it takes time to realize that the incidence of strikes were declining, and certainly people like Wagner knew that the situation created by P.R. 44 could only be temporary.

44   F. Block, "Beyond Corporate Liberalism," 24 Social Problems 352 (1976–77). See also, J. Weinstein, *The Corporate Ideal in the Liberal State: 1900–1918* (Beacon 1968).

The perception that the purpose of the New Deal was to preserve capitalism and the existing economic order was shared by the Communist party and a small group of liberals. Labor unions and the Socialist party generally supported the NLRA, but few, it seems, were unaware of the nonradical thrust of Roosevelt's administration. Its remonstrations against strikes and its lack of overt support for union organization helped give the program an antiunion look, a view strengthened by the administration's failure to make NIRA §7(a) an effective instrument. The creation of the National Labor Board, and indeed the Wagner Act itself, was seen by some as designed to overcome and discourage strikes. This perception was one of the reasons that apparently led the national board of the ACLU to come out against the Wagner Act, a decision that not only placed the union in strange company but that was to be reversed later in the 1930s. See C. Daniel, *supra* note 40.

In addition, a few liberals and communists felt that an act stemming from a capitalist society could only strengthen employers. First, the act, given the employer's control over production and eventually over employment, could hardly equalize bargaining power. Second, governmental regulation itself would pressure a general continuation of the status quo. Ultimately, and perceptively, the critique stated that the NLRB would "discourage strikes in favor of less disruptive methods of resolving conflicts." Mary Van Kleeck, cited in Daniel at 72. Finally, governmental intervention would "transform the labor movement into a mere appendage of a nascent fascist state." See Daniel at 119.

45   *Skocpol* at 163.

The massive shift of power to the state in the Depression was justified by liberals as necessary to protect individual rights, a reversal of traditional civil libertarian views. Civil liberties were seen as involving protection by the state rather than simply protection against the state. But the usefulness of New Deal legislation was that it also focused upon private power and the extent to which it affected lives and liberty as much as governmental power.

The liberal response to radical critics of the NLRA was clearly set forth in Senator Wagner's letter to the ACLU: "Whether we will it or not, government in every country is going to be forced to play a more important role in every phase of economic life, and for that reason it seems to me more useful to attempt to direct the nature of that role rather than merely to state the truism that government is likely to be influenced by the forces in society that happen to be the strongest. Certainly these forces cannot be checked by governmental self-limitation nor do I believe that governmental action in such matters over a decently long period of time serves to check the struggles that labor must carry on by extra-governmental means" [Robert F. Wagner to Roger N. Baldwin (April 5, 1935), 780 ACLU Papers].

46   *Skocpol* at 164.
47   P. H. Burch, Jr., "The NAM as an Interest Group," 4, no. 1 Politics and Society 100–105 (1973).
48   *Skocpol* at 168–69.
49   *Id.* at 188.
50   *Id.* at 183.

3   SITDOWNS, SLOWDOWNS, AND THE NARROWING OF FEDERAL PROTECTION

1   Quoted in Fleming, "Significance of the Wagner Act" at 40, in *Labor & the New Deal*, M. Derber & E. Young, eds. (U. of Wis. Press 1957).
2   Karl Klare argues that one effect of these decisions is that unions are encouraged to act as restraining influences on their members. Klare notes that it was not inevitable that unions would play this type of institutional role, but such a result follows once unions were deemed responsible for the establishment of industrial peace as well as responsible to their members. Klare, "Judicial Deradicalization of the Wagner Act and the Origins of Modern Legal Consciousness, 1937–1941," 62

Minn. L. Rev. 265, 318–25 (1978) [hereinafter cited as *Klare*]. It is no doubt true that unions have long acted as brakes to rank-and-file discontent, and the post-1935 federal law surely was less draconian than either state or federal law prior to 1935. Although institutional factors are probably as important as legal concerns, the threat of injunctions or damages prior to 1935 may have made such restraint reasonable. It is also true that unions have long expressed a desire to limit strikes and other weapons, at least in the absence of approval from the international. This desire stems not so much from leader conservatism, or from a desire for the centralization of authority, but is based on painful experience with ill-timed or ill-conceived rank-and-file action. The attempts of the early UAW to control militant locals parallels efforts by Polish Solidarity to centralize decisions concerning strike activity and to end wildcat strikes. New York Times, Nov. 17, 1980, at A12.

3   Southern Steamship Co. v. NLRB, 316 U.S. 31 (1942).

4   See Cox, "The Right to Engage in Concerted Activities," 26 Ind. L. J. 319, 325–33 (1951).

5   It is possible to analogize the employer's right to use self-help in these cases, despite the availability of the NLRB, to the Board's protection of "unfair labor practice" strikers who could have filed charges rather than engage in a strike. See House Rep. No. 510, 80th Cong., 1st Sess. 37–40 (1947).

6   NLRB v. Fansteel Metallurgical Corp., 306 U.S. 240 (1939).

7   See, *e.g.*, Hart & Pritchard, "The Fansteel Case: Employee Misconduct and the Remedial Powers of the National Labor Relations Board," 52 Harv. L. Rev. 1275 (1939); *Klare* at 322–25.

8   Levinson, *Labor on the March* (University Books 1956) [hereinafter cited as *Levinson*]; Bernstein, *The Turbulent Years* at 457–73, 519–51 (Houghton Mifflin 1970).

9   *Id.* at 143–68; see also S. Fine, *Sit Down: The General Motors Strike of 1936–37* (U. Mich. Press 1969).

10 American sitdowns occurred as early as 1906 when the IWW sat-in at General Electric in Schenectady, N.Y. The device was also used in other countries, especially in the 1930s. See *Levinson* at 169–70.

11 *Levinson* at 169. The economic growth during this period was the highest during the decade. Montgomery notes that annual GNP rose in 1937 to a level approximately that of 1929 but by 1939 there were 10.4 million unemployed, 9 million *more* than in 1929. D. Montgomery, *Workers' Control in America* at 162 (Cambridge U. Press 1979).

12 See J. R. Green, *The World of the Worker: Labor in Twentieth-Century America* at 157 (Hill & Wang 1980). As Jeremy Brecher noted in *Strike* (Fawcett 1974), sitdowns dramatized that factories or other social institutions cannot run without the cooperation of those upon whose activity it depends. This type of rank-and-file activity continued even after recognition. The General Motors contract, like the others that followed, conceded control over the pace and organization of production to management, but organized workers continued to engage in slowdowns and other concerted actions to humanize the workplaces and to reduce the speed-up. As one Fisher Body worker declared in the euphoric days of March 1937: "the inhuman speed is no more. We now have a voice, and we have slowed up the speed of the line. And [we] are now treated as human beings, and not as part of the machinery." Quoted in Green at 157.

13   *Levinson* at 185–86.

14   " 'Quickie' strikes forced managers to revise piece rates and pay for 'down time, to slow assembly lines, to correct unsafe or unhealthy conditions, and to sack unpopular foremen." Montgomery, *supra* note 11, at 163; see also, 178, no. 36. These battles, fought with rank-and-file weapons, won power not wage gains, and their importance to workers should not be overlooked.

15   *Levinson* at 177.

16   *Id.* The Wagner Act was held constitutional in NLRB v. Jones & Laughlin Steel Co., 301 U.S. 1 (1937).

17   *Levinson* at 169, 179–85. Most CIO unions attempted to centralize control over *all* economic pressure activity. There is considerable support for the argument that the creation and success of the CIO represented a triumph more of tactics than of principles which differed from those held by the AFL. The emergence of John L. Lewis as the leader of the industrial union movement suggests that, unlike earlier movements for industrial unionism, the goal was not to create a movement for basic social change. D. Brody, "The Emergence of Mass Production Unionism" at 224–37, in *Change and Continuity in Twentieth-Century America*, Braeman, Bremner, Walters, eds. (Ohio State U. Press 1964).

18   New York Times, Nov. 17, 1980, at A12.

19   Montgomery, *supra* note 11, at 164. The American experience is in no way unique. Thus, a French court ruling on the expulsion of strikers, relied upon the right of ownership as "inviolable and sacred, . . . among the indefeasible rights of man." Legal provisions protecting concerted actions "cannot permit the occupation of places of work nor constitute the abolition of the right of ownership or even a momentary obstacle to the said right; whereas the aforesaid occupants [the sit-down strikers] have neither claim nor right." T. C. Chateau-Thierry, July 11, 1936, G.P. 1936 2.235. Moreover, the labor contract gives employees no right to occupy the place of work. T. C. Pau, July 9, 1936, G.P. 1936 2.237. See Bernard Edelman, "The Legalization of the Working Class," 9, no. 1 Economy and Society 51 (1980). Edelman concludes that the workers' right to enter the workplace arises solely from contract, and this right ceases when the contract is suspended by strike. The contract, then, gives the worker no " 'right' other than the right to sell his labour-power and to receive the 'price' in the form of wages." The price, or wage, then, grants the worker all that he or she is entitled to receive. For an American parallel, see the discussion of *Teamsters* v. *Daniel* in chap. 11.

20   Montgomery, *supra* note 11, at 166. Similar deradicalization or cooptation stemming from the aid or support of the state has been noted in Cloward & Piven, *Poor Peoples' Movements* (Pantheon 1977).

The reliance by the union movement on the aid and protection of the federal government may have been shortsighted as some have argued, but there may have been no realistic alternatives during the 1930s. The power and organized resistance to unionism of American employers has been often recognized, and leaders remembered that the temporary expansion during World War I was substantially aided by the National War Labor Board. Surely this view was reinforced as well as reflected in the Railway Labor Act of 1926 and the Norris-LaGuardia Act of 1932. The NIRA, which caused initial organizing successes, "heavily influenced Lewis' decision to take the initiative that led to the C.I.O." Brody, *supra* note 17, at 244.

21   The narrowing of the allowable scope of economic warfare, for instance, to the employer-employee relationship, is not a new phenomenon. In drastically curtailing the scope of the Clayton Act, an act that purportedly relaxed the strictures of the Sherman Anti-Trust Act in regard to unions, the Supreme Court stated that "Congress had in mind particular industrial controversies, not a general class war." Duplex Printing Co. v. Deering, 254 U.S. 443, 472 (1921).

As it was used in the late nineteenth century, and in some other countries even now, the term "labor movement" implies a wide variety of different forms of organization and activity, including reform, revolutionary, and cooperative organizations. In the United States, however, the union "has become the one surviving agency of working-class action," although its character is determined by law to a considerable extent. The unions' survival is a tribute to the determination of American workers, just as its existence as the one surviving working-class agency is a "stunning tribute to the power and pervasiveness of American capitalism. . . ." D. Montgomery, *supra* note 11, at 171.

22   S. 1958, 74th Cong., 1st Sess. at 16.

23   Millis & Brown, *From the Wagner Act to Taft-Hartley* at 191 (U. of Chicago Press 1950).

24   NLRB v. Fansteel Metallurgical Corp., 306 U.S. 240 (1939). Prior to *Fansteel,* the appellate decisions were not uniform. See R. Downing, "The Federal Courts and Labor Relations Policy, 1936–1954: A Study of Judicial Decision-Making" at 43–44 (Ph.D. diss., U. of Ill. 1956), U. of Michigan Microfilms 19, 814.

25   In 1942, the Supreme Court (disagreeing with the Board and Third Circuit) also held that maritime workers—who struck aboard ship, even though their vessel was moored in a safe domestic port and the strike was provoked by an illegal refusal to bargain—were in violation of the federal mutiny act. As a result their actions were not protected by the NLRA. The Court admonished the Board not to be so "single-minded" in effectuating the policies of the act as to ignore other equally important congressional objectives. Southern Steamship Co. v. NLRB, 316 U.S. 31, 47 (1942). Four judges dissented, believing the Board's decision reasonably within its discretion.

26   NLRB v. American News Co., 55 NLRB 1302 (1944).

27   Gross uses this case to show how the new chairman, Herzog, was sensitive to public relations, and moved the Board to the right. Ironically, although former chairman Millis strongly objected, the trend to the right had begun with the Millis board. J. Gross, *The Reshaping of the National Labor Relations Board: National Labor Policy in Transition, 1937–1947* (SUNY Press 1981).

28   Millis apparently was willing, given *Fansteel,* to distinguish between inquiry into the legality of actions, the means, and the propriety of objectives.

29   NLRB v. Thompson Products, Inc., 70 NLRB 13, *vacated,* 72 NLRB 886 (1947).

30   NLRB v. Elk Lumber Co., 91 NLRB 333 (1950).

31   See H. Braverman, *Labor & Monopoly Capital* at 97 (Monthly Review Press 1974).

32   See D. Montgomery, *supra* note 11. See also S. Mathewson, *Restriction of Output among Unorganized Workers* (Viking Press 1931).

33   See, *e.g.,* D. Rodgers, *The Work Ethic in Industrial America: 1850–1920* at 165–68 (U. of Chicago Press 1978); D. Nelson, *Managers & Workers: Origins of the New Factory in the United States, 1880–1920,* chap. 3 (U. of Wis. Press 1975).

Restrictive practices (limitations on labor supply, apprenticeship ratios, etc.) are defined as those union rules that "prevent management from achieving the most efficient utilization of resources of labor and machinery given existing technology and wage rates." A. Aldridge, *Power, Authority & Restrictive Practices: A Sociological Essay on Industrial Relations* at xi (Blackwell 1976). To preserve the pejorative flavor of the phrase, it is sometimes admitted that some work rules can be reasonable if they shield workers against conditions that would be considered socially undesirable. As Aldridge notes, restrictions on managerial freedom of action need not produce inefficiency, even if we can always be sure to recognize efficiency. In any case, efficiency is not the only value in the employment relationship. In addition, some practices promote other values—decent wages, hours, sanitary conditions, safety. Aldridge at 35–37, 43–67. These values cannot be weighed against costs to the employer because some situations involve subjective costs to employers and in others the values to employees may be unmeasurable.

Moreover, managers can be wrong in their perceptions of efficiency. Studies suggest that some restrictive practices may actually promote efficiency. Aldridge at 33; D. F. Roy, "Efficiency & 'The Fix' " at 359, 377–78, in *Industrial Man*, T. Burns, ed. (Penguin 1969). Thus, a device may be restrictive *to* management even though it's not a restriction *on* management. Indeed, the creation by workers of their own production systems may not necessarily result in processes that attempt to undermine managerial interests. See M. Burawoy, *Manufacturing Consent* at 79–94 (U. of Chicago Press 1979). The existence of production games or "making out" may simply be a sign that managerial interests are not adversely affected. Evidence exists that management sometimes actively assists in or even creates patterns of output restriction. Mathewson, *supra* note 32, chap. 2 (Viking Press 1931).

34 From J. R. Commons, ed, *Trade Unionism and Labor Problems*, 2d series, at 148–49 (Ginn 1921).

35 Rodgers, *supra* note 33, at 168.

36 Yet, as my grandmother would say, "where is it written" that workers must work up to their physical, emotional, and psychological maximum?

37 See J. Atleson, *et al., Collective Bargaining in Private Employment*, chap. 1 (BNA 1978).

38 C. Gregory, *Labor and the Law*, chap. 3 (2d rev. ed. 1961).

39 Vegelahn v. Guntner, 167 Mass. 92, 44 N.E. 1077 (1896).

40 NLRB v. Elk Lumber, 91 NLRB 333, 337 (1950).

41 NLRB v. Insurance Agents Int'l. Union, 361 U.S. 477 (1960).

42 Lodge 76, IAM, v. WERC, 427 U.S. 132 (1976).

43 Automobile Workers v. WERB, 336 U.S. 245, 264 (1949).

44 Cox, "The Right to Engage in Concerted Activities," 26 Ind. L. J. 319, 339 (1951).

45 *Id.*

46 The illogic of the law's condemnation of partial strikers, a response similar to the approach to slowdowns, is noted in Getman, "The Protection of Economic Pressure by Section 7 of the National Labor Relations Act," 115 U. Pa. L. Rev. 1231–40 (1967).

47 Of course, the courts often do this, although the balancing process is generally disguised. For instance, intent is required but waived when actions are inherently

discouraging or inherently destructive of union rights. This is simply another way of saying that if the impact on statutory rights is great enough, employers' actions will be enjoined despite the presence of good faith or the absence of antiunion animus.

48 Lodge 76, IAM v. WERC, 427 U.S. 132, 152 (1976).

49 Getman, "The Protected Status of Partial Strikes After Lodge 76: A Comment," 29 Stan. L. Rev. 205 (1977).

50 K. Lopatka, "The Unprotected Status of Partial Strikes after Lodge 76: A Reply to Professor Getman," 29 Stan. L. Rev. 1181, 1188 (1977). The Court, as noted, did state that certain weapons "disabled [the employer] from any kind of self-help." 336 U.S. 264. In addition, the Court also seemed to believe that it was unfair to apply pressure without actually striking. The Court cited C. G. Conn., Ltd. v. NLRB, 108 F.2d 390, 397 (7th Cir. 1930), which stated that one could not "be on strike and at work simultaneously."

51 The legislative history is admittedly thin. Id. at 1188, n. 57.

52 Id. at 1189–90.

53 Id. at 1189, n. 62.

54 One distinction between the disapproval of slowdowns and the approval of strikes is that a strike can be likened to a quit. The right to cease work can be protected, although the law still limits strikes in certain ways, because of the myth of equality between worker and employer. This notion was suggested to me by Staughton Lynd. This notion helps explain the recognition of strikes but, of course, does not attempt to explain the approbation leveled at slowdowns.

55 C. G. Conn. Ltd. v. NLRB, 108 F.2d 390 (7th Cir. 1939).

56 See NLRB v. Montgomery Ward & Co., 157 F. 2d 486, 496 (8th Cir. 1946).

57 See Cox, supra note 44, at 337–38; Getman, supra note 46, at 1195.

58 Cox, supra note 44, at 338.

59 See, e.g., NLRB v. Swift Co., 124 NLRB 394 (1959), enf'd, 277 F.2d 641 (7th Cir. 1960). Of course, such action by individual employees clearly falls outside the protective ambit of the act.

60 Republic Aviation Corp. v. NLRB, 324 U.S. 793, 803 (1945). See also, NLRB v. Peyton Packing, 49 NLRB 828 (1943), enf'd, 142 F.2d 1009 (5th Cir.), cert. den., 323 U.S. 730 (1944).

61 NLRB v. Peyton Packing, 49 NLRB 828, 843 (1943).

62 This limitation generally applies to department stores where, it is assumed, solicitation upsets the mood and decorum of the selling floor. See, e.g., May Dept. Stores, 59 NLRB 976 (1944), enf'd as modified, 154 F.2d 533 (8th Cir. 1946), cert. den., 329 U.S. 725.

63 NLRB v. Babcock & Wilcox, 351 U.S. 105 (1956).

64 See Diamond Shamrock Co. v. NLRB, 443 F.2d 52 (3d Cir. 1971); G. T. E. Lenkurt, Inc., 204 NLRB 921 (1973).

65 See R. Pfeffer, Working for Capitalism at 75 (Columbia U. Press 1979).

66 In a similar vein, arbitrators have held that just cause for discipline may exist in a limited range of circumstances for actions while off duty and away from the work premises. See Elkouri & Elkouri, How Arbitration Works at 616–18 (BNA, 3d ed., 1973).

67 Eastex, Inc. v. NLRB, 437 U.S. 556 (1978).

68   Hudgens v. NLRB, 424 U.S. 507, 522, n. 10.

69   NLRB v. Babcock & Wilcox, 351 U.S. at 112.

70   This argument is explicitly presented in the Burger-Rehnquist dissent in *Eastex*, although they focus primarily upon the appropriateness of protecting employee distribution of material which is seemingly unrelated to the employment relationship. ". . . Congress never intended to require the opening of private property to the sort of political advocacy involved in this case." The dissenters refer to state law which prescribes the conditions under which persons may enter private property and the conditions under which a licensee exceeds the scope of the license. 437 U.S. 579–80 (J. Burger, dissenting). "Thus," conclude the dissenters, "the employee efforts to distribute political material is deemed a trespass under Texas law." The dissenters, however, make no attempt to apply the relevant Texas law, nor do they explain how "employees" gain the right to distribute material which is clearly employment-related on plant premises. They merely conclude that sometimes a property right must be "subordinated" by governmental enactment.

71   NLRB v. Babcock & Wilcox, 351 U.S. at 113.

72   NLRA, Section 2(3).

73   Duplex v. Deering, 254 U.S. 443 (1921).

74   Norris-LaGuardia, Section 13(c), 29 U.S.C.A. 113(c).

75   NLRA, Section 7.

76   Mr. Justice White, in his *Eastex* concurrence, seemed also dubious about this distinction. He did not understand why an "employer need permit his property to be used for distributions about subjects unrelated to his relationship with his employees simply because it is convenient for the latter to use his property in this manner and simply because there is no interference with 'management interests.' Ownership of property normally confers the right to control the use of that property." 437 U.S. at 579 (White, concurring). The dissenters also asserted that property rights, not management interests, govern the owner's right to establish the conditions under which one may remain on the premises. See Sears v. San Diego Dist. Council of Carpenters, 98 S. Ct. 1745 (1978).

77   See *Klare* at 284–85. Cox, "The Duty to Bargain in Good Faith," 71 Harv. L. Rev. 1401, 1408 (1958).

78   I agree with Klare that individual cases presented the Court with a variety of possibilities, but I am doubtful that the Court was compelled to create "a new legal consciousness" in order to justify its results over a range of decisions. *Klare* at 292. The "new" consciousness looks suspiciously like the old outlook, a conclusion I hope at least to suggest is reasonable. Consciousness, as I perhaps faintly understand the concept, involves an outlook on the world that limits the way in which problems are defined, filtering out certain questions and certain ways to resolve them. But many of the decisions discussed here could, with some change in language and style, emanate from a nineteenth-century bench. Some "of course" answers have seemingly remained the same.

79   B. Ramirez, *When Workers Fight: The Politics of Industrial Relations in the Progressive Era, 1898–1916*, chap. 5 (Greenwood 1978); D. Nelson, *supra* note 33; D. Montgomery, "Workers' Control of Machine Production in the Nineteenth Century," in *Workers' Control in America, supra* note 11.

80   See Aldridge, *supra* note 33.

81   See D. Montgomery, *supra* note 11.

82   D. Brody, *Steelworkers in America: The Nonunion Era* at 1–54 (Cambridge U. Press 1960); B. Soffer, "A Theory of Trade Union Development: The Role of the 'Autonomous' Workman," 1 Labor History 141–63 (1960).

83   Quoted in S. Meyer III, *The Five Dollar Day: Labor Management & Social Control in the Ford Motor Company, 1908–1921* at 42 (SUNY 1981).

84   *Id.* at 42–43. Meyer notes that pictures of the time frequently show skilled workers wearing white shirts and ties at their machines, while unskilled workers wear the more conventional blue collar or traditional immigrant clothes.

85   D. Montgomery, *supra* note 11, at 101–2. See also Meyer, *supra* note 83, at 116–17. Group setting of production rates and resistance to time-study investigators have long been noted in the auto industry. J. S. Peterson, "Auto Workers and Their Work, 1900–1933," 22, no. 2 Labor History 231–32.

86   D. Rodgers, *supra* note 33, at 155. See also D. Nelson, *supra* note 33; D. Walkowitz, *Worker City, Company Town* (Illinois U. Press 1978).

87   Ramirez, *supra* note 79, at 90.
      Stephen Meyer notes that "output restriction had deep roots in the working-class shop culture." At the time, most employers believed that only skilled workers, particularly those associated with the trade-union movement, were capable of concerted or systematic output restrictions. Thus, employers charged unions with a "conscious conspiracy to impede American industrial progress." In 1904, however, Carroll D. Wright, the United States Commissioner of Labor, reported that some restrictions on output "have been in existence as trade customs or traditions for many years, and when, with modern shop equipment, the employers begin to infringe on the traditions, the union comes in to formulate and preserve them." Quoted in Meyer, *supra* note 83, at 86.

88   Quoted in Ramirez, *supra* note 79, at 90. For a strikingly similar evaluation of piece rates in a Hungarian tractor factory, see M. Haraszti, *A Worker in a Worker's State* (Universe 1978).

89   Stephen Marglin has argued that the formation of factories was not a result of the technological superiority of large machinery but, rather, that the form increased discipline over workers which had the effect of lowering costs. Indeed, many factories preceded the introduction of power equipment. At least partially, therefore, factories were designed for purposes of social control, *e.g.*, to control output and workers' hours. Workers who may have previously worked at home at their own pace now had the choice of not working at all or working on employers' terms, as much as 12–14 hours a day and 6 days per week. Employees still earned a subsistence wage but worked twice as much per week. Production could be increased, even doubled, without new technology. The older system, that of "putting out," permitted workers to work at their own rhythms and, often, at home. Prior to the formation of factories, the law was used in eighteenth-century England to prescribe the time period in which domestic woolen workers had to complete and return work. The factory's disciplinary potential was greater because it reduced the worker's choice to only one, whether or not to work at all. Marglin, "What do Bosses Do? The Origins and Functions of Hierarchy in Capitalist Production," 6 Review of Radical Political Economics 60–112 (1974). See also Clawson, *Bureaucracy & the Labor Process*, chap. 2 (Monthly Review Press 1980).

90   E. P. Thompson, "Time, Work-Discipline, and Industrial Capitalism," 38 Past and
      Present 72 (1967). Ignorance of past practices of work lead many to assume that
      current problems of absenteeism are somehow new and at variance with long-
      standing cultural norms. In addition to high turnover in automobile plants, "a
      casual attitude toward attendance on the job was also characteristic of the pre-
      union work force." Peterson quotes a Ford executive complaining of absenteeism
      in 1916. J. Peterson, *supra* note 85, at 230.
         Stephen Meyer has demonstrated that the modern concern with absenteeism
      has antecedents in American history. Absenteeism and turnover severely dis-
      rupted the new Ford methods and techniques of production. As the new assembly-
      line technology was introduced at Ford, the rates of absenteeism and turnover
      reached incredible proportions. In 1913, the daily absences in the Highland Park
      plant amounted to 10 percent of the total work force. In the same year, the rate of
      labor turnover reached 370 percent. Both forms of behavior, Meyer notes, were re-
      sponses to conditions in the Ford plant. Absenteeism often translated into short
      vacations or rest from the tedium of the assembly line. Turnover, on the other
      hand, often reflected dissatisfaction with changes in the conditions of work and
      the character of the workplace. For the officials, absenteeism and turnover forced
      management to hire extra men to account for absentees and to bear the cost of
      breaking in new workers to replace those who quit. In 1913, a 10 percent rate of ab-
      senteeism meant that, on the average, from 1,300 to 1,400 persons were absent
      from their place on the production line. A 370 percent turnover rate meant that
      Ford managers had to hire more than 52,000 workers to maintain a workforce of
      about 13,600 persons. Meyer, *supra* note 83, at 83.
91   E. P. Thompson, *supra* note 90, at 56, 73. For one modern example (of possibly
      hundreds), see C. Denby, *Indignant Heart: A Black Worker's Journal* at 138–41
      (Black Rose 1979).
92   Thompson, *supra* note 90, at 61.

4   THE DEFINITION OF EMPLOYEES' REAL INTERESTS

1   Klare, "Judicial Deradicalization of the Wagner Act and the Origins of Modern Le-
     gal Consciousness, 1937–1941," 62 Minn. L. Rev. 281, no. 53 (1978).
2   Cox suggests that the Wagner Act's stress on union organization and collective
     bargaining was seen as a way to avoid direct judicial or governmental interference
     with labor-management relations. Such regulation was to be avoided because
     there was "no consensus of opinion, about the property of labor's various objec-
     tives or of the weapons with which they are pursued." Cox, "The Right to Engage
     in Concerted Activities," 26 Ind. L. J. 323 (1951). The passage of a statute does not
     remove the occasion for policy judgments, as this book seeks to demonstrate.
3   NLRA, Section 1, 29 U.S.C. Section 151 (1970).
4   See C. Gregory, *Labor and the Law*, chap. 3 (2d rev. ed. 1961).
5   Berry v. Donovan, 188 Mass. 353 (1905).
6   In one case, the court was led to refuse an injunction sought by a group of workers
     who were being systematically frozen out of construction by larger unions who
     could also perform the work. Although the defendants' actions would have drastic
     effects upon the plaintiffs' skills and job prospects, the court saw the conflict as

"competition" between two groups of workmen for the same work. Pickett v. Walsh, 192 Mass. 572 (1906). Ironically, the court's doctrines led it to protect the one type of dispute, *i.e.*, a work assignment or jurisdictional dispute, that has generally been regarded as the most wasteful.

7   Gregory, *supra* note 4, at 72–73.

8   176 Mass. 492, 57 N.E. 1011 (1900).

9   See comments and questions on *Plant* v. *Woods* in Atleson, *et al.*, *Collective Bargaining in Private Employment* at 34–36 (BNA 1978).

10   Berry v. Donovan, 188 Mass. 353 (1905). See also Folsom v. Lewis, 208 Mass. 336, 338 (1911); Fashioncraft, Inc. v. Halpern, 313 Mass. 385 (1943); Reves v. Scott, 324 Mass. 600 (1949).

11   See, *e.g.*, Bowen v. Matheson, 96 Mass. (14 Allen) 499 (1867); see also Gregory, *supra* note 4, at 31–51. Doctrinally, the decision at least focuses on the relevant issue—"justification"—instead of assuming that abstract, formal reasoning would resolve the issue. Compare, *e.g.*, Vegelahn v. Guntner, 167 Mass. 92, 44 N.E. 1077 (1896).

12   Attempts by employers to exclude new entrants to a field or to squeeze out other competing employers were broadly justified as long as they were in the pursuit of self-gain and as long as the means used did not fall within a category of tort or crime. See Gregory, *supra* note 4. Labor unions did not receive the same protection when they acted in pursuit of their own self-interest until the late nineteenth century and, then, only in some states. Unions were using the only weapons at their disposal, for instance, the right to withhold labor or the right to persuade others to cease to purchase struck goods. In the early labor antitrust cases, the courts did not stress, and of course did not balance, the interests of the defendant employees in causing economic harm. See Meltzer, "Labor Unions, Collective Bargaining, and the Antitrust Laws," 32 U. Chi. L. Rev. 659, 662 (1965). Nor did the Court explicitly concern itself with the quantitative impact of particular boycotts on supply and price in interstate markets.

13   The impetus to mutual assistance was reflected in the CIO pledge that ended with a promise "to help and assist all brothers in adversity, and to have all eligible workers join the union that we may all be able to enjoy the fruits of our labor; and that I will never knowingly wrong a brother or see him wronged, if I can prevent it." Cited in Levinson, *Labor on the March* at 299 (University Books 1956). Although the CIO pledge was written subsequent to Section 7 of the NLRA and 7(a) of the NRA, it reflected the spirit of solidarity long recognized in the ranks of labor. The motto of the Noble Order of the Knights of Labor was more terse: "An injury to one is the concern of all." Levinson, *id.* at 297. See generally, N. Ware, *The Labor Movement in the United States, 1860–1895* (Quadrangle Books 1964). The impetus toward solidarity receives less publicity generally than Samuel Gompers's famous statement that the aim of labor was to gain "more and more—and then more." This voraciousness, of course, is generally, and unfavorably, contrasted to the motivation of all other Americans who are perfectly happy to strive for less and less.

14   See, *e.g.*, National Protective Ass'n. v. Cumming, 170 NY 315 (1902). See, generally, Gregory, *supra* note 4, chap. 3.

15   Gregory, *supra* note 4, at 81–82.

16   *Id.* at 109–10.

17   Duplex Co. v. Deering, 254 U.S. 443 (1921).

18   U.S. v. Hutcheson, 312 U.S. 219 (1941).

19   Norris-LaGuardia, Section 13(a) (emphasis added).

20   NLRA, Section 2(3) (emphasis added).

21   The political need to at least recognize the reality of strikes, and thus, picketing as well, may explain the protection accorded to employees who respect picket lines created by other unions either at their place of work or at other locations. See NLRB v. Union Carbide, 440 F.2d 54 (4th Cir. 1971). In the latter situation, a truck-driver refusing to deliver goods at a struck plant would seem to be remaining "at work" and yet be determining what part of the assigned work he will perform. In similar cases, as already noted, decisions have made it clear that workers may not remain at work "and at the same time select what part of their allocated tasks they [care] to perform of their own volition . . ." NLRB v. Montgomery Ward & Co., 157 F.2d 486 (8th Cir. 1946). Yet, the "partial striker" who respects a picket line is protected even though, unlike the slow-downer, the employee is not even participating in a dispute with his or her own employer. The irony is rarely mentioned by decision makers.

22   NLRB v. C. K. Smith & Co., Inc., 569 F.2d 162, n. 1 (1st Cir. 1977). Other circuits have directly held that employees who respect picket lines have no direct stake in that dispute and are, therefore, not engaged in protected concerted activity. NLRB v. Illinois Bell Tele. Co., 189 F.2d 124 (7th Cir. 1951); NLRB v. L. G. Everist, Inc., 334 F.2d 312 (8th Cir. 1964). Three circuits, however, agree with the NLRB that such refusals are protected. See NLRB v. Alamo Express, Inc., 74 LRRM 2742, 430 F.2d 1032 (5th Cir. 1970); Teamsters, Local 657 v. NLRB, 70 LRRM 2480, 429 F.2d 204 (D.C. Cir. 1970); NLRB v. Rockaway News Supply Co., 30 LRRM 2119, 197 F.2d 111 (2d Cir. 1952) aff'd, 345 U.S. 71 (1953). See also NLRB v. Difco Laboratories, Inc. 427 F.2d 170 (6th Cir. 1970).

23   428 U.S. 397 (1976).

24   428 U.S. at 429 (J. Stevens, dissenting).

25   Smith, "The Supreme Court, Boys Market Labor Injunctions and Sympathy Work Stoppages," 44 U. Chi. L. Rev. 321, 342 (1977). But see Freed, "Injunctions Against Sympathy Strikes: In Defense of *Buffalo Forge,*" 54 N.Y.U. L. Rev. 289 (1979).

26   Eastex, Inc. v. NLRB, 437 U.S. 556, 563 (1978).

27   The Court maintained, however, that these citations should not be read as approval of the results reached in any of these cases. *Id.* at 565, n. 13.

28   See *id.* at 556.

29   Norris-LaGuardia Act, Act of March 23, 1932; 47 Stat. 70 (1932), 29 U.S.C. Section 102 (1964).

30   S. Rep. No. 163, 72 Cong., 1st Sess. 9 (1932).

31   The case, G. & W., Electric v. NLRB, 360 F.2d 873 (7th Cir. 1966), is expressly rejected by the Court. Eastex v. NLRB, 437 U.S. 556, 567, n. 17.

32   Eastex v. NLRB, 437 U.S. 556, 570, n. 20; also see cases cited at 568, n. 18.

33   Getman, "The Protection of Economic Pressure by Section 7 of the National Labor Relations Act," 115 U. Pa. L. Rev. 1195, 1221 (1967).

34   The "political expression" exception in *Eastex* has led to further litigation, and recent General Counsel decisions on appeals or requests for advice, although seem-

ingly consistent with the views of the Court, show the chilling potential of the decision. See, Report on Case-Handling Developments at NLRB, 101 LRR 360 (Aug. 27, 1979). The vagueness of the doctrine makes it difficult for employers to predict the extent to which they can regulate employee speech. In one case the General Counsel refused to issue a charge because the "bulk of the material was highly political and inflammatory in nature," even though a "small portion" was arguably protected by Section 7. *Id.* at 361. The material in question related to the discharge of an employee employed elsewhere, and the lack of immediate connection to the employer's own work environment was deemed relevant in balancing the speech interest against the employer's management interest. The cases will turn on slippery notions such as the "inflammatory" nature of the contents and whether the interests involved are "attenuated" from the employees' interest *qua* employees. Endorsements of political candidates seem generally protected if the *content* of the material refers to labor-related issues, and, at least so long as the material refers to *domestic* labor-related issues, the material will not be considered a "purely political tract."

In a brilliant critique of postwar academic thinking about collective bargaining, focusing upon the dominant "consensus" or "liberal pluralist" school, Walter Korpi notes that one of the central tenets was that the bargaining system institutionalized conflict much like the electoral process institutionalized political conflict. One of the legal notions that seems to flow from this conception is that collective bargaining serves a governing role and the collective agreement becomes a type of constitution. Yet, somewhat inconsistently, if conflict is to be controlled it is also necessary to separate political and industrial conflict. Industrial conflict must be seen as separate from the conflicts of political society. Thus, one's industrial class position becomes separate from one's political class. W. Korpi, "Industrial Relations and Industrial Conflict: The Case of Sweden," in *Labor Relations in Advanced Societies: Issues and Problems*, B. Martin and E. Kassalow, eds. (Carnegie Endowment for International Peace 1980).

The pluralists, it should be noted, may only have been continuing an older tradition. Thus capitalism itself defines a wide variety of economic activities as the "market" and, therefore, private. As private, the pursuit of wealth is unencumbered by political restraints. Marx, for instance, noted that "modern capital . . . has . . . shut out the state from any influence on the development of property." K. Marx, "The German Ideology: Part 1" at 150, in *The Marx-Engels Reader*, R. Tucker, ed. (W. W. Norton & Co. 1972).

This economic precept is often violated in practice, and private matters often become public when it is of value to so treat them. The ideal remains firmly embedded, and perhaps more strongly so in America than anywhere else.

35 See Hudgens v. NLRB, 424 U.S. 507 (1976); Marshall v. Barlows, Inc., 436 U.S. 307 (1978).

36 437 U.S. at 579 (J. White, concurring).

37 See, *e.g.*, NLRB v. Burnup & Sims, 379 U.S. 21 (1964).

38 NLRB v. Union Carbide, 440 F.2d 54 (4th Cir. 1971), citing NLRB v. Southern Greyhound Lines, 426 F.2d 1299 (5th Cir. 70).

39 NLRB v. Union Carbide, 440 F.2d at 55–56.

40 I would assert that respect of a picket line for any reason is a "concerted" act and

mutual aid is the result, and, therefore, the action should be protected in all cases. The fourth circuit, however, will not protect those employees who refuse to cross a picket line out of fear rather than principle. The court, I believe, is simply wrong in its belief that one who "respects" a picket line "by reason of physical fear makes no common cause, contributes nothing to the mutual aid or protection, and does not act on principle." The latter phrase is partly tautological, although the preservation of one's safety may well be highly principled to some. The court has merely distinguished, perhaps, between principles. Yet it is not clear why an employee need act out of principle in order to be protected. In no other area of labor law do we ask whether action is based upon principled solidarity or perceived needs of self-protection.

41 See, generally, Schatzki, "Some Observations & Suggestions Concerning a Misnomer—'Protected' Concerted Activities," 47 Texas L. Rev. 378, 393 (1969).

42 NLRB v. Peter Cailler Kohler Swiss Chocolates Co., 130 F.2d 503 (2d Cir. 1942).

43 See Getman, *supra* note 33, at 1222.

44 NLRB v. Peter Cailler Kohler Swiss Chocolates Co., 130 F.2d 505–6 (2d Cir. 1942).

45 See. H.R. Rep. No. 245, 80th Cong., 1st Sess. (1947) in 1 Legis. Hist. of LMRA, 1947 at 297 (1948); S. Minority Rep., No. 105, 80th Cong., 1st Sess. 1947 in 1 Legis. Hist. of LMRA, 1947 at 463, 481–82 (1948). Moreover, the debate over the Landrum Griffin Act of 1959 makes clear that such action would *remain* protected. See Getman, *supra* note 33, at 1227–28.

46 As in other areas used in these articles, I have not attempted to survey the entire territory or to develop a comprehensible rule or approach. In traditional legal scholarship, this would require an article for each area. Thus, the subject of picket lines alone has resulted in many long articles. See, *e.g.*, Carney and Florsheim, "The Treatment of Refusals to Cross Picket Lines: By-Paths and Indirect 'Crookt' Ways," 55 Cornell L. Rev. 940 (1970). The authors in 1970 found "only" three articles and a number of student comments on the subject. *Id.* at 940, n. 1.

47 R. Gorman, *Basic Text on Labor*, 318–19 (West Pub. 1976).

48 *Id.* at 321–22. A single concerted refusal to work overtime is protected "if it is a concerted activity directed at changing employee working conditions, or employer policy." NLRB v. Gulf-Wandes Corp., 101 LRRM 2373, 2375 (5th Cir. 1979). Employees will be subject to discharge if the work stoppage is "part of a plan or pattern of intermittent action which is inconsistent with a genuine strike or genuine performance by employees of the work normally expected of them by the employer." NLRB v. Polytech, Inc., 195 NLRB 695 (1972). It is still true, however, that a series of intermittent work stoppages or refusals to work overtime will be deemed unprotected even though the actions are in support of bargaining demands.

49 See, generally, Atleson, "Work Group Behavior & Wildcat Strikes: The Causes and Functions of Industrial Civil Disobedience," 34 Ohio St. L. J. 751, 772–76 (1973); Gould, "The Status of Unauthorized & 'Wildcat' Strikes Under the NLRA," 52 Cornell L. Q. 672 (1967).

50 See, *e.g.*, NLRB v. Shop-Rite Foods, Inc., 430 F.2d 786 (5th Cir. 1970). The Supreme Court's decision in *Emporium Capwell*, while not a wildcat case, suggests strong opprobrium for rank-and-file activity outside of, or in conflict with, formal union demands.

51 The basic notion at work here also seems to underlie the rule recognized by most arbitrators and, presumably, in most collective bargaining agreements, *i.e.*, the employee must follow work orders, unless, perhaps, they order action that is unsafe or illegal, and may protest only via the grievance system. See Atleson, "Threats to Employee Health and Safety: Employee Self-Help Under the NLRA," 59 Minn. L. Rev. 647, 675 (1975).

52 The union as an institution is not necessarily harmed by a wildcat. See, generally, Atleson, *supra* note 51.

53 Schatzki, "Majority Rule, Exclusive Representation, and the Interests of Individual Workers: Should Exclusivity be Abolished," 123 U. Pa. L. Rev. 897, 915–16 (1975).

54 NLRB v. Draper Corp., 145 F.2d 199 (4th Cir. 1944).

55 NLRB v. Shop-Rite Foods, Inc., 430 F.2d 786 (5th Cir. 1970).

56 Even with this focus, the NLRB is arguably wrong in assuming that differences in means or timing may not be as significant as differences in goals. See Gould, *supra* note 49.

57 Atleson, *supra* note 49, at 814–16, 782–83, 790–92, 778–80.

58 *Id.* 810–11 (footnotes omitted).

59 Mastro Plastics Corp. v. NLRB, 350 U.S. 270 (1956).

60 Lucas Flour v. Teamsters Local 174, 369 U.S. 95 (1962); Gateway Coal v. UMW, 414 U.S. 368 (1974).

61 The continued vitality of *Mastro* is threatened by the current stress on resolution of contractual disputes through arbitration even though the employer's action might be deemed a statutory violation. See, *e.g.*, Carey v. Westinghouse, 375 U.S. 261 (1964); NLRB v. Collyer Insulated Wire, 192 NLRB 837 (1971).

62 Schatzki, *supra* note 57, at 915–18.

63 See NLRB v. Washington Aluminum, 370 U.S. 9 (1962), for the suggestion that wider latitude might be granted to unorganized workers.

64 The frustration of courts facing wildcats that are not deterred by existing legal doctrine is shown by those cases holding unions contractually liable under no-strike clauses for failing to exert every reasonable effort to end such walkouts. See, *e.g.*, Eazor Express, Inc. v. Teamsters, 357 F. Supp. 158 (W.D.Pa. 1973), *modified* and *affirmed*, 520 F.2d 951 (3d Cir. 1975); Note, 89 Harvard L. Rev. 601 (1976).

65 Cox, *supra* note 2, at 332–33.

66 I do not mean to suggest that Cox is unaware of these problems. Hidden in his article is a surprising suggestion that some other solution should be found for the present practice that reads into concerted activities "moral and economic limitations for which . . . [decision makers] lack accepted standards." Thus, Cox would bar only "violence, mass picketing and related misconduct which both our labor laws and general criminal statutes have uniformly condemned." *Id.* at 339.

67 UAW, AFL v. Wisconsin Employment Relations Board, 336 U.S. 245 (1949); see Cox, *supra* note 2, at 323.

68 Cox, *supra* note 2, at 324–25.

69 "This provision [8(b)(4)(A)] could not be literally construed; otherwise it would ban most strikes historically construed to be lawful, so-called primary activity." Local 761, I.U.E. v. NLRB, 366 U.S. 667 (1961).

70 NLRB v. Fruit and Vegetable Packers, Local 760, 377 U.S. 58 (1964); see also NLRB

v. Drivers, Local 760, 377 U.S. 84 (1964); see also NLRB v. Drivers, Local Union, 362 U.S. 274 (1960).

71 See, *e.g.*, National Woodwork Mfr's Ass'n. v. NLRB, 386 U.S. 612 (1967); NLRB v. Fruit and Vegetable Packers Union, 377 U.S. 58 (1964).

72 Klare, *supra* note 1, at 267. It should be noted that American unions have not generally been concerned with radical transformations in workplace decision making. Ronald Radosh has argued that the CIO was as committed to corporate liberalism as the AFL, and may well have been more of a force for the stabilization of capitalism than a rebellion against it. Radosh, "The Corporate Ideology of American Labor Leaders from Gompers to Hillman," 6 Studies on the Left 66–88 (Nov.–Dec. 1966); Radosh, *American Labor and United States Foreign Policy* (Random House 1969). See also J. Weinstein, *Ambiguous Legacy: The Left in American Politics* (New Viewpoints 1975).

5   STATUS ASSUMPTIONS AND THE "COMMON ENTERPRISE"

1   NLRB v. Local 1299, IBEW, 346 U.S. 464 (1953).

2   *Id.* at 472–73.

3   *Id.* at 472.

4   Quarterly Report of The General Counsel, 100 LRR 260 (1979).

5   NLRB v. Patterson Sargent, 115 NLRB 1627, 1629 (1956).

6   See A. Fox, *Beyond Contract: Work, Power & Trust Relations* (Faber & Faber 1974) (hereinafter cited as *Fox*); P. Selznick, *Law, Society & Industrial Justice* (Russell Sage 1969).

7   Masters were given complete control over apprentices, usually for seven years. For the indentured servant, who also suffered under a number of serious legal restrictions, the contract time was usually much shorter, ranging from a low of three to a high of about five years. Contracts for apprenticeships and indentured servants bound the person for a period of years and severely circumscribed the ability to exercise personal rights. After the termination of the contract an apprentice or servant would in all likelihood become either a journeyman, which could mean entering into another possible transitional status leading to independent artisan, or a day laborer, whose economic dependency on the master was permanent as long as he or she remained unable or unwilling to move. See H. Wellenreuther, "Labor in the Era of the American Revolution, a Discussion of Recent Concepts and Theories," 22, no. 4 Labor History 573, 584–85 (1981).

8   R. Morris, *Government and Labor in Early America* (Harper 1946). See also R. Morris, ed., *The Emergency of American Labor, The U.S. Dept. of Labor Bicentennial History of the American Worker* (1976); Morris, Preface to 3, 4. J. Commons and E. Gilmore, *Documentary History of American Industrial Society* (1958). It is estimated that 17 percent of Philadelphia's work force was unfree at the outbreak of the Revolution. Salinger, "Colonial Labor in Transition—The Decline of Indentured Servitude in Late Eighteenth-Century Philadelphia," 22, no. 2 Labor History 165 (1981).

9   E. Foner, *Tom Paine and Revolutionary America* at 43 (Oxford 1976).

10 "The American Revolution did not put an end to the use of indentured labor. The war disrupted the operation of the system by temporarily curtailing immigration,

but the servant trade revived in the early 1780's . . . [T]he system persisted in use, although on a limited scale, into the nineteenth century." David Galenson, *White Servitude in Colonial America* at 178 (Cambridge U. Press 1981).

11 D. B. Davis, *The Problem of Slavery in the Age of Revolution, 1770–1823* at 87, 88, 89 (Cornell U. Press 1975).

12 *Id.* at 254. See also J. Glickstein, " 'Poverty Is Not Slavery': American Abolitionists and the Competitive Labor Market" at 195, in *Antislavery Reconsidered: New Perspectives on the Abolitionists*, L. Perry and M. Fellman, eds. (Louisiana Press 1979).

13 Davis, *supra* note 11, at 259.

14 *Id.* at 358. Despite the weakness of historical evidence, Davis's monumental work offers fascinating connections between slavery and free or bound labor. "The increase in the importation of slaves [into the South] was matched by a decrease in the importation of indentured servants and consequently a decrease in the dangerous number of new freed men who annually emerged seeking a place in society that they would be unable to achieve." E. S. Morgan, "Slavery and Freedom: The American Paradox," 59 Journal of American History (June 1972), cited in Davis at 260–61. Thus, blacks in the South at least took the place of lower-class whites who were threatening to certain elements. The common fear of the landless poor could not be focused upon a limited and visible group.

Northern workers, some time later during the Jacksonian period, could rail against their situation as "wage slavery." But, as Davis argues, the same workers were "notoriously unsympathetic to the abolitionist cause, which they tended to view as a distractive maneuver of the capitalists." Davis at 275.

15 Wedderburn, *The Worker & The Law* at 10–11 (Penguin 1965).

16 *Id.* at 32.

17 R. Morris, *Government and Labor, supra* note 8, at 518.

18 F. Meyers, *Ownership of Jobs* at 112 (U. of Calif. Press 1964). A nice example of the difference of cultural perceptions is reflected in T. Hareven and R. Langenbach, *Amoskeag: Life and Work in an American Factory City* (Pantheon 1978). One of the causes of the ultimate demise of the huge Amoskeag Mill was the transfer of an $18 million cash reserve accumulated by the company in good times to a holding company pursuant to a 1925 reorganization. The transfer left the manufacturing company with "insufficient cash for modernizing and properly maintaining the large plant and effectively sealed the doom of the Manchester operation." *Id.* at 302. The workers viewed the reserve as a fund created by their labor upon which they had a claim.

19 Wedderburn, *supra* note 15, at 95.

20 See Recommendation 119 of the ILO, cited in *id.* at 97.

21 See, *e.g.*, Summers, "Individual Protection against Unjust Dismissal," 62 Vir. L. Rev. 481 (1976).

22 T. Cochran & W. Miller, *The Age of Enterprise* at 238 (Harper & Row, rev. ed. 1961).

23 Marshall v. Barlow's, Inc., 436 U.S. 307 (1978).

24 *Id.* at 313.

25 *Id.* at 339 (J. Stevens, dissenting).

26 *Id.* at 329.

27   NLRB v. Babcock & Wilcox, 351 U.S. 105 (1956).

28   See Hudgens v. NLRB, 424 U.S. 507 (1976), and Central Hardware v. NLRB, 407 U.S. 569 (1972).

29   Specific concerns, such as littering, for instance, could be handled by narrower rules which would not prohibit all informational activities.

30   It is possible to read cases such as *Jefferson Standard* in a narrow fashion, although I believe the implicit values in the language quoted above are the most significant part of the decision. The Court stressed that the handbills did not refer to any labor condition or issue in dispute and did not request public support. "The fortuity of the coexistence of a labor dispute affords these technicians no substantial defense." 364 U.S. at 476. The Court was itself aware that this "fortuity" might well lead to some "future concession" by the employer. The handbills, however, did not disclose this possible purpose. The Court approved the Board's holding that the attack was separate from the dispute, purportedly in the name of the public rather than the employees. This bizarre assumption was noted by the dissenters, and they suggested that the decision was based primarily on the product disparagement ground, with the additional irritant that the attack was, in the majority's words, "initiated while off duty, upon the very interests which the attackers were being paid to conserve and develop." *Id.* The employees are "paid" to do more than perform work, yet, as later material will show, employers are only obliged to pay for such labor.

An ironic footnote to *Jefferson Standard* was added in the 1962 *Washington Aluminum* decision in which the Court referred to the "disloyal" product disparagement in that case as being "unnecessary to carry on the workers' legitimate concerted activities." NLRB v. Washington Aluminum, 370 U.S. 16–17 (1962). The irony is that the Court in *Washington Aluminum* held that the "reasonableness of the workers' decision . . . is irrelevant to the determination of whether a labor dispute exists."

31   See, *e.g.*, Sullair P.T.O. Inc. v. NLRB, 106 LRRM 2705 (7th Cir. 1981), where the Board could not "condone [the] use of such vulgarities directed at management."

32   American Tel. & Tel. Co. v. NLRB, 521 F.2d 1159 (2d Cir. 1975).

33   See, *e.g.*, Atlantic Steel Co., 245 NLRB 814 (1979); Thor Power Tool Co., 148 NLRB 1379, *enf'd*, 351 F.2d 584 (7th Cir. 1965); Hawaiian Hauling Service, Ltd., 219 NLRB 765 (1975).

34   Atlantic Steel Co., 245 NLRB 814 (1979). Arbitrators have tended to confirm rather than challenge the assumption that employees have an obligation of fealty and deference to their supervisors and employers. No area more clearly reflects this view than the discipline accorded employees who "bad mouth" supervisors. Many agreements, it must be noted, and unilaterally promulgated employer rules provide penalties for employees who use uncivil or obscene language or who otherwise exhibit disrespectful behavior. It is not uncommon for employees to receive suspensions for such utterances as "go to hell" or for calling a supervisor a "fatso." Arbitrators generally attempt to distinguish rough "shop talk" from personally demeaning references, but it is not at all clear why the latter type reference, no matter how unfortunate, should be a matter of discipline. Unions claim that supervisors are rarely punished for reviling an employee, whereas the reverse seems increasingly common.

Arbitrators routinely permit a wider latitude of speech by stewards or union officials while engaged in grievance administration or bargaining. Obviously, wide-open debate is necessary in such situations in order for union officials to effectively carry out their representational role.

This distinction is based upon the notion that employees, or even officials when not acting in an official capacity, do not possess personal equality with management. Thus, an employee who responded to a supervisor's order to speed up her work with "Dammit, I can't!" received a two-week suspension from work. The suspension was upheld because the arbitrator found the employer's rule against profanity reasonable even though the discharge, without the rule, was deemed to be unreasonable in light of modern usage. The language of arbitrators makes clear that such discipline is proper because rough language constitutes "an affront to managerial authority . . ." L. Stessin, New York Times, July 1, 1979, at F 3; see also, *Steelworkers Handbook on Arbitration Decisions* at 325–26 (Pike & Fischer, 1970).

35   Often, employees are misled about changes in the enterprise. See, *e.g.,* UAW v. NLRB, 470 F.2d 422 (D.C. Cir. 1972).

36   A. Wallace, *Rockdale: The Growth of an American Village in the Early Industrial Revolution* at 54–55 (Knopf 1978). Wallace's evidence demonstrates that rules of discipline in pre-1850 enterprises differ little from rules of order in modern firms. Thus, the regulations of the Matteawan Company in 1846 prohibited workers from leaving "their work without permission of the overseer" or from talking "except on subjects relative to their work." Even outside the work environs, intemperance or gross impropriety was prohibited, and regular attendance "on some place of divine worship" was required.

6   MANAGERIAL CONTROL AND THE FEAR OF ANARCHY

1   NLRA Section 502, 28 U.S.C. Section 143 (1970).
2   Atleson, "Threats to Health and Safety: Employee Self-Help Under the NLRA," 59 Minn. L. Rev. 647, 658–59 (1975).
3   See Roadway Express, Inc. v. NLRB, 217 NLRB 278, *enforced,* 527 F.2d 853 (4th Cir. 1976); Combustion Eng., Inc., 224 NLRB 542 (1976).
4   414 U.S. 368 (1974).
5   Atleson, *supra* note 2.
6   Gateway Coal Co. v. UMW, 414 U.S. 368, 386 [1974].
7   Atleson, *supra* note 2, at 686.
8   As the comedy group Beyond the Fringe has noted, a judge, unlike a miner, rarely need fear a roof cave-in—"Judges are rarely troubled by falling coal—it's a feature of guild-hall life" (Beyond the Fringe, Capitol Records, SW 1792).
9   Atleson, *supra* note 2, at 700–703.
10   *Id.* at 701.
11   414 U.S. at 386.
12   Atleson, *supra* note 2, at 700–701.
13   *Id.* at 701–2. It is painfully ironic to note the hundreds of cases in which employers are charged with discriminatory discharges, for instance, in organizational situations where the impact upon statutory interests is often severe. The legal inquiry

focuses upon the employer's "motive," and the impact on employees is irrelevant.

14 The Court's argument that an objective test is needed to avoid the administrative problems of a subjective test is probably disingenuous. See *id.* at 700–701.

15 Curtis Mathes Mfg. Co., 145 NLRB 473, 482, n. 6 (1963).

16 The impact of *Mackay* is also felt in the health and safety area. Thus, even if the walkout is held within Section 502, and impliedly within Section 7, it is still arguable that the employer may be able to replace the employees permanently. The better argument is that walkouts within Section 502 were singled out for special treatment and represent conduct that is protected over and above economic walkouts. This special and unique treatment suggests that employees engaging in such walkouts should be treated more like unfair labor practice strikers.

17 First National Maintenance Corp. v. NLRB, 452 U.S. 666 (1981).

18 As Neil Peck has suggested, risk is a subjective matter, not one of factual determination. Letter to author.

19 The 1973 UAW-GM strike involved the UAW's desire to prohibit compulsory overtime. It is quite possible that the length of the strike was due in large part to GM's perception that this demand was far more of a threat to its authority than a wage or pension-fund increase.

20 See, generally, R. Edwards, *Contested Terrain: The Transformation of the Workplace in the Twentieth Century*, chap. 1 (Basic Books 1979) [hereinafter cited as *Edwards*].

21 See *Edwards* at 30–47; K. Stone, "The Origins of Job Structures in the Steel Industry," in *Labor Market Segmentation*, Edwards, Reich, & Gordon, eds. (Heath 1975); D. Brody, *The Steelworkers in America: The Non-Union Era* (Harvard U. Press 1960); D. Montgomery, *Workers' Control in America* (Cambridge U. Press 1979); T. Hareven and R. Langenbach, *Amoskeag: Life and Work in an American Factory City* at 155 (Pantheon 1978).

22 D. Montgomery, "The Workers' Search for Order in the Late Nineteenth Century," lecture given at State University of New York at Buffalo, February 16, 1978.

23 *Edwards* at 31–32.

24 See D. Nelson, *Managers & Workers: Origins of the New Factory System in the United States 1880–1920* (U. of Wis. Press 1975). Stone, *supra* note 21, at 323.

25 *Edwards* at 48–67.

26 Stephen Meyers has noted that foremen represented 2 percent of a Detroit sample of workers in 1891, and clerks and inspectors were not even listed. By 1917, foremen, clerks, and inspectors constituted 14 percent of the total number of employees in the Ford plant. The new foreman did not supervise an entire shop but only directed the operations of a particular department. He had become a "production man." In short, he became a disciplinarian. S. Meyer, *The Five Dollar Day: Labor Management & Social Control in the Ford Motor Company, 1908–1921* at 55 (SUNY Press 1981).

27 *Edwards* at 52.

28 Hobsbawm has noted a parallel development in the 1860s and 1870s in Europe. Because large-scale enterprises could not be effectively guided by the models of the family or of small craft businesses, enterprise adopted military and bureaucratic models. The military model was adopted in some industries in various countries either because of pride in military structures or because other models of manage-

ment simply did not exist. Uniforms, among English railway workers, and military titles, among railroad executives, are fairly clear examples of an appeal to military structures. Similarly, appeals to loyalty to the firm, paralleling military appeals to patriotism, were quite common—in the United States as well. Such appeals were useful given a doctrine that wages were to be kept as low as possible. Thus, wages could not be an adequate incentive. Some perhaps could be motivated by the chance of becoming middle class, but the realism of this hope was certainly fading in this period. E. J. Hobsbawm, *The Age of Capital, 1848–1875* at 237–40 (Mentor 1979).

29   Quoted in Meyer, *supra* note 26, at 68.

30   *Edwards*, chap. 6; S. Brandes, *American Welfare Capitalism, 1880–1940* (U. of Chicago Press 1976); D. Brody, *supra* note 21; J. Weinstein, *The Corporate Ideal in the Liberal State: 1900–1918* (Beacon Press 1968).

31   Paternalism at companies such as Ford failed because it did not achieve its principal object, the control of workers. Although Ford successfully wrested production control from skilled workers and deskilled work tasks and routines, labor problems persisted. Ironically, Ford had destroyed traditional means of work discipline such as craft traditions and union apprenticeship systems. Ford responded with a sophisticated system of social control, culminating in the creation of the Sociological Department to mold norms by going beyond the workplace and into the homes and communities of its workers. It was thought in the progressive era that home environment and not innate moral qualities determined work attitudes and habits. Labor problems persisted and welfare programs were expensive. Paternalism was superceded by tougher, more authoritarian controls. See Meyer, *supra* note 26, at 195–99.

32   *Edwards* at 98. As Stanley B. Mathewson demonstrated in his famous study of restriction of output among unorganized workers, both union and nonunion employees found many ways to fool the time and motion study of men with their ever-present stopwatch. Even among unorganized workers without union work rules Mathewson found that restriction of output remained "deeply entrenched in the working habits of American working people." Scientific management had simply failed "to develop that spirit of confidence between parties to labor contracts" which was essential to the scheme Taylor had in mind. The efforts of scientific managers to obtain more efficiency and productivity had been "offset by the ingenuity of workers developing restrictive practices." Mathewson, *Restriction of Output among Unorganized Workers* (Viking Press 1931).

33   The primary issue was control rather than efficiency. Efficiency, it should be noted, may not be always a value-free term. Efficiency can be increased by lowering wages, thereby reducing labor input while maintaining the same production levels. Alternatively, workers can be induced to produce more without increasing pay.

34   *Edwards* at 99. See, in general, Noble's description of the origins of the engineering profession in *America by Design* (Knopf 1977). Taylorism involved a stress on the division of labor and the fragmentation of work into narrow tasks, each minutely timed, a process already underway in many parts of industry. The position of the worker is clearly stated: "The workman is told minutely just what he is to do and how he is to do it, and any improvement he makes upon the orders given

him is fatal to success." Taylor, *The Act of Cutting Metals* (ASME 1906), cited by
M. Cooley, in "Computerization—Taylor's Latest Disguise," 1, no. 4 Economic
and Industrial Democracy at 525 (Nov. 1980). His system would relegate "the entire mental parts of the tasks in hand to the managerial staff." Taylor, *Shop Management* (1903), cited by Cooley at 525.

35 Montgomery, *supra* note 21, at 26.

36 See *id.* citing F. J. Roethlisberger & W. J. Dickson, "Management and the Worker:
Technological vs. Social Organization in an Industrial Plant" at 16–17, Harvard
Business Research Studies 9 (1934). New classification systems, like Ford's, provided a ladder for social mobility within the factory. Workers were granted an
automatic wage increase as soon as they reached a specific standard of efficiency.
If the worker increased his skill, he moved on to the next grade of skill. One result
was that the worker could only blame himself if he failed to maximize his earn-
ings. This system made the worker internalize the self-discipline required for industrial efficiency in the mechanized plant. See Meyer, *supra* note 26, at 102–3.

37 Montgomery, *supra* note 21, at 27.

38 Quoted from J. R. Commons, *et al.* at 267, *Industrial Government* (New York
1921). Robert Ozanne has argued that Commons's views cannot be equated with
those of Taylor, and he notes that the quote used by David Montgomery is taken
from a discussion of worker-owned businesses and producer cooperatives created
after losing strikes in the nineteenth century. Commons believed that most of
these businesses failed, but management in those which succeeded soon altered
the form of the business to limit ownership, thus excluding new employees from
stock ownership. Ozanne, "Trends in American Labor History," 21 Labor History
518 (1980). Ironically, both Montgomery and Ozanne rely upon Commons's next
statement that if some workers do "shoulder responsibility, it is because certain
individuals succeed, and then those individuals immediately close the doors, and
labor, as a class, remains where it was." Montgomery seems to have the better argument, for even if the class "remains where it was," Commons nevertheless concludes that labor as a class can never manage industry. Such a position is perfectly
consistent with the limited, "job-consciousness" perception of workers by the
Commons-Perlman school.

39 Montgomery, *supra* note 21, at 27.

40 H. Aitken, *Taylorism at the Watertown Arsenal* (Harvard U. Press 1960).

41 *Edwards* at 102.

42 *Id.* at 105–10.

43 *Id.* at chaps. 7 and 8.

44 *Id.* at 110, 128–29.

45 Edwards provides a welcome response to organizational theorists who recognize
technical efficiency, but not worker control, in the design of the labor process.
Edwards, however, has been criticized for overstressing worker control as the preeminent motivation behind capitalist planning, and for underplaying the "importance of the drive for internal efficiency and the concern with eliminating external
uncertainties." The use of older methods of control or the creation of new devices
"may be often in response to heightened competition, shifting state regulation,
economic crises or internal problems of coordination." D. R. Van Houten, Book
Review, 1, no. 4 Economic and Industrial Democracy 584 (Nov. 1980). Van

Houten also notes that subtle controls such as departmental divisions of labor which creates interaction, a shared language, and a world view may have more of an effect than the rules themselves. Van Houten also argues that Edwards ignores informal organization with its patterns of accommodation by overstressing the effect of formal structures.

46   P. Mantoux, *The Industrial Revolution in the Eighteenth Century* 206 (1928; Harper & Row, reprint ed. 1962).

47   Testimony of Newcomb Carlton, Mass. State Board of Labor and Industries, Boston, Mass. June 16, 1916. Cited in C. Craypo, "The Impact of Changing Corporate Structure and Technology on Telegraph Labor, 1870–1978," 3, no. 3 Labor Studies Journal 295 (1979).

48   *Edwards* at 131.

7   THE SCOPE OF MANDATORY BARGAINING

1   C. Summers, "Industrial Democracy: America's Unfulfilled Promise," 28 Clev. St. L. Rev. 29, 41 (1979).

2   Steelworkers, Local 1330 v. U.S. Steel Corp., 492 F. Supp. 1, 103 LRRM 2925, 2931–32 (D.C. Ohio, 1980).

3   First National Maintenance Corp. v. NLRB, 452 U.S. 666, 676 (1981).

4   See Report of the Senate Committee on Education and Labor, May 1, 1935 (S. 1958).

5   Thus the act as noted in its statement of policy was designed to "eliminate the causes of certain substantial obstructions to the free flow of commerce . . . by encouraging the practice and procedure of collective bargaining and by protecting the exercise by workers of full freedom of association, self-organization and the designation of representatives of their own choosing, for the purpose of negotiating the terms and conditions of their employment or other mutual aid or protection." 49 U.S. Stat. 449 (1935). See, generally, H. Millis and E. Brown, *From the Wagner Act to Taft-Hartley* (U. of Chicago Press 1950).

6   See, generally, B. Ramirez, *When Workers Fight: The Politics of Industrial Relations in the Progressive Era, 1898–1916* (Greenwood Press 1978).

7   *Id.* at 21. Ramirez suggests that some operators favored the rise of the UMW and looked upon some early strikes as necessary to relieve the market of coal and, thus, bring about an increase in coal prices. The first interstate labor agreement was signed by operators and the United Mine Workers in 1897 in the midwestern competitive field. The mine owners were anxious to stabilize labor costs and reduce them as a competitive factor. They recognized the UMW, conceded the eight-hour day, and allowed for a check-off of union dues. In return the owners gained conciliation machinery designed to regulate competition over wages and to provide arbitration in the wage disputes. See also, J. R. Green, *The World of the Worker: Labor in Twentieth Century America* at 51 (Hill and Wang 1980).

8   Marcus Hanna, *Marc Hanna, His Book* at 32 (Boston 1904); see Ramirez, *supra* note 6, at chap. 4; Weinstein, *The Corporate Ideal in the Liberal State: 1900–1918* (Beacon 1968).

9   J. Commons, *Myself* at 170 (Macmillan 1934).

10   See also statement by Senator Wagner, 73d Cong., 2d Sess., May 15–16, 1935, at 319.

11   301 U.S. 1 (1937).

12   NLRB v. Jones & Laughlin Steel Corp., 301 U.S. 1, 45–46 (1937).

13   Klare, "Judicial Deradicalization of the Wagner Act and the Origins of Modern Legal Consciousness, 1937–1941," 62 Minn. L. Rev. 265, 302 (1978).

14   See, *e.g.*, Vegelahn v. Guntner, 167 Mass. 92, 44 N.E. 1077 (1896).

15   S. Perlman, "Labor and the New Deal in Historical Perspective" at 367 in *Labor & the New Deal*, M. Derber & E. Young, eds. (U. of Wis. Press 1957).

16   W. Leuchtenburg, *F. D. Roosevelt and the New Deal* at 153 (Harper 1963) [hereinafter cited as *Leuchtenburg*].

17   *Id.* at 151.

18   I. Bernstein, *The New Deal Collective Bargaining Policy* at 116 (U. of Calif. Press 1950). Bernstein also suggests that many legislators, convinced of the act's unconstitutionality, were willing to shift the onus of defeat to the Supreme Court.

19   *Leuchtenburg* at 336.

20   As noted earlier, the Wagner Act is actually not a part of the New Deal program. Roosevelt was not a supporter. He did not seem to understand or sympathize with organized labor's problems, nor did he seem to recognize the possible political dividends in sponsoring prolabor legislation. B. Bernstein, "The New Deal: The Conservative Achievements of Liberal Reform," in *Towards a New Past: Dissenting Essays in American History*, B. Bernstein, ed. (Pantheon 1968). Roosevelt did not support Wagner's bill until passage was assured. See I. Bernstein, *supra* note 18, at 274; *Leuchtenburg* at 150–51. Secretary of Labor Perkins admitted that she had "little sympathy with the bill." 7 Columbia Oral History Memoir, 138, 147, quoted in *Leuchtenburg* at 151.

21   Conklin, *FDR and the Origins of the Welfare State* at 55 (Crowell 1967).

Conklin argues that a type of "welfare" capitalism has become the established system in America, a system that sounds—but is not—daring and progressive. *Id.* at 54. Private property and free enterprise, "meaning the private right to manage the means of production" or "private property," were indispensable components of the faith. Everyone should have the right to own and manage or at least to share in the ownership of management of productive property. The "faith survived but not the sustaining environment." *Id.* at 55. An "ersatz type of opportunity—to work for other men, to sell one's labor to those who did own and manage property—replaced an earlier dream of farm or shop, along with an ersatz type of property—common stock, or claims on profits, but no real role in management." The Depression, of course, wiped out even these substitutes for millions.

Conklin argues that the "meager benefits of Social Security were insignificant in comparison to the building system of security for large, established businesses." *Id.* at 75. The New Deal tried to frame institutions to protect capitalism from major business cycles. "Although some tax bills were aimed at high profits, there was no attack on fair profits or even on large profits." There was no significant leveling by taxes and the proportionate distribution of wealth remained.

William Bremner has argued that the New Deal relief programs reflected traditional cultural norms such as self-help and individual initiative. Innovations, he argues, tended to be restricted to the "confines of the capitalistic order." Bremner, "Along the 'American Way': The New Deal's Work Relief Program for the Unemployed," 63 Journal of American History 636 (1976).

22   The obligation to bargain in good faith over "wages, hours, and other terms and conditions of employment" is also provided in Section 8(d), added in 1947. There seems to be no meaningful difference between the scope of the two phrases.

23   See, *e.g.*, NLRB v. Wooster Div. of Borg-Warner, 356 U.S. 342 (1958).

24   This is the explanation given by Senator Wagner for the inclusion of specific unfair labor practices 8(2)–8(5) following the all-inclusive, generic 8(1). 73d Cong., 2d Sess., May 15–16, 1935.

25   Houde Engineering Co., 1 NLB 87 (March 3, 1934).

26   Cox & Dunlop, "Regulation of Collective Bargaining by the National Labor Relations Board," 63 Harv. L. Rev. 389 (1950). The language of both the original 8(5)—"subject to the provisions of section 9(a)"—and the use of "or" in the key phrase in 9(a) is "more consistent with the notion that the employer is not to bargain with the minority unions about any of the listed subjects of bargaining than it is with the conclusion that he must bargain with the majority union about each and every subject embraced by the phrase." *Id.* at 396–97. Moreover, "[t]here is not a word in the hearings, in the committee reports, or in the debates to suggest that the Act would define the subjects of collective bargaining and give the Board power to resolve the issue in disputed cases." *Id.* at 395. See also Statement of Senator Walsh, 79 Cong. Rec. 7659–60 (1935); Sen. Rep. No. 573, 74th Cong., 1st Sess. 595 (1935).

27   Summers, "Past Premises, Present Failures, and Future Needs in Labor Legislation," in Buffalo Law Review (forthcoming).

28   Cox and Dunlop, *supra* note 26 at 396.

29   *Id.* (my emphasis).

30   See Wilson & Co., 19 NLRB 990 (1940); Singer Mfg. Co., 24 NLRB 444 (1940). See also J. H. Allison & Co., 70 NLRB 377 (1946).

31   The Railway Labor Act required that carriers make "every reasonable effort to make and maintain agreements concerning rates of pay, rules, and working conditions. . . ." Section 2, First. This phrase, preceding the Wagner Act, is somewhat similar, but the language is even less susceptible of a reading that deems the phrase one of limitation. In the National Industrial Recovery Act, providing for codes of competition, the president had the authority to prescribe "the maximum hours, minimum wages and other working conditions necessary for effectuation of the Act." H.R. 5755. Nevertheless, the similarity was noted. 1 Leg. Hist. of NLRB 256 (Testimony of Mr. Beyer). Section 7(b) of the NIRA authorized the president to give every opportunity to employers and employees to contract for hours, pay, and other working conditions.

32   The notion that employers had an affirmative obligation and not merely a negative one to avoid bad-faith bargaining began early. In an early NLB case the Board held that employers had to "exert every reasonable effort to reach an agreement on all matters in dispute. . . ." National Lock Company, 1 NLB 15 (1934). See also Houde Engineering, 1 NLRB 35 (1934), perhaps the most well-known early case on the subject.

33   Eagle Rubber Co., 1 NLRB 157 (1934). See Bernheim & Van Doren, eds., *Labor & Government* at 217–19 (McGraw-Hill 1935).

34 See P. Ross, *The Government as a Source of Union Power* at 64–71, 96–100 (Brown U. Press 1965).

35 Claire Knitting Mills, Inc., 2 NLRB 469 (1935). The case involves the all-too-common situation of employer concealment and misrepresentation in cases of termination. Employee and union representatives were told that the company was "merely disposing of some surplus machinery." 2 NLRB 470. The Board had no difficulty in finding that the move was improper, at least in the absence of prior bargaining with the union. The question of the inclusion of such items as the power to move a plant seems not to have arisen.

36 1 Legis. Hist of NLRA at 1419 (1948). Wagner's concern may have been that an explicit good faith bargaining requirement would intensify opposition to his bill, making it more "vulnerable to charges that the law would require an employer to make an agreement with the union and that agreement be written, referred to at the time as compulsory arbitration." See J. Gross, *The Making of the National Labor Relations Board* at 137 (SUNY Press 1974).

37 See, *e.g.*, 1 Legis. Hist. of NLRA at 1455 (Chairman Biddle of the NLRB); at 1517 (Garrison, first Chairman of NLRB); at 1612 (Handler, former General Counsel, NLB).

38 Ross, *supra* note 34, at 77–78.

39 Ross's book convincingly undercuts the arguments used by important scholars, *e.g.*, Smith, Cox, and Fleming, that the legislative history was so indifferent to the duty that it should be narrowly construed. Ross, however, does not support his criticism of Cox for arguing that the Board was not to have the power to resolve issues over the scope of bargaining. The evidence, as reviewed by Ross, does indeed show support for a broad reading of good faith, but there was little if any discussion about the *subjects* within the area of compulsory bargaining or—important for my purpose here—no guide as to how lines were to be drawn. One could read the legislative history, as perhaps Ross does, to argue that the absence of discussion over subjects means that *all* subjects raised must be given equal respect. Ross, however, strongly supports the distinction between mandatory and nonmandatory subjects.

Nevertheless, it is important to note that members of the first NLRB played an active role in drafting the Wagner Act, a fact that lends support to the notion that the decisions of the first NLRB apply or at least aid in defining the limits of the obligation to bargain. See Gross, *supra* note 36, at 130–48. Board Chairman Biddle directed the Board's legal staff, particularly Calvert Magruder, Philip Levy, and Phillip G. Philips, to work closely with Senator Wagner's legislative counsel in the preparation of the bill. One member of the legal staff, Philip Levy, succeeded Leon Keyserling as Senator Wagner's legislative counsel in 1937. He later stated that "the Board through its staff was by far the largest outside contributor to the development of the details [of the Wagner Act] on both procedure and substance." Quoted in Gross, *supra* note 36, at 131. The Board, for instance, had held as early as 1936 that the employer had a duty to make "every reasonable effort to arrive at an understanding which, if reached, must be embodied in an agreement." St. Joseph's Stockyard Company, 2 NLRB 39, 51 (1936). This holding, found in numerous decisions of the old Board, would reasonably carry over in the interpretation of Section 7 and Section 8(5) of the Wagner Act.

40   See, *e.g.*, Farmer, dissenting in *Borg-Warner,* 113 NLRB 1306; Harlan, dissenting
     in *Borg-Warner,* 356 U.S. 342, at 352.
41   See A. Cox & J. Dunlop, *supra* note 26, at 389.
42   Klare, *supra* note 13, at 293–310.
43   Cox & Dunlop, *supra* note 26, at 389, 397.
44   *Id.* at 405–7, 418–25. See also S. Lynd, "Government without Rights: The Labor
     Law Vision of Archibald Cox," 4 Ind. Rel. L. J. 483 (1981). Lynd views Cox as re-
     versing the normal paradigm that perceives government as protecting rights. In-
     stead, Cox stated that the "purpose of the original Wagner Act was to facilitate the
     organization of unions and the establishment of collective bargaining relation-
     ships." Cox & Dunlop, *id* at 389. Unions and bargaining, therefore, become ends
     in themselves; employee rights are only means to these ends. Presumably, these
     rights are also dispensable once the governmental structure is established.
45   Cox, "The Duty to Bargain in Good Faith," 71 Harv. L. Rev. 1401 (1958). One fa-
     mous quote suggests some caution in reading the scope of the act. Senator Walsh
     stated: "[L]et me say that the bill requires no employer to sign any contract, to
     make any agreement, to reach any understanding with any employee or group of
     employees. . . . Let me emphasize again, . . . all the bill proposes to do is to escort
     them to the door of their employer. . . . What happens behind those doors is not in-
     quired into . . . he [the employer] is obliged to sign no agreement; he can say 'Gen-
     tlemen, we have heard you and considered your proposals. We cannot comply
     with your request'; and that ends it." 2 Legis. Hist. of NLRA at 2372–74 (1948).
     Walsh's persistent effort to state what the bill did not do led Philip Levy, who
     played a leading role in the preparation of the Wagner Bill, to say that this was "the
     kind of thing that Walsh did too much of in the legislative history. He was always
     making speeches about what the law did not do. By the time he got through saying
     all the things it did not do there wasn't a hell of a lot left for it to do." Quoted in
     J. Gross, *The Reshaping of the National Labor Relations Board* at 29 (SUNY
     1981).
46   NLRB v. Wooster Div. of Borg-Warner, 356 U.S. 342 (1958).
47   The argument for a broader reading of mandatory subjects is presented by H. Wel-
     lington, *Labor & the Legal Process,* chap. 2 (Yale U. Press 1968).
48   See, *e.g., id;* but see Ross, *supra* note 34.
49   NLRB v. Fibreboard, 379 U.S. 203 (1964).
50   Ross, *supra* note 34, at 281.
51   See, generally, annotations collected in 12 ALR 2d 266, and R. Gorman, *Basic Text
     on Labor Law* at 496–531 (West Pub. 1976). See also, *e.g.,* Cross & Co. v. NLRB,
     174 F.2d 875 (1st Cir. 1949); Inland Steel v. NLRB, 77 NLRB 1 (1947).
52   See, *e.g.,* Cross & Co. v. NLRB, 174 F.2d 875 (1st Cir. 1949).
53   See, *e.g.,* Penello v. UMW, 88 F. Supp. 935 (D.D.C. 1950) (closed-shop provision).
54   Douds v. ILA, 241 F.2d 278 (2d Cir. 1957) (bargaining for an inappropriate unit). See
     also NLRB v. Borg-Warner, 356 U.S. 342 (1958).
55   See Gorman, *supra* note 51, at 531.
56   Cleveland Newspaper Publishers Assn., 51 L.A. 1174, 1181 (Dworkin 1969).
57   Fairway Foods, 44 L.A. 161 (Soloman 1965).
58   National Lead Co., 43 L.A. 1025, 1027–28 (Larking 1964). See, generally, Elkouri &
     Elkouri, *How Arbitration Works* at 412–550 (BNA, 3d ed. 1973).

59 See, *e.g.*, Edwards, *Contested Terrain* (Basic Books 1979); K. Stone, "The Origins of Job Structures in the Steel Industry," in *Labor Market Segmentation*, Edwards, Reich, & Gordon, eds. (Heath 1975).

60 L. Hill & C. Hook, *Management at the Bargaining Table* at 56 (McGraw-Hill 1945).

61 Cox and Dunlop, *supra* note 26, at 389, 391.

62 *Id.* at 391.

63 Quoted in J. Gross, *supra* note 45, at 17.

64 379 U.S. 203 (1964).

65 Justice Stewart stresses that the language of 9(a), and after 1947, 8(d), are words of limitation. The House bill in 1947 did contain a list of subjects to be included within the scope of bargaining, but this bill was rejected in favor of the Senate version which continues the original meaning of 9(a). Justice Stewart's contention that the legislative history would not support the inclusion of "any subject which is insisted upon as a prerequisite for continued employment" is itself not supportable.

66 379 U.S. 223.

67 See, generally, Gorman, *supra* note 51, at 509–23.

68 H.R. 3020, Section 2(11), 80th Cong., 1st Sess. (1947).

69 H.R. Rep. No. 245, 80th Cong., 1st Sess., 71 (1947) (minority report).

70 H.R. Conf. Rep. No. 510, 80th Cong., 1st Sess., 34–35 (1947).

71 See Atleson, *et al.*, *Collective Bargaining in Private Employment* at 36–37 (BNA 1978).

72 "Another object of the conspiracy, which was no less harmful, was to deprive the public at large of the advantages to be derived from the use of an invention which was not only designed to diminish the cost of making certain necessary articles, but to lessen the labor of human hands." Hopkins v. Oxley Stove Co., 83 F.912 (8th Cir. 1897). The coopers' conception of the value of machines which lessened the labor of their own hands differed substantially from the courts. The coopers' concerns with labor-saving machinery is discussed in I. Yellowitz, *Industrialism and the American Labor Movement* at 71–74 (Kennikat Press 1977).

73 Auto Workers, Local 864 v. NLRB, 470 F.2d 422 (D.C. Cir. 1972).

74 See, *e.g.*, Ozark Trailers, Inc., 161 NLRB 561 (1966); Royal Plating, 152 NLRB 619 (1965); Morrison Cafeterias Consol., Inc. v. NLRB, 431 F.2d 254 (8th Cir. 1970); see, generally, R. Rabin, "*Fibreboard* and the Termination of Bargaining Unit Work: The Search for Standards in Defining the Scope of the Duty to Bargain," 71 Colum. L. Rev. 803 (1971); Rabin, "The Decline and Fall of *Fibreboard*," N.Y.U. 24th Ann. Conf. on Labor 237 (1972).

75 Ozark Trailers, Inc., 161 NLRB 561, 567 (1966).

76 Adams Dairy, Inc., 350 F.2d 108, 111 (8th Cir. 1965).

77 Although there is some doubt that *Fibreboard* really hinders managerial freedom, we are here concerned with the underpinnings of the doctrine. It is true that in most cases of terminations, mergers, or sales, the union is not informed of the planned change or is actually misled. To the extent that bargaining can reach unexpected results or stimulate fresh approaches, mandating bargaining can conceivably alter the outcome.

78 See, generally, R. Rabin, "*Fibreboard* and the Termination of Bargaining Unit

Work," 71 Colum. L. Rev. 803 (1971).

79   470 F.2d 422 (D.C. 1972).

80   470 F.2d 424.

81   General Motors Corp. v. NLRB, 191 NLRB 951, 952 (1971). See also Summit Tooling Co., 195 NLRB 479 (1972). But see Royal Typewriter Co., 209 NLRB 1006 (1974), enf'd, 533 F.2d 1030 (8th Cir. 1976).

82   Rabin, "*Fibreboard* and the Termination of Bargaining Unit Work," 71 Colum. L. Rev. 827 (1971).

83   See M. Bernstein, "The NLRB's Adjudication-Rule Making Dilemma Under the Administrative Procedure Act," 79 Yale L. J. 571 (1970).

84   See, *e.g.*, H. Braverman, *Labor & Monopoly Capital: The Degradation of Work in the Twentieth Century* (Monthly Review Press 1974); R. Edwards, *Contested Terrain* (Basic Books 1979); A. Zimbalist, ed. *Case Studies on the Labor Process* (Monthly Review Press 1979).

85   D. Noble, "Social Choice in Machine Design: The Case of Automatically Controlled Machine Tools" at 18–19, in *Case Studies on the Labor Process*, Zimbalist, ed. (Monthly Review Press 1979).

86   See, *e.g.*, Renton News, 136 NLRB 1294 (1962); Apex Linen Serv., 151 NLRB 305 (1965).

87   First National Maintenance Corp. v. NLRB, 452 U.S. 666 (1981).

88   H. R. Conf. Rep. No. 510, 80th Cong., 1st Sess., 34–35 (1947). The same Congress, however, made it difficult for the NLRB to "study" industrial practices, at least in regard to economic analysis. Section 4(a) stated that "nothing in the Act shall be construed to authorize the Board to appoint individuals for the purpose of . . . economic analysis."

89   First National Maintenance Corp. v. NLRB, 452 U.S. at 676.

90   *Id.* at 676. Blackmun's statement of the test begins with the following phrase: "in view of an employer's need for unencumbered decision making. . . ." Moreover, "bargaining over *management* decisions that have a substantial impact on the continued availability of employment should be required only if the benefit, for labor-management relations and the collective bargaining process, outweighs the burden placed on the conduct of the business." *Id.* at 676. The statement deftly turns the explicit purpose of the Wagner Act on its head. The purpose of requiring bargaining was to encourage workplace democracy even though management decision making might thereby be "encumbered." The statement is only sensible if it is limited not to all management decisions, but only to those involving the "core of managerial prerogatives." Even so, such a statement of the "balance" merely restates the basic question.

91   *Id.* at 679.

92   Blackmun argues that if bargaining is required, the union will seek to delay or halt the closing. It may offer "concessions, information and alternatives that might be helpful to management or forestall or prevent the termination of jobs." Unaccountably, Blackmun states that it is unlikely that requiring bargaining "will augment this flow of information and suggestions." Apparently, since unions can still bargain over the "effects" of the closing, bargaining over the decision itself would not alter the union's role or chance of success.

93   See K. Klare, "Labor Law as Ideology: Toward a New Historiography of Collective Bargaining Law," 4 Ind. Rel. L. J. 450 (1981).

94   B. Ramirez, *supra* note 6.

95   *First National Maintenance,* among other recent decisions, seems contrary to one of the dominant themes in recent legal thought. The goal of many labor decisions, echoing one of the important aims of the Wagner Act, is to institutionalize labor conflict, encouraging bureaucratic or institutional means of resolving workplace conflict. In *First National,* however, the Court *excludes* a concededly important matter from the scope of mandatory bargaining. Similarly, in the recent NLRB v. Bell Aerospace Company, 416 U.S. 267 (1974) and NLRB v. Yeshiva University, 444 U.S. 672 (1980) (discussed in chap. 11), the Court held that "managerial" employees are not to be treated as protected by the NLRA and that the professors of Yeshiva are managerial. As Karl Klare has noted in regard to these decisions, they appear to be "a marked deviation from the integrative, cooptation approach" followed since the end of World War II. K. Klare, "The Bitter and the Sweet: Reflections on the Supreme Court's Yeshiva Decision," Socialist Review (forthcoming).

8   VALUATION IN OTHER GUISES

1   29 U.S.C. Section 158(2)(3) (1958).

2   NLRB v. Erie Resistor, 373 U.S. 221 (1963).

3   American Shipbuilding v. NLRB, 380 U.S. 300 (1965).

4   Textile Workers Union v. Darlington Mfg. Co., 380 U.S. 263 (1965).

5   NLRB v. Great Dane, 388 U.S. 26 (1967).

6   See, *e.g.,* Getman, "Section 8(a)(3) of the NLRA and the Effort to Insulate Free Employee Choice," 32 U. Chi. L. Rev. 735 (1965); Christensen and Svanoe, "Motive and Intent in the Commission of Unfair Labor Practices: The Supreme Court and the Fictive Formality," 77 Yale L. J. 1269 (1968).

7   Christensen & Svanoe, *supra* note 6.

8   Getman, *supra* note 6.

9   See, *e.g.,* 2 Legis Hist. of the NLRA 1949, at 2332–33 (remarks of Senator Wagner; S. Rep. No. 573, 74th Cong., 1st Sess. (1935) in 2 Legis. Hist. of the NLRA 2309; H.R. Rept. No. 969, 74th Cong., 1st Sess. (1935); see also Christensen and Svanoe, *supra* note 6, at 1323–25.

10   379 U.S. 21 (1964).

11   NLRB v. Burnup & Sims, Inc., 379 U.S. 21, 24 (1964).

12   Textile Workers Union v. Darlington Mfg. Co., 380 U.S. 263 (1965).

13   NLRB v. Darlington Mfg. Co., 325 F.2d 682 (4th Cir. 1963).

14   See Summers, "Labor Law in the Supreme Court—1975," 75 Yale L. J. 64–65 (1965) (footnotes omitted).

15   *Id.* at 66.

16   *Id.* at 66–77.

17   NLRB v. Great Dane, 388 U.S. 26 (1967).

18   "That there was discrimination seems hardly contestable whatever definition of that term is used. . . ." Christensen and Svanoe, *supra* note 6, at 1307.

19   The rights granted by the act are deemed "public rights," meaning that the Board

possesses vast discretion in the handling, settling, or litigation of complaints. Private parties may not litigate substantive rights but are restricted to challenging the General Counsel's failure to file a charge, a discretion that courts have shown great reluctance to review. Moreover, only the NLRB can enforce an order that is obtained. See Amalgamated Utility Workers v. Consolidated Edison Co., 309 U.S. 261 (1940). Thus, the rights under the act are not personal, nor does the act provide a private administrative remedy. Rather, "it is the Board's order on behalf of the public that the court enforces." *Id.* at 269. Remedies, too, are based upon the effectuation of public policy rather than the compensation for individual injury. Many of these notions flow quite easily from the language of the act.

It is possible to argue, as does Karl Klare, that the "public right" doctrine along with other doctrines, such as the Board's broad power to define appropriate bargaining units under Section 9, "created an intellectual justification for the dependency of labor on the state, thereby reinforcing the cultural hegemony of liberal political theory. This dependence hindered labor from conceiving of itself, or acting, as an autonomous movement capable of fundamentally transforming the established social relations of production." Klare, "Judicial Deradicalization of the Wagner Act and the Origins of Modern Legal Consciousness, 1937–1941," 62 Minn. L. Rev. 265, 317–18 (1978) (footnote omitted). As Klare notes, however, the labor movement was in fact dependent upon government support in the 1930s, due both to the relative power and opposition of enterprise and to the views of its own leaders. Much of the Left was strongly in favor of state action. It is interesting that the hesitation came from the AFL, which was then in the slow process of shedding its voluntaristic views.

20   The phrase is Justice Frankfurter's. NLRB v. Radio Officers Union, 347 U.S. 17, 56 (1954) (J. Frankfurter, concurring).

9   THE BARGAINING ENIGMA

1   Fibreboard Paper Products Co. v. NLRB, 379 U.S. 203, 225–26 (1964).

2   *Id.* at 226 (J. Stewart, concurring).

3   See, *e.g.*, Davidson, "Government Role in the Economy: Implications for the Relief of Poverty," 48 Urban Law Journal 1 (1970).

4   J. K. Galbraith, "The Economic Image of Corporate Enterprise," at 5, in *Corporate Power in America*, R. Nader & M. Green, eds. (Grossman 1973).

5   See, *e.g.*, Lloyd v. Tanner, 407 U.S. 551 (1972); Hudgens v. NLRB, 424 U.S. 507 (1976); Sears, Roebuck & Co. v. NLRB, 436 U.S. 180 (1978).

6   Fibreboard Paper Products Co. v. NLRB, 379 U.S. 203, 220–21 (1964).

7   H.R. Conf. Rep. No. 510, 80th Cong., 1st Sess., 34–35 (1947).

8   H. Wellington, *Labor & the Legal Process* at 72 (Yale U. Press 1968). Moreover, Section 8(d) states an affirmative obligation over certain topics. It need not be read as a prohibition of bargaining over *other* lawful matters. See NLRB v. Borg-Warner Corp., 356 U.S. 342, 357–58 (J. Harlan, dissenting).

9   Cited in N. W. Chamberlain, *The Union Challenge to Management Control* at 2 (Harper & Bros. 1948).

10   The actual validity of this challenge is far from clear. The presidents of both AFL

and CIO signed their names in 1945 to a new charter for labor and management, to which the United States Chamber of Commerce is likewise a party, containing among other policy statements the following: "the inherent right and responsibility of management to direct the operations of an enterprise shall be recognized and preserved." New York Times, March 29, 1945, quoted in Chamberlain, *supra* note 9, at 4.

11   Golden & Ruttenberg, *The Dynamics of Industrial Democracy* at 330 (Harper & Bros. 1942).

12   D. Brody, *Workers in Industrial America & Essays on the Twentieth Century Struggle* at 178–79 (Oxford 1980). Much of this discussion is based upon chap. 5 of Brody's book, which deals with bargaining in the 1940s [hereinafter cited as *Brody*].

13   E. Wight Bakke, *Mutual Survival* at 7 (Yale Labor & Management Center 1946).

14   Quoted in *Brody* at 176. It is true that union bargaining efforts after the war focused primarily upon wages and fringe benefits. Such action is understandable given galloping inflation and changing patterns of consumption. In 1944, 43 percent of strikes focused upon wages and hours, while 40 percent centered upon other issues, from the speed of production to unsafe working conditions. By 1946, the percentage of strikes concerned with wages climbed to 45 percent and those concerned with other issues fell to 23 percent. This might suggest that workers had abandoned issues of control over production in order to emphasize purchasing power and security, and unions seem to have interpreted past strikes this way. J. R. Green, *The World of the Worker: Labor in Twentieth Century America* at 196 (Hill & Wang 1980). Large corporations could concede wage increases to powerful unions, because these costs could be spread throughout the industry, thus disadvantaging smaller competitors, and such costs could also be passed on in monopoly or oligopoly sectors.

15   See, *e.g.*, *Brody* at 175–76.

16   National Labor Management Conference, November 5–30, 1945, Division of Labor Standards, U.S. Dept. of Labor, Bull. 77, 1946, at 53–56. Quoted in *Brody* at 175–76.

17   Quoted in N. W. Chamberlain, *The Labor Sector* at 342 (McGraw-Hill 1965).

18   The continuity of such views in American history is truly impressive. Judge Edwards in 1936 could refer to societies of journeymen as being of "foreign origin, . . . mainly upheld by foreigners." People v. Faulkner, 4 Commons & Gilmore, *A Documentary History of American Industrial Society* at 315 (1958).

19   As David Brody explains, the aggressive bargaining stance of unions in the postwar era was defeated in large part by managerial resistance. *Brody* at 185. General Motors, for instance, refused Walter Reuther's famous demand to "open its books," would not discuss prices, and refused to submit disputes to arbitration. "To preserve what it considered to be management prerogatives, GM had taken a 113-day strike, accepting losses of nearly 89 million dollars (of which 52.9 million was recovered through tax credits) and, most important, conceded its headstart to competitors in the race for post-war markets." *Brody* at 183–84.

Brody suggests that unions may not have placed as high a value on these issues as management. Yet, the information set out by Brody reveals that the union de-

sire to stress wage issues was largely due to the general economic situation, especially galloping inflation and intraunion political dynamics, rather than to a theoretical acceptance of exclusive managerial authority.

It is possible that the basically conservative nature of American unions led
them to seek security rather than participation in the 1950s. The Pacific Long-
shore Agreement of 1959, for instance, may be an example of a choice of income
security over employment security, leaving management free to make key capital
decisions. Slichter, Healey, & Livermash, *The Impact of Collective Bargaining* at
458 (Brooking 1960); *Brody* at 194. Again, however, the explanation may also reflect the traditional refusal to consider matters of relative power as motivating
union behavior.

20   Chamberlain, *supra* note 9 at 319. "Virtual unanimity of opinion exists among the
union leaders that any managerial decisions or authority threatening the security
of workers must be regulated." *Id.* at 89.

21   See D. Rodgers, *The Work Ethic in Industrial America, 1850–1920* (U. of Chicago
Press 1978); I. Yellowitz, *Industrialism & the American Labor Movement* (Kennikat Press 1977).

22   Apprenticeship was often used by employers to increase the number of apprentices so as to increase the labor pool, thus reducing the bargaining position of
skilled labor. Attempts by unions to control or terminate such programs often followed. Yellowitz, *supra* note 21, at 85–104, 141.

23   *Id.* at 4–5; D. Montgomery, *Workers' Control in America* (Cambridge U. Press
1979).

24   Yellowitz, *supra* note 21, at 5.

25   Montgomery, *supra* note 23, at 21–46, 63–74.

26   Wellington, *supra* note 8, at 84.

27   Chamberlain, *supra* note 9, at 89–100, 118–28; see also 129–40.

28   *Id.* at 131–42.

29   See Richard C. Wilcox, "Industrial Management's Policies Towards Unionism" at
278–79 in *Labor and the New Deal*, M. Derber and E. Young, eds., (U. of Wis. Press
1957).

30   *Id.* at 279–80.

31   See Chamberlain, *supra* note 9, at 129–57. Of course, all groups feel such losses
when exclusive decision-making authority is challenged.

32   See also *id.*, chap. 2.

33   *Id.* at 133. Employer opposition to collective efforts by employees have been motivated at least as much by concerns of authority and prerogative as by more immediate balance-sheet costs. Thus, one employer in 1886 could explain his firm's
intransigence and its willingness to suffer at least short-term economic disadvan-
tage, by explaining that the firm "would be surrendering ourselves into the control of our workmen by yielding at present. It is not a question of a slight advance
in wages merely, but there is a principle at stake which is of far more importance."
Letter from Charles Huston and Sons, quoted in J. Skaggs & R. Ehrlich, "Profits,
Paternalism, and Rebellion: A Case Study in Industrial Strife," 44, no. 2 Business
History Review 174 (1980).

34   Chamberlain, *supra* note 9, at 178.

35   S. D. Brandes, *American Welfare Capitalism, 1880–1940* (U. of Chicago Press 1976).

36   See Gutman, *Work, Culture & Society in Industrializing America* (Vintage 1977).

37   I. Bernstein, *The Lean Years: A History of the American Workers, 1920–1933* at 187 (Houghton Mifflin 1960; Penguin Books 1966). See also Ozanne, *Century of Labor-Management Relations* at 245 (U. of Wis. Press 1967); M. Derber, *The American Idea of Industrial Democracy, 1865–1965* at 260 (U. of Illinois Press 1970). Welfarism and unionism were indirectly related on scales of expansion and contraction. Brandes, *supra* note 35, at 32. Some argue that "welfare" activities were not common but were limited to a handful of employers. See *id.* at 7, n. 14. Some corporations, International Harvester for instance, instituted welfare schemes for public-relation purposes and especially to appear as a "good" trust and thereby elude antitrust prosecution. Ozanne, *Century of Labor-Management Relations* at 80–81.

38   Wihaprade, a welfare advocate of The Plymouth Cardage Co., cited at Brandes, *supra* note 35, at 27.

39   Quoted in Chamberlain, *supra* note 9, at 134 (emphasis added).

40   *Id.* at 135.

41   *Id.* at 137, 138, 139.

42   *Id.* at 141.

43   *Id.* at 156.

44   Chamberlain, *The Labor Sector, supra* note 17. See also Chamberlain, *The Union Challenge to Management Control, supra* note 9, at 20–27.

45   Chamberlain, *The Labor Sector, supra* note 17, at 314–15.

46   *Id.* at 343.

47   See Chamberlain's earlier doubts in *The Union Challenge to Management Control, supra* note 9, at 27–28.

48   For an interesting parallel, consider the response of faculty to demands of students in the 1960s for a democratization of the academy.

49   Klare, "Judicial Deradicalization of the Wagner Act and the Origins of Modern Legal Consciousness, 1937–1941," 62 Minn. L. Rev. 265, 321 (1978).

50   *Id.* Yet, Ronald Schatz's study of the union's emergence in General Electric and Westinghouse plants indicates that the "rank and file in these plants was not seething with revolt." The "1930's appear as a decade of real but limited protest." Union organizers were, at least initially, "quite isolated from other workers," and male organizers tended to be more highly skilled and accustomed to greater freedom in the plants as well as to higher pay. A higher proportion of female activists were children of activists, and others lived in nontraditional families. R. Schatz, "Union Pioneers: The Founders of Local Unions at General Electric and Westinghouse, 1933–1937," 66, no. 3 Journal of American History 586 (1979). See also Schatz, "American Electrical Workers: Work, Struggles, Aspirations, 1930–1950" (Ph.D. diss., U. of Pittsburgh 1977).

51   Klare, *supra* note 49, at 321.

52   See J. H. M. Laslett, "The American Tradition of Labor Theory & Its Relevance to the Contemporary Working Class" at 3, in *The American Working Class: Prospects for the 1980's,* I. L. Horowitz, John C. Leggett, M. Oppenheimer, eds. (Trans-

action Books 1979) [hereinafter cited as *Laslett*].

53   See H. Braverman, *Labor & Monopoly Capital* (Monthly Review Press 1974); Montgomery, *supra* note 23.

54   J. Commons, "American Shoemakers, 1648–1895: A Sketch of Industrial Evolution," 24 Quarterly Journal of Economics 39 (Nov. 1909).

55   C. Craypo, "Introduction—Special Issue on the Impact on Organized Labor of Changing Corporate Structure and Technology," 3, no. 3 Labor Studies Journal 195 (1979).

56   S. Perlman, *A Theory of the Labor Movement* at 6, 199 (Kelley 1929).

57   See *Laslett* at 16. This parallels Ely Chinoy's finding that auto workers tend to redefine American values of mobility and success to mean security, albeit outside of work. Chinoy, "The Tradition of Opportunity and the Aspirations of Automobile Workers," 57 American Journal of Sociology (March 1952).

58   S. Perlman, quoted in *Laslett* at 16.

59   Montgomery, "To Study the People: The American Working Class," 21 Labor History 485, 500 (1980).

60   Perlman, *supra* note 56, at 214, 239–40.

61   *Laslett* at 17, 18.

10   THE INTEREST IN THE MOBILITY OF CAPITAL

1   John Wiley & Sons v. Livingston, 376 U.S. 543 (1964).

2   NLRB v. Golden State Bottling Co., 4 ⋈ U.S. 168 (1973).

3   NLRB v. Burns International Security Services, 406 U.S. 272 (1972).

4   John Wiley & Sons v. Livingston, 376 U.S. 543 (1964).

5   The Court in *Wiley*, in a footnote, referred to New York law, which provided that in merger situations the surviving corporation was liable for the debts of the terminated enterprise. The employer also based part of its argument upon New York law, but this was ignored too. Nevertheless, the Court in *Burns*, to be discussed subsequently, has distinguished *Wiley* since the merger then occurred "against a background of state law."

6   John Wiley & Sons v. Livingston, 376 U.S. at 548.

7   See, *e.g.*, Doppelt, "Successor Companies: The NLRB Limits the Option—and Raises Some Problems," 20 De Paul L. Rev. 176, 183–84 (1971).

8   NLRB v. Burns Int'l. Security Services, 182 NLRB 348 (1970).

9   John Wiley & Sons v. Livingston, 376 U.S. 543, 549 (1964).

10   See, *e.g.*, E. Kassalow, *Trade Unions and Industrial Relations: An International Comparison* at 132 (Random House 1969).

11   See, *e.g.*, Textile Workers v. Lincoln Mills, 353 U.S. 448 (1957); United Steelworkers v. American Mfg. Co., 363 U.S. 564 (1960); United Steelworkers v. Warrior Gulf, 363 U.S. 574 (1960).

12   Wellington has noted that the Court demonstrates great interest in free collective bargaining, and thus the exertion of economic strife in the bargaining area, while stressing the value of peaceful resolution of disputes if arbitration is a possible avenue. Wellington, *Labor & the Legal Process*, chap. 3 (Yale U. Press 1968).

13   406 U.S. 272 (1972).

14 Indeed, one writer argues that not only would *Wiley* have compelled Burns to arbitrate, but an arbitrator would probably have held that the contract survived! See Slicker, "A Reconsideration of the Doctrine of Employer Successorship—A Step Toward a Rational Approach," 57 Minn. L. Rev. 1051, 1098–99 (1973).

15 NLRB v. Burns Int'l. Security Services, 406 U.S. 272, 287–88. There was no suggestion that Burns would have been deterred by the contract's survival, but the Court was concerned with a broad freedom for capital. The Court ignored the possibility that successor employers could bargain with the predecessor union prior to the change of ownership in order to seek arrangements and concessions it deemed vital. See C. Morris & W. Gaus, "Successorship and the Collective Bargaining Agreement: Accommodating *Wiley* and *Burns*," 59 Vir. L. Rev. 1359, 1384 (1973). In many merger situations, bargaining rather than arbitrating occurs. Instead, the Court stressed a federal policy in free collective bargaining under the NLRA, a policy which given the result in *Wiley* apparently contains less force in the arbitration sphere.

16 Of the many scholarly attempts to criticize or rationalize these decisions, see Morris and Gaus, *supra* note 15, at 1359; Slicker, *supra* note 14, at 1051; Swerdlow, "Freedom of Contract in Labor Law: *Burns, M. K. Porter*, and Section 8(d)," 51 Texas L. Rev. 1 (1972).

17 The Court's statements of policy hamper any attempt to limit *Burns* to its facts although the Court did stress that, unlike *Wiley*, there was no merger, no exchange or sale of assets, and no direct dealing at all between the two employers.

18 NLRB v. Burns Int'l. Security Services, 406 U.S. 272, 288–89.

19 Morris & Gaus, *supra* note 15, at 1386 (1973).

20 John Wiley & Sons v. Livingston, 376 U.S. at 549 (1964).

21 If an arbitration provision survives a merger, even though the union does not represent a majority of the successor's employees, presumably the arbitrator might find that the entire agreement or parts of it survive also. If so, the *Burns* holding that the new employer is not bound by the contract under the NLRA seems inconsistent. At least the contrary approach hardly seems irrational. Policies under the NLRA and Section 301 could conceivably differ, however, and some contrary strains already exist.

22 See, *e.g.*, H. K. Porter v. NLRB, 397 U.S. 99 (1970).

23 *Id.* at 108.

24 See Local 174, Teamsters v. Lucas Flour, 369 U.S. 95 (1962); Gateway Coal v. UMW, 414 U.S. 368 (1974).

25 417 U.S. 249 (1974).

26 *Id.* at 257–65.

27 NLRB v. Burns Int'l. Security Services, 406 U.S. at 294.

28 This argument is made by Morris & Gaus, *supra* note 15, at 1394.

29 *Id.* at 1360, nn. 7, 8. Confusion, however, still reigns because results that seem based more upon policy considerations than consent still occur in arbitration cases. In 1977, for instance, the Court held that an employer may have a duty to arbitrate a dispute based upon events that occurred *after* the expiration of the collective agreement. Nolde Bros. v. Bakery Workers, 430 U.S. 243 (1977).

30 Lion Dry Goods v. Retail Clerks Local 128, 369 U.S. 17 (1962); John Wiley & Sons

v. Livingston, 376 U.S. at 551, n. 5.

31   See Morris and Gaus, *supra* note 15, at 1379–80.

32   *Id.* at 1360–61.

33   See Howard Johnson Co. v. Detroit Local Joint Executive Board, 417 U.S. 249, 256.

11   THE EMPLOYMENT RELATION AND THE PREMISES OF LABOR LAW

1   Teamsters v. Daniel, 439 U.S. 551 (1979).

2   *Id.* at 560.

3   *Id.*

4   NLRB v. Bell Aerospace Co., 416 U.S. 267 (1974).

5   NLRB v. Bell Aerospace, 219 NLRB 384, 385 (1975).

6   NLRB v. Packard Motor Car Co., 330 U.S. 485 (1947).

7   *Id.* at 494.

8   Vegelahn v. Guntner, 167 Mass. 92, 44 N.E. 1077, 1081 (1896). The use of "capital" and "labor" was widespread, although courts did not always perceive a competition to exist between the two forces.

9   NLRB v. Packard Motor Car Co., 330 U.S. 485, 493, 494–95. The Senate concurred. S. Rep. No. 105, 80th Cong., 1st Sess. (1947). Douglas also noted that the act was designed for workers whose rights to organize had not been recognized, thus causing strife and unrest. Foremen, managers, or vice presidents had created no similar history. *Id.* at 496–97. See. H. R. Rep. No. 245, 80th Cong., 1st Sess. 13–17 (1947).

10   D. Noble, *America by Design: Science, Technology and the Rise of Corporate Capitalism* (Knopf 1977).

11   In other areas it could be argued that the union is recognized as an agency separate from the employees it represents, carrying out a federal role. Aside from the fact that unions do tend to serve as disciplining and mediating influences on the rank and file, the law has encouraged such roles. The result is to further blur the "owner-employer" conflict by deeming the basic combatants to be management and unions. Thus, unions, presumably restrained and responsible, may pressure management, but individuals or informal groups of employees are restrained from "mau-mauing" the flak catchers. (I will be eternally grateful to Tom Wolfe for this phrase—T. Wolfe, *Radical Chic & Mau-Mauing the Flak Catchers* [Bantam 1971].)

12   NLRB v. Yeshiva University, 444 U.S. 672, 677 (1980). A penetrating analysis of this case can be found in Klare, "The Bitter and the Sweet: Reflections on the Supreme Court's *Yeshiva* Decision," Socialist Review (forthcoming).

13   444 U.S. at 676.

14   *Id.* at 680–81.

15   The Board, for instance, presented a functional argument. The faculty, while participating in academic governance, it argued, was exercising professional judgment. Such judgment is neither expected "to conform to management policies [nor] judged according to their effectiveness in carrying out those policies." Thus, it argued, there was no danger of a divided loyalty because faculty are expected to seek "professional values rather than institutional interests." *Id.* at 683–84.

16   This is not to say that a factory model ideally fits the university. As the Board has noted, the university and its collegiality concept does not "square with the tradi-

tional authority structures with which th[e] Act was designed to cope in the typical organizations of the commercial world." Adelphi University, 195 NLRB 639, 648 (1972).

17   Ironically, although guards are specially treated in the NLRA, they are *not* excluded from the act's coverage, although potential conflict might exist. They must belong, if at all, to a union representing only guards, even though membership in a union could arguably affect their values. Perhaps guards are different from managers because of their relatively low status in the hierarchy, and thus they are not treated as representatives of capital. Oddly, however, this is the way they would be generally perceived.

18   It is true that Justice Powell mentions the danger of "divided loyalty," but it is unclear what he means or why he believes unionization will create the "danger . . . [of] divided loyalty." Bargaining, after all, has existed in many institutions for many years and will continue to do so, for instance, in public colleges in many states. Loyalty may indeed be required for managers, but such assumptions merely beg the question. The Court seems to assume that professors are managers because their interests and those of the administration are the same. Again, the expectations of the employers, not the interests of the employees, are given predominant weight.

19   NLRB v. Bell Aerospace Co., 416 U.S. at 283.

20   Klare, "The Bitter and the Sweet," *supra* note 12, at 213. As Klare notes, it has become common for the Court to stress the interest in industrial peace, ignoring goals of industrial democracy, economic redistribution, and equality of bargaining power. Thus, Justice Marshall could say in 1975 that the rights of employees granted by Section 7 "are protected not for their own sake but as an instrument of the national labor policy of minimizing strife. . . ." Emporium Capwell v. WACO, 420 U.S. 50, 62 (1975).

21   The limited functions of collective bargaining have been clearly asserted by scholars. David Feller, for instance, views collective bargaining as only the method, but not the occasion, for creating managerial rules. Bargaining, therefore, establishes a method for securing consent to these rules. Feller, "A General Theory of the Collective Bargaining Contract," 61 Cal. L. Rev. 720–24 (1973). For an excellent critique of this view and the Court's postwar use of ideology, see K. Stone, "Law and Class Conflict in the Post-War Era," 90 Yale L. J. 1509 (1981).

22   A. D. Chandler, Jr., *The Visible Hand: The Managerial Revolution in American Business* at 493 (Belknap Press 1977).

23   A. Fox, "Work Roles and Relations in the Wider Social Setting," chap. 4, *Beyond Contract: Work, Power & Trust Relations* (Faber & Faber 1974).

24   C. Spencer, *Blue Collar: An Internal Examination of the Workplace* at 92 (Lakeside Charter Books 1977).

25   See Fox, *supra* note 23, at 246.

26   F. Tannenbaum, *A Philosophy of Labor* (Knopf 1950).

27   Fox, *supra* note 23, at 190.

28   *Id.* at 220.

29   S. Lynd, "Investment Decisions and the Quid Pro Quo Myth," 29 Case Western L. Rev. 396 (1979).